A Legacy of Faith in 55 Days

A mother learns that Gods love is greater than hers

By

Jelana Hobbs

authorHOUSE

1663 LIBERTY DRIVE, SUITE 200
BLOOMINGTON, INDIANA 47403
(800) 839-8640
www.authorhouse.com

© 2005 Jelana Hobbs
All Rights Reserved.

No part of this book may be reproduced, stored in a retrieval system, or transmitted by any means without the written permission of the author.

First published by AuthorHouse 12/01/04

ISBN: 1-4184-8533-0 (sc)

Library of Congress Control Number: 2004095315

Printed in the United States of America
Bloomington, Indiana

This book is printed on acid-free paper.

IN Loving Memory of
JOSHUA HOBBS
February 20, 1987 - July 18, 2001

*It's been 3 years since your passing and
everyday I'm assured you are happy.
Our last days together often I think of,
and hold very dear to my heart, the
gift you gave, a prayer sent to
see me saved.
Thank you for such great love,
until we meet again.*
I love you, Joshua
Forever and a day
Mom

JOURNEY

A Legacy of Faith in 55 Days

Wednesday May 23rd 2001, it was a typical day for us; the time was flying by fast.

Joshua had been sick earlier in the week, and that meant all rest and no physical activities. He was so excited to return to school, he knew he would be allowed to see his friends and play outside again.

I had picked Joshua up from school, and already knew what we were going to do. From the moment he shut the truck door. It was just minutes after 3:00 p.m., everything going as planned.

I had always planned everything in advance. I didn't like surprises. And I liked having everything on a timely schedule. When things didn't go as planned, I became irritated and frantic. A feeling that the life I was living was going to end. I felt I was a failure if I didn't have everything in perfect order

I had told him on the way home we had to stop at the grocery store; I needed a few items for dinner that evening. Joshua was quite easy to please. As we left the store, I said one more stop, as I looked toward him and seen him frown I said do you want your hair-cut? He said, yes. Joshua smiled ear to ear when he seen his hair-stylist, he didn't mind that she was a few minutes behind. What about my schedule? I thought. As we sat await Joshua had a way of making me smile, just watching him made it all o.k.

It wouldn't be too bad, Joshua wasn't getting a lot cut, more of a trim to keep his hair out of his eyes. Finally, his turn within minutes we were done. Now we can rush home, making up for those minutes my lost time!

My brother had planned on meeting me at the house at 4:00 p.m. I wasn't sure if I was going to make it. Just in time, as we arrived at our home my brother pulling in right behind us. Wow

Now were rushing in the house, Joshua maneuvering to let his dog Bear out. I'm following right behind setting the bags of groceries down. My brother going around to the back of the house, setting up to finish the plowed area he had started earlier that mourning. I had started to put away the groceries that I had purchased when my brother had called for me to come around back. I was playing close attention to the minutes flying by; I had answered his question and rushed back to the kitchen.

Joshua patiently waiting to ask if he could stay out until 6:00 p.m. that was much later than I usually let him. As he reached in the refrigerator to grab him a Coke, I was hesitant to allow him this extra time, I felt the less time I allowed him to rome, the less likely he would be able to do what I didn't want him doing.

Joshua was required to check-in within 45 minutes to 1 hour from leaving the house. If he didn't follow that rule, he wouldn't be allowed to go out, for the rest of the evening, and if I had to go look for him he would be grounded for the rest of the week.

TRAGEDY

As I looked at him, in amazement taking a moment and realizing he's almost grown. He's only 14, yet he stands at 5'8, and 114 lbs. I answered yes, and I grabbed him and hugged him and said I love you, Joshua. He said love you to mom. He was excited that he was given more time to be with his friends.

I had no idea how long it would be before I would be able to take hold and hug him again.

Joshua hurriedly moved towards the front door, to make sure that I didn't change my mind, about the later time. I couldn't help from watch him, there was an oddity feeling that I had, I can't describe the exact feeling that was going on inside. I had this feeling for quite some time. It was stronger today than it had been and I didn't know why.

I wanted to tell Joshua that he couldn't go, there was no reason why, and I sure didn't want him mad at me, so I let him go.

He ran around to the side of the house, I had continued to watch him, grabbing his bike, my brother calling for me again in the back, and I'm thinking what could it be now?

I continued to have this feeling, this thought, as I hurried to answer my brother, I didn't realize that would be the last time that I would see Joshua ride.

By the time I was able to get back to the front of the house, Joshua was already gone. I had stepped out and looked; I couldn't call him back, even if I wanted too he was already gone.

I felt sad, and said he's alright. You're just being over protective again! He's visiting his friends; I went in to prepare dinner for us, and said to myself Jelana what is the matter with you? I didn't have an answer at the time.

Minutes had passed and I had this big ache in my heart, the clock read 4:16 p.m. within seconds there were multiple sirens going off. It sounded as if they were everywhere. There was probably an accident that took place on the Interstate. I was in the house; it was hard for me to determine how close or far away that they really were.

As I proceeded to prepare dinner, I was startled by a huge knock on my front door. The knock was so great; I thought they were going to beat down my door.

I opened my front door to a woman who was in a semi-frantic state. She asked if I was Joshua's mom. I said, yes. She said Joshua's just been hit, it doesn't look good Jelana!

I asked where he was, my knees starting to shake, he was 5 blocks away. I said I'm on my way not knowing what to expect. As I turned away I called upon Jesus, and asked him to please help him, be with him Lord as I walked thru the house, going to the back to get my brother.

I knew from my experience as a little girl, that you could call upon Jesus at any time with an open and sincere heart and he will come to you, he had been there for me and brought me through many times.

I was living a life of destruction, yet I was asking for God to help Joshua until I could get there not for me, for him I pleaded.

I was feeling a little distraught as I called upon my brother and shared the news.

Neither of us realizing how serious it would be; My heart pounding with every breath as we hurried to get to the seen.

I wanted to drive yet I knew I wouldn't be able to. I had so many feelings going on inside.

I felt that I could get out and run faster than the truck was actually going. I didn't move on the way there. I did keep saying, Lord please be with him, please Lord let him be o.k.

As we pulled into the blocked off seen, police cars and lights going off every-where. Crowds of people gathering around I stepped out of the truck calling Joshua's name,

He'll be alright as long as I can get to him I thought. I'll protect him! I can help him.

I took off running towards the paramedics, officers, and firemen wanting to get to my son. Joshua I screamed as I reached the place where I seen him lay, face down and the mini-van lay on top of him.

As I fought the officials trying to keep me away from him, and then one said let her through. I broke away with all my might and looked at him so helplessly.

I dropped to my knees immediately and said Joshua I'm here, Lord please. I closed my eyes and felt overwhelmed inside, Lord I know that you can help him, I'm not worthy to ask anything of you, I prayed. Please Lord, we need you. Whatever you ask of me I will do, as I was humbled in the sight of the Lord, believing for the first time and truly meaning every word.

Please God do something. I can't help him Lord, you can. I opened my eyes as I was a few feet away from him, I reached over and touched his leg and said I'm here Joshua, I'm here. Please don't leave me! Lord I know that you can give life back to him as you did me.

As I watch him lay under, staff was communicating with one another. on how to get the van off of him, without causing more injury to him.

He was so helpless. I was really starting to feel the anxiety building up within me I felt as if I couldn't breathe. Time had past and I had seen them place a jack under the backside of the front wheel tire, and within seconds it was cranked to lift the van off of him.

As the jack worked it compressed more pressure down, that appeared to push out the last breath that he may have had. As I watched every move, the front wheel tire being parallel in the middle of his back. Finally having the van lifted off of him at last.

As the paramedics reached over, turning him over it was then that I probably looked like I had seen a ghost. Joshua had blood coming from his nose, ears, and mouth and I knew it wasn't a good sign. God please I screamed, don't take him away from me, please Lord not my baby, I will do anything Lord.

As I was made to stand as they rushed to care for him that is when it really hit me hard.

I started to cry, and shake, moving around wanting to be with him. I couldn't catch my breath I was hurting on the inside!

I was told that Joshua wasn't responding and that he was about to be life-lined (flown by helicopter) to Methodist Hospital the states best Trauma Center.

I wanted to go; I didn't want to be away from him, I had to be with him I said. Please let me go with him.

Joshua's situation was critical and I wouldn't be allowed to fly with them. I was afraid Joshua was going to leave me. I was hysterical. I was told if I didn't calm down that they would have to call an ambulance for me, and take me in. I couldn't allow that to happen, I would be separated from him.

Every second feeling like it was going to be our last.

Lord give me the strength as I prayed, you know our circumstance, please Lord don't take him away he is all that I have! I had never been placed in a situation like this, I couldn't think of my life without him. Not now, not ever, even in a time like this!

Some of my family had arrived at the scene and was trying to help calm me; I was so upset and thinking about what I had just seen it made me feel like I had to throw up. I knew I hadn't had anything to eat, and I was shaking vigorously and had no control and I felt like I was hyper-ventilating.

I had such numbness and a deep pain; in my heart and I was having a very difficult time dealing and coping with the circumstance.

FAITH

We had to move quickly, I had to be reunited with him I wanted Joshua to know that I hadn't given up on him. Although my physical reaction was like others that had experienced trauma or the same thing that I just did.

All of us scuffling around to leave the scene, they hadn't seen what I had seen. I wasn't going to let go of him, I needed him and he needed me. Our love for one another was intertwined, I believed.

My brother drove back to the house so we could lock up, and put a few things away. I felt as if I had been caught up in the wind, I felt like I could collapse if I'd had the time or the chance. It wasn't about me, Joshua needed me and timing was everything. We hurried to leave not taking any more time than was needed. Jimmy was shook up, like I was.

I knew that from what I had just seen, it would be a while before we would see home again.

God had already stepped in, and was in control from the very beginning. His love lifted me as he had both of us in the palm of his hand.

As we journeyed on the road, I continually prayed the best that I could, it wasn't much because I couldn't think, I remember saying Lord please, I will be good. I can't do it without him Lord, I need him, please don't take him, I love him. I had seen three rainbows in the sky and it didn't phase me at the time I was overwhelmed inside.

God knew what he was going to do, and had enough confidence in me to help carry his plan and works through.

Every second counting, I had faith and believed that God was going to give us a second chance. He would see us through this, believe in what you ask, I remember my grandmother saying to me.

Whatever it takes not realizing the sacrifice that I would have to make.

Finally we had arrived at the hospital, as we pulled in everyone else right behind us. All of us running in, and approaching the Emergency Desk, the receptionist standing to help assist us.

I told her I was Joshua's mom, she said who? I said Joshua the boy who's just been life-lined. I turned to look at the time it read 5:02 p.m. Maybe we took to long. She picked up the phone to tell the Emergency Staff that I was there, immediately a set of double-doors opened and a Charge Nurse approached us and took us back to a quiet room.

We were asked to sit, I was shaking, my knees were knocking, and tears were rolling, I was scared it was hard for me to sit at a time like this. Everyone was sitting and for a moment I was too.

As we sat a Chaplin came and asked to have prayer with us. This room was so quiet you could've heard a pin drop. As everyone bowed there heads in prayer, I focused on seeing Joshua again, please Lord don't take him I will do anything I pleaded quietly.

I wasn't listening to the Chaplin, I needed to see Joshua, Joshua needed to hear my voice and know that I wasn't giving up on him!

I wanted to pray with Joshua not them. I was told the accident was a lot for him, and they would allow me to go back and see Joshua as soon as they could. I believe this was my last chance given by God.

Joshua was waiting on me and I needed to have the opportunity to go back and pray again with him to be with him.

My belief in God was that strong. I knew early in life he had spared me and given life to me and that what he had done for me he would do for Joshua believing and trusting in him.

I would soon learn that this was the chosen time to full fill what God had called me to do.

As we were waiting I stood standing and shaking, my sister Donna grabbed me and hugged me and said he's going to be alright as I had tears well up in my eyes. I had complete confidence in her about every decision that I've ever made and she said I love you, as I did her too. She knew that I was scared and how much Joshua meant to me, my life was based on him.

As we stood waiting the ER Nurse came in (Stephanie) and said Ms. Hobbs I can take you back to see your boy if you calm down. I nodded my head in agreement; I can't take you back with you shaking this way she said. I immediately wiped my eyes and stood straight, "I'm ready" having that need to see, be, and pray with him and I'm sure it was part of my mothering instinct. God had already stepped in; I was given a super-natural calm and didn't realize that it was God given at the time.

I made a pact to myself not to react distraught or stressed like that again. However God knows what we will go through or repeat through given circumstance.

She told my sister that if I did alright she would come to get her in a little while. I was given a hug one more time, before Stephanie and I left the room. I wasn't sure what to expect, I did feel God's presence.

I remember the sound of another set of double-doors opening, it was so quiet there wasn't any distraction, I had visited other hospitals before, and I had never had an experience like this one before.

PAST

There were many doctors and nurses standing in the hallway, just outside of Joshua's room. You could here our foot steps as we were walking towards them and we were wearing tennis shoes. As we walked it seeming to be an empty floor, where is everyone I thought? In amazement were the only ones on this floor how odd.

As we walked side by side Stephanie approaching the group, I was asked by a physician if I still wanted to pray with him and I said yes. There was some commotion as I turned to my right looking in on this. There was several staff standing back as there was Joshua lying so lifeless without a stitch of clothing on him or a sheet to cover him. He didn't have anything connected to him, my first thought is they knew I was coming back; I wouldn't want Joshua to awake and be embarrassed because of this. Cover him, please. Immediately the male doctor in charge was having me escorted out and said she's not aloud to be back here, get her out of here now!

I became hysterical, I looked at this man and asked him, are you a parent? If you are then you would know where I'm coming from, I just want to be with my son and pray with him please! I was being pushed outside of the room and begging God to have mercy on him, and me. I said I'm here Joshua, please don't leave me! Stephanie tried to comfort me, I started to shake and I wasn't able to tolerate anyone's touch it was too much. I know that from having to leave that room they had already given up, but God didn't he was with us, I felt something going on deep down inside of me. And I wasn't going to give up or give in letting go of my son.

As I paced the floor waiting, having no place to run or escape begging God for one more chance, making it right this would be my final time. Many had tried to tell me that the accident had been to serious, yet I believed God was going to use us, my focus was on Joshua.

Ironically the doctor had changed his mind and said he would give me a minute with Joshua that is all that I needed that is all that I asked.

As I entered in he was now covered up, he had oxygen on and was hooked up to a machine which had a symbol of a heart beat and read the number 23.

I stepped as close to him as I could and said Joshua I'm here. And I leaned over and kissed him, I said I wanted to let you know that I've gave you to God, I've seen the light and I know you have too. And my tears started to flow I love you, I need you, please don't leave me. Don't let go!

I then sang to him the first few verses of Amazing Grace, believing God was helping us. And said Jesus loves you Joshua and I do to. I was then asked to leave; I repeated to him how much I loved him and needed him.

Joshua I'm right here, we will get through this together believe it with me ok.

I found myself not saying or making any promises to God, moments of silence. My heart was heavy and I knew that in times past, I had never finished what God had asked.

God have your will; have your way. I didn't know how much he was doing from the very first day, and how much praise I would give him, also building trust and truly believing in him. In every step of the way

As I walked back to reunite with family again, Stephanie said that I could have one family member to come back with me to see him. Everyone was there, I chose Donna she was strength when I felt weak. She had been there for me, Joshua trusted in her too. If there was a situation that Joshua didn't confide in me with he would confide in Donna (my sister) with knowing that he could trust to tell her anything.

We walked back hand in hand, as we approached his room her eyes filling with tears as mine did. I prayed with Joshua again asking God to hear me, remembering his word, believing that if two shall gather together in his name asking and believing in what they asked for then what they ask for shall be given in Jesus name. I couldn't quote the scripture at the time but I did remember this verse. I had seen it work many times in the past.

I sang Jesus Loves Me (you) yes I know, I wanted God to love him, as he had shown me. All of those scriptures that I had tucked away for so long were coming out of me so openly.

Donna had shared with him how much he meant to her and how much we needed him to be with us.

Time was up and we were asked to leave, neither one of us giving up on him.

I had felt something going on with me, something I couldn't explain. As we slowly walked back, Would God reach out to me and hear my plea for help and have mercy on me as a sinner? Yes. Only by invitation and he already had.

All along I was asking God for a conformation and he didn't have to say anything or use anyone because for every second, minute, and hour was a conformation.

What I was feeling and believing wasn't in question for me; I wouldn't be able to explain it at the time and others may have had a hard time understanding why I was strong in mind this way, God chose me and not them and one day they would understand.

I had been living a life of destruction as a sinner yet I had yielded my vessel to be a part of God's wonderful plan. I believed Joshua was going to be alright and God was about to show me and all of them. As we grow in Gods word we soon learn that he chooses the least to do the greatest task, because we don't look to man but to him. And I know that I'm not able to do anything without him.

Minutes passing, walking, standing and waiting. Finally we received the best news; Joshua had just been transported to the East Wing, 8th Floor he was in the Intensive Care Unit. Yes, the situation was critical but he was moved from the ground floor up. A journey began a moment of celebration and everyone being Thankful an open invitation for God to work.

I believe that from the very moment the accident took place that it threw Joshua in a deep sleep and God came to Joshua as he did with Daniel and he reached out and touched him immediately resting in Gods hands. And then God said Joshua there is work for you to do, and sent him back to finish what was asked of him and he would use me for others to see the completion.

I imagine the crown given to those who suffered, that others may receive salvation a life turning destination.

It was getting late and we hadn't had the opportunity to go back and see him. I started to feel overwhelmed inside; I needed to see him I wanted to make sure that he was alright.

I needed to be with him, to love him, touch him, hold him and thank him for coming back to me.

Lord please make the way for me to be with him and he did!

There were many of us waiting, wondering when we would be allowed to go back and see him? How much longer was asked repeatedly.

I had a lot of mixed emotion and was ready to see him. I started to ask about every 20 minutes, I began to feel overwhelmed inside and ask why they are keeping me from him. Within minutes the receptionist came to me and said she would take me back to see him, for a few minutes. And then all of us could. I was so happy!

This was a time God chose to give all of us a remembrance of what he had done that would last each of us a lifetime.

As she took me back through two sets of double-doors and we walked the hall, we quickly turned to the 1st room on the right, there he was. I was so glad to see him and to hold his hand even though I knew it would only be for a minute or two it felt good to see him and know he was breathing.

I told him how much he meant to me and how much I loved him. I was so glad that he hadn't given up.

I told him that I knew God had done this and that he was resting in his hands. I will give God the praise continually!

Joshua had tubes down his nose, mouth, the left side of his chest, and at the end of his bed. He was given oxygen to help him breath. Joshua had numerous ivies on both sides of his arms, bandages on both arms and even on his chest. Joshua had bruising and a blue discoloration from his head half way down his chest and 2 monitors attached to him for every breath, and every move. He was alive and that meant everything.

He loved me as much as I did him and he wasn't going to leave me, I was so happy. He was going to be alright I continued to believe this. I told him I would be right back everyone else had been waiting to see him, I hurried to get them and have everyone come back.

We had to gather around him and pray for him and encourage him, in my heart I felt this to be necessary to do immediately. Nothing else would do to show my appreciation for what God was doing.

A sign of hope, our faith as a family started to grow.

All of us hurried back, walking around to make a circle around his bed, my mom's preacher leading us in prayer. I believed in what we were asking for the angels to come down and repair and mend every inch of him to make him whole again and they did. And as the prayer ended it was Lord have your will, have your way and God did all the way. **Everything that had taken place wasn't just for me; it was for all of us to believe.**

As we were leaving Joshua's room I felt the connection to see this through

This journey was based on God, Joshua and I to remember the good that would come from this. To leave a Legacy of Faith I didn't know God had already started the conditioning process with me. He works so mysteriously.

Signs had already been given and always in three's. The rainbow, (Gods promise) the Eagle, (Freedom) and a bright star (represents life). And this was just the beginning everyone had seen these signs including me on day one.

In my heart I felt that Joshua knew I was holding on and out of love God used Joshua and this time to make a change in my life. A commitment that I made that would last a lifetime.

We were going to overcome this as we had many circumstance in times past, but you have to have God on your side to do just that.

God knew that I was willing to do whatever it took and whatever was asked, I made that statement repeatedly. I didn't want to loose Joshua, not just for me but for all of us is what I asked.

Teach me Lord, I am willing!

FORGIVENESS

I hadn't even asked Jesus to forgive me or come back into my life and save me to be born again. This was just the beginning for him to come in and start to move he already knew when and what I would do.

I had ran from being a Christian all of my life, feeling I wouldn't and couldn't live up to Gods expectations and that I had failed him too many times and that there was a responsibility, and obligation that comes with it.

God was merciful to except me just the way I was. He took me when I felt the least wanted or favored in anyone eyes.

He knew what my life had been and what kind of past I had and He knew and had confidence that he could change everything about me and eventually he would just one step at a time.

And it would all be good because it was in his time and not mine.

That is Gods wonderful gift of love to all of us who seek him and desire to find favor and delight in his eyes, to understand his ways and not ours.

I believe Joshua was an angel sent back to help us learn to have faith as a family and to earn jewels for his beautiful crown seeing to my salvation.

God used Joshua to open our hearts and to give us this time to heal and to see and realize how wonderful and loving he is to each of us. Miracles take place daily and Joshua was willing and did what was asked of him, immediately I did too.

Our time was up and everyone had started to leave his room, most were leaving for the evening all of us had a since of relief to see him alive and breathing. To me that was the best news for the evening. I knew everyone was watching me and if I had broken down they would have to!

Everyone had said and planned to come up early in the mourning to see how he was doing, as I gave everyone hugs and kisses good-bye.

I was surprised when my mom had said she had planned on staying with me for the night.

I wondered why, I had resentment towards many within my family

It shouldn't take an accident to show your concern on how a loved ones doing. Or offer to help when one faces tragedy, that being the only time when you want to help.

How could anyone expect me to open up to them when they hadn't been a part of our daily lives for the longest time?

STRENGTH

A Legacy of Faith in 55 Days

At the time I had a lot of emotions going on, and I wasn't an easy person to get along with. I know that I wasn't liked by many families and of Joshua's friends. Immediately there was a whole lot of changing going on, and God would make me loveable and kind to all of them.

God chose me to show them that he can use the least of us to do the most for him.

All of had been used to holding onto all of the negativity in times past, remembering all of the pain and hurt that others had caused and the bad conversations that had taken place and been said.

Joshua and I both felt like an outcast to our family for the longest time!

The only two that never made us feel that way was Donna and Chris.

God had a lesson to give me; he was waiting for the right time and he knew it wouldn't be long. To Forgive; forgiveness had to start immediately or else I wouldn't be allowed to leave a testimony. At the time I didn't understand the necessity of forgiveness completely until now.

As we were placed in a quiet room for the evening, my mom was nestled on one side of the room and I was on the other. I found myself not wanting to sleep, I lay awake tossing and turning continually going for more cups of coffee, it was so strong and it was early in the mourning.

It was around 4:30a.m. I knew it wouldn't be long before I would have the opportunity to go back and see him. I had to rest I would need it for later on as our time progressed. My mind continually going and saying What If?

There were voices outside our quiet room, and the sounds of double doors opening. It was around 6:45 a.m. and we realized it was time for us to get up.

Immediately upon arising thanking our Lord Jesus Christ for giving us another day and asking for him to be with us throughout every minute of this day. I wasn't sure what to ask yet I knew he had already showed us that he was with us. I believed he was taking care of everything.

The receptionist had arrived early to inform us no one would be allowed to go back in the Intensive Care Unit and visit until 8:00 a.m. That seemed like a long way away considering we had only minutes to visit with him from the night prior. I asked her if she would go back and see him, and let me know that he was alright? And she did. I was relieved at the news however I wanted to see him too.

I appreciated the training given to these receptionist, most of the families are highly stressed when they first arrive at the hospital and the receptionist works continually to help keep the families calm. They do a great job!

It was going to be a little while before we could go back, my mom and I went downstairs to smoke a few cigarettes we had very few words with one another. At the time I didn't mind it was better that way.

As we were walking back I had asked if we could stop in the chapel to pray. I felt the need to have continual prayer for Joshua and we did.

Every time I walked in the chapel I would drop to my knees as the stained glass depicted a mother handing her child back to Jesus. I hadn't understood the full meaning.

I remembered the significance of having two or more gathered together asking and believing in Christ name as a child having that seed planted and now it was starting to grow it is quoted in Matthew.

I believed if I was willing to give Joshua to Jesus to heal him then he would give him back to me whole and complete again. And I wouldn't be separated from him. I was compromising for my benefit and not Gods.

I have realized that there are conditions that go with Gods promise and we have to be willing to except them.

As we entered the 8th Floor many of our family was there to greet us, everyone anxious to see Joshua again. I was mixed with emotions and then I heard Gods voice boldly say "Have I not forgave you and heard your prayer? I said, yes. He said to me forgive those as I have forgiven you. I was in immediate agreement saying yes Lord whatever you ask I will do. I was willing to learn. I had a mini study guide (The Upper Room) it had a lesson given on forgiveness to.

Finally given the opportunity to go back and see him as everyone patiently waiting there turn.

I was so happy to see him and to let him know how much he was loved Joshua I said you are a miracle and I'm going to say a prayer with you,

I want you to realize how blessed and thankful I am that God gave life back to you.

I'm so Thankful that God gave you and me one more chance and as you heal you will hear me say it many more times.

I was afraid to touch him or hold his hand; I didn't want to hurt him. I reassured him that I would be with him every step of the way and I was.

A Legacy of Faith in 55 Days

I told him that there were many who were waiting to see him and that we would have to take turns. I went to get them individually hurrying to get them back so I would have more time with him.

I constantly feared he would leave me if I wasn't there for him. Was I willing to do whatever was asked, when I was asked by our Master?

I said yes but I really wanted it to benefit me. God knows the ones he can use and the ones who are willing to suffer for his name sake not everyone would talk or think positive in a time like this. To lift up his name, and to continually say whatever it takes.

I made myself give hugs and pats and say Thank You and found as I was reaching out to them they were reaching out to me.

Everyone wanted to help, everyone was waiting to do something and most of all **everyone believing in God and in Joshua in one accord that says it all.** For the non-believer this feeling and belief in God would last for a short while, a non-believer will think negative when the situation looks good.

Our family in belief and faith was being strengthened by every moment of this day. There was much work that needed to be done with each of us.

Throughout the day and multiple conversations there were many that told us Joshua was pronounced D.O.A (dead on arrival) on the police scanner and to us that was just a saying. We had already seen Joshua and there were no signs in our minds of anything of that nature God had already moved.

We had asked everyone to have faith and pray this time for his recovery. And to remember Gods love that he was showing to all of us.

I knew in my heart God was having his way and I wouldn't take part with any negative conversation.

God was patient with us and he wasn't doing bad things but good for all of us to see. A preparation for what was then and what was to come!

It is only through Gods love that will truly set you free and allow you to see and hear everything differently.

Joshua had a puncture wound on his left elbow and ex-ray showed part of his bone chipped away causing a fever that wouldn't go away.

There was sign of infection that had concerned a doctor and he recommended surgery immediately.

HEALING

Joshua had already been through so much I had to know if this surgery was really necessary.

The decision was made in agreement with the doctor and soon Joshua would be wheeled to surgery. I was told that if Joshua's fever continued to rise this could cause serious brain injury.

I was so scared, the plan was to go in and flush the area adequately and then place a pin where his elbow bent. This would eliminate the infection and reduce his fever and allow full movement of his left arm and that was what was needed.

The staff had scurried to take Joshua down; I walked with him to the set of operating doors. I had asked them to give me a minute and I ran back to get a Bible to place it with him, Joshua and I both believed in Gods word and as I hurried back and placed it beside him, I told him what he had in the palm of his hand.

I remember many times in the past if Joshua had a bad dream or was frightened at night he would place a Bible under his pillow or in his bed and would say that he was no longer scared and if it was real bad Joshua would ask me to pray with him.

I told Joshua that I was waiting for him and this was needed of him. I love you Joshua as I know you love me please dont leave me, there are many praying for you. Hang in there ok, I'm right here.

Everyone was patiently waiting. We had to see this through we had to prove what God was doing.

It took 2 hours as I watched every door that opened and the many doctors that walked the floor waiting to see and talk with the right one, the one who had worked with Joshua. Finally there he was (surgeon) as I approached him so eagerly to see how Joshua was doing and waiting to go back and see him.

I spoke with the surgeon and he stated they went in and flushed the area and planned on putting a pin in it the following day. They had to wait 24 hours to see how the incision would do, but Joshua came through successfully! That was great news. I didn't like that idea that we were going to go through this again, yet it was something that we would have to do.

I had to trust and obey and remember that God had got us through today.

I was ready to see him and was told that he was being transported back to the 8th Floor and that I would be able to see him immediately. I wanted to run to get to him to see him and, as I moved being so Thankful for the success of this operation.

None of us deserved what God was giving us, he was so good to comfort us and grant our request. To be told that Joshua was coming out of the anesthesia without complications was a relief to.

I had the opportunity to go back first to see how he was doing, I was told by staff this was a very critical time and he needed rest with minimal distractions.

I was so happy to see him as I had tears rolling down, I reached for his hand and thanked him and I told him how proud of him I was and I knew that God was taking care of him. I leaned over and kissed his hand and thanked the Lord for him again.

I wanted to hold him, he was my baby regardless of how old or big he was and I wanted him to feel safe. I know in my heart Joshua felt safe because he knew he had already been placed in Gods hands.

I didn't know that God had already prepared his place and that Joshua was already working to full fill Gods plan.

I managed to find a way to get to his head, I gave him little kisses and told him how much I loved him and how much he meant to me and he had scared me. But I was ok because he had stayed with me.

I would go and get the others they had been patiently waiting and they wanted to see him to. And this was a time that I didn't want to be stingy but to share him with the others I knew that was the right thing to do.

I made it a point to hurry in everything I did, I never liked leaving him for more than a few minutes.

All of us hurrying back to see and be with him, being so thankful that we weren't limited to what we had been asking for or receiving and believing.

I could see the doubt and fear that was upon each ones face yet we made it a point to hold together, being reminded this was a great request that we had asked and it was going to take time each of us having need of patience.

I depended on God and Joshua and they were depending on me. Psalm 23 came back to me and I knew that this scripture was strengthening me. I thought it was to help Joshua and not me for he was the one that was walking through the valley of the shadow of death and we shall not fear...

Joshua believe it with me I repeated.

Evening had come and everyone sighed with relief Joshua had just made it through the first 24 hour stay.

TRUST

Visiting hours would soon be over and the hallways were starting to calm down and everyone was starting to go home. Family had made plans to come up again the next day.

It would be 2 hours before I could go back to see him, this gave the staff time to give him extensive breathing treatments that was done frequently throughout the evening, attend to his multiple wounds and give a sponge bath and if he had time rest in between.

I was feeling tired yet I felt I couldn't sleep because if Joshua needed me I had to be there for him. I wanted to be ready and there for him at all times and after carefully watching the clock it was almost 8:00p.m. I would soon be able to reunite with him.

This was a busy floor there were many families there hurting and mourning over a loved one. Everyone waiting patiently minutes seem like hours when you're made to wait.

Finally it was 8:00p.m. I hurried back to be with him only to be asked to step back they weren't done with Joshua yet and it would be a little while longer. My heart felt crushed, I didn't like being separated from him.

I didn't like what I had seen it was my first time to see how the RT's (Respiratory Therapist) work with ICU patients. I wasn't sure it was a good idea to beat on his chest when they had said he had 4 to 6 broken ribs.

As his mom I was concerned with what they were doing and after all that he had been through I sure didn't want anyone miss-handling or hurting him. I had to believe they were helping him and I definitely wanted Joshua to get better. As I stepped out and I paced back and forth not interfering with what they were doing. Finally having the opportunity to be with him I was so happy to see him he was a miracle to all of us and I was holding onto him.

I had a chair pulled up to him and had been gently holding his hand, and I had sung Jesus loves you and I was doing a lot of thinking. I felt God reaching out to me I knew he loved me to it was heartfelt.

I had tried resting my head on the metal bed rails but it didn't seem to relaxing. He was sleeping and I thought maybe I'll fix me a cot in the corner of his room if he starts to move I will be right there for him. As I walked a few steps away Joshua began to stir and his monitor started to sound.

I moved close to him and told him everything was ok, I was right there I'm not going anywhere to relax and calm down as I caressed him softly!

That reaction meant so much to me because I knew that he knew that I was right there with him and I needed reassurance too.

A Legacy of Faith in 55 Days

God knows what we have need of at all times. Joshua's nurse came in and asked what happened I told her and she looked at me and smiled as she checked him over and watched his monitors read normal again. As I watched him and thinking where does the time go, it didn't seem like that long ago when he had been born I loved him so much I needed more time with him he's only fourteen he needs me and I need him.

I waited for quite a while and then I had decided it was time for me to make things right. I told Joshua I was going downstairs to the Chapel to pray, I think he knew what I was going to do. And I told him to be good and not to do anything.

I didn't like the life I had been living; I was living a lie and was teaching Joshua to follow lead. Until now God was changing everything.

I was about to make a lifelong change to do it willingly to surrender my soul and ask for forgiveness to ask Jesus to come into my heart and renew my mind remembering what he did and died for and that he had risen that would last a lifetime and thanking him for being so merciful that right there I was feeling the connection and I had truly felt forgiven.

I had to know that Joshua already knew the feeling that could only be given by Jesus Christ as his Lord and Savior.

I heard a voice plainly say God wouldn't have moved in his life like he did if Joshua hadn't already accepted him. I was so happy to hear this and had a peace carrying with me to let me know everything was going to be alright and I was going to have to trust without hesitation.

I didn't want to even think about taking another day without having Jesus on our side at all times.

I didn't realize until later on that God had already prepared Joshua, and God does everything in perfect harmony and timing.

I believe with all of my heart just weeks before the accident Joshua had said the sinner's prayer he hadn't shared it with others because of his past they may not have believed him and he wasn't one to argue with anyone.

He didn't share it with his family or friends because he thought they would laugh at him or make fun of him and they wouldn't understand unless they were in the same spiritual rim.

And if he was looking for an example through any of us we were sinners and he wouldn't receive sound doctrine from us because lifestyle and truth are twisted to accommodate ones sin.

SALVATION

He was a beginner trying to understand what God wanted of him and was seeking his will privately.

Joshua knew his life would soon end because he had made mention to others prior to the accident.

I seen a definite change in him even though I wasn't sure what was causing it or how long it would last but it was a good change. And as God moved from the very beginning this was a conformation of his divine intervention and mercies.

I know that Joshua made confession by a television broadcast done early in the mourning, God showed this to me after arriving home from the hospital which was much later in our stay. It was not yet time for me to see this; it was for Joshua's ears to hear, and eyes to see at the time and not mine.

This was a conditioning time and preparation process for me and God had confidence in Joshua to help others seek him especially me that's what he had need of and he believed in me. Amazingly

Had Joshua been praying for me and he hadn't said anything? I believe he did and out of his prayer God had mercy with me and used me to help others and to show his mighty healings to leave a Legacy of Faith in 55 days.

It was time for me to head back and I was so relieved and glad. I loved being Joshua's mom and having this extra time. As I entered in Joshua's room feeling nervous, I approached him and felt that he knew what God was doing even though no words was flowing. There was a definite connection.

I was eagerly waiting for him to recover and as I sat and held his hand I knew it was going to take time and this was just the beginning. I let him know how scared I was, I had never showed him or told him.

He was going to get better and we may be in the hospital for a little while, but when we get home I was going to do things a lot different than I had been.

I said I would never take having him for granted ever again and I meant it. Joshua do you know how much I love you? I would do anything for you if I had the opportunity! I would switch you places and give my life for yours; it should've been me and not you.

I knew that what God was doing for us nobody else could.

I believe he already knew!

The minutes and hours were long as I stay and watched his every move, longing to keep that connection that we had going. These were baby steps for me I had to trust and learn to listen for instruction.

I was soon asked to leave it was 6:00 a.m. and they were going to start with the mourning activities, this was for everyone not just me.

I was so tired yet the adrenalin was still going I was afraid to sleep.

As I told Joshua over and over how proud of him I was I would be around the corner waiting to hang in there for me. God was taking good care of him, even though I had to step out it would only be for 2 hours that no matter what I wasn't going to leave him and that God was with him.

I was uptight because I knew he was scheduled to have another surgery today and he would be put under anesthesia again and you take a risk when you do that within the time frame that we did.

I had to be Thankful we were given another day and this was just the beginning of our hospital stay.

After talking with others sharing this floor I had discovered some had been there for 4 months or more. I couldn't imagine what that would be like because I thought within a few weeks we would be released. This was wishful thinking without knowing what Gods decision would be.

Many family members started to come up all of us were waiting patiently. We had discussed what some of the other families were going through and prayed with some of them individually.

Finally the clock struck 8:00 a.m. and we started to head back. We began to circle around Joshua's bed and asking God to repair and mend every inch of him to please make him whole again. And as Joshua was being prepared for surgery let him remember that we were waiting on him and to let him feel Gods presence and protection. Amen

Everyone was asked to leave as they planned to take him back for surgery, I was the only one given the opportunity to walk back with him before he went through the surgery doors. I enjoyed having these extra minutes with him it was reassurance for me.

I was blessed to have this availability to stay with him. Yet a part of me felt like I couldn't breathe, especially when I was separated from him.

I prayed with him again and leaned over and kissed his hand. I said I'm right here Joshua waiting on you, your going to be alright believe it with me.

TRANSFORMATION

One of the staff said you're a good mom! I looked at her and said I wish he would tell me that, I'd do anything to here his voice right now. She smiled as I had to say by, I'll see you in a little bit as he was rolled back. I walked away holding my tears back and then I was asked if I was going to be alright? I responded as long as he is I would be.

I'm not sure how long I was gone; I went back to reunite with family and wait. It would be at least 2 hours before we would be able to see him. We decided to take a small break; I hurried what if they got done early as I paced back and forth nervously.

I had many available to help me yet I felt they couldn't possibly understand and I was having a problem with trust again.

I wasn't ready to open up with anyone. And I knew that if I broke down they would to.

I had to keep my self together for this was a test for me as it was for Joshua to finish with what God has asked of us.

The side doors flew open any minute Joshua's surgeon would come out; I scrambled to remember which one it was and then there he was I approached him eager to hear and listen every word he had to say. He stated the initial plan was to go in and flush the incision and place a pin in where the elbow bent.

However the ex-rays showed he wouldn't need a pin in, what he had thought was a bone that chipped away was really debris from the scene and the area wasn't large enough to do anything other than flush and clean.

Joshua had reached his growing peak so it wouldn't hurt anything. I was so relieved and Thankful God was showing us that he was working with him and was mending and repairing every inch of him inside out. Joshua's incision was closed and he was sent back to his room for recovery.

All of us were eager to go see him and connect with him. I was the first one to have a few minutes with him and to let him know how proud of him I was and I thanked him again.

I loved him so much and that no matter what we were going to see this through.

I had to get the others they had to see he was stable and made it through too.

God was moving through the hearts of each one of us individually.

As everyone had visited I stepped out and as I did Joshua's doctor had asked if she could speak with me for a moment privately.

Her office was just a few steps away I agreed. I listen to her tell me she had only seen a miracle take place like Joshua's one other time in 25 years of practice. As she told me about a young college boy coming home for spring-break, he was hit by a drunk driver and they said he was killed on impact.

They contacted this boy's mother and she said keep him alive until she could get there, not to give up on him, the staff had thought maybe she didn't realize what they had just told her and shared her sympathy. But upon her request they kept him on life support until she arrived.

As the mother walked in being greeted by staff wanting to see and pray for her boy as time would allow. They took her back and immediately she walked towards him holding a tattered Bible in her hand believing in her son's recovery and as she seen he lay immediately dropping to her knees pleading for God's mercies and asking him not to take her boy away.

She opened up her Bible and began to read and believed in Gods promise because she had been living for him. Within minutes her boy opened his eyes and started responding and 2 days later was sent home. Wow!

Joshua's doctor didn't have to tell me that, I'm so glad she did. As I looked into her eyes them filling with tears as mine did. She had compassion and wanted to encourage me. She said she shared that with me because Joshua's case had been more traumatic than that one, but when she heard that I had prayed at the scene and came to the hospital having the same request that that mother did she was immediately reminded and had to let me. She knew the power of prayer and had the faith and belief too. Everyone had given up except for the mother, she knew and seen that I hadn't given up on Joshua.

This was a conformation for me in what God was doing for all of us, and to continue believing he would take care of us.

I had a large lump in my throat however when I was asked if I had any special request I said I would like some music therapy, I heard it was very helpful in situations like this.

She agreed and said she would have someone come see me and provide this for us.

I asked if I could return to see Joshua I didn't like being away from him. She said if you need anything just let me know, I agreed.

I shared the news with family and friends wanting to encourage them as everyone smiled with delight to hear the news

I didn't want anyone saying or acting as if God wasn't doing enough because God had already given us so much and they knew.

PROTECTION

A Legacy of Faith in 55 Days

Everyone smiling and having feelings of joy as Jan the music therapist came in. I felt it necessary to keep music playing it was symphony in the beginning but we would soon be given a Christian CD that we would play throughout our entire stay. I listened carefully to every word finding it was helping me to heal more than anything. As I was able to stay and watch Joshua it strengthened me even though I felt weak.

All of us were given the opportunity to view his ex-rays shown; they were displayed as you entered his room. It was amazing to see how rapidly all of his tests were changing even though we hadn't been there very long.

Everyone had faith as Hebrew 11:1 (KJV) Now faith is the substance of things hoped for, the evidence of things not seen.

Many surgeons were on standby waiting for more trauma to take place with Joshua, his first 72 hours would be the most critical time. If he makes it some would say.

Man couldn't take credit for what God was doing and had already done. I would say Joshua was doing great and that we would be over comers of all of this you'll see regardless of what the circumstance was in front of me.

There were some focusing heavily on what the machines were reading and it seemed to be a distraction and this was the beginning. There were some who wanted the doctor's report and not the report of the Lord's. I didn't want anything negative to be discussed in Joshua's room regardless of whom maybe speaking. I desired everyone to think and speak positive for once for some this would be a real challenge.

I felt if Joshua or myself were encouraging or influencing others believing and trusting in God then we didn't need anyone turning around what God had done. It was very early in our recovery yet I believe it was necessary for me to request openly to the doctor's that Joshua's condition and medical records to be discussed with myself only.

To be over comers you can't allow negative conversation to have part of Gods healing! I wanted everyone to say and believe everything was going to be alright, like me.

I appeared to be bold with everyone visiting, and if one started to break down I would walk them out of his room. And I would say as his mom if I'm not allowed to cry in front of him then no one else can, I hope you understand.

Visiting hours were soon over and everyone was leaving. I was tired and wanted to get a few hours sleep, yet I found myself staying with him. In fear of what would happen if I left him. It was 6:00p.m. And I new staff would ask me to leave it would only be for 2 hours yet that seems like eternity when every second and minute is being accounted for.

This was a good time for me to shower and brush my teeth, I was really feeling down; I needed a little rejuvenation all of us do sometimes. I continually thanked God for what he was doing and had done for me. Remember Gods Love that will last you lifetime.

The clock said 8:00p.m. And I quickly returned to Joshua's room letting him know where I had been and what I had done. And that he was doing great!

Joshua seemed to be resting quite peacefully and I thought maybe I should go to my assigned room and sleep for a few hours to. Yet I found myself lingering around to make sure he was going to be alright, I enjoyed watching him breathe that was a good sign.

Every so often his machine would make a beep and I thought maybe he was sleeping to sound. I would say breathe Joshua breathe and his chest would go up and down every time I said it. The respiratory therapist came in and said that's not what was causing the machine to sound. Either the paper roll was about out or there wasn't enough moisture coming through the plastic tube he was alright and that was a relief he was breathing with consistency.

I stayed beside him until approximately 4:00 a.m. and then I said Joshua I'm going to my room to sleep for a few. Tomorrow will be another long day. I prayed with him and asked God for his safety and being so thankful for this time. I told him to continue to sleep, that I would be around the corner and not to do anything until I returned. As I left him to get some sleep Joshua seeming so at peace.

I was exhausted and as soon as I entered my sleeping room and I lay my head to rest, and said God there are so many that has request. Please Lord Comfort each family that is in distress as I tried to remember the names of those I had met. Lord please let me feel at rest and let him stay with me ok.

And then I fell asleep.

I awoke to noises outside of my room and wandered what time it was, I quickly scurried to find a clock and found it was almost 8:00a.m.

I was so upset with myself for being away from him that long I had only meant to be away for a short while. I couldn't wait to visit with him again.

The double-doors opened and I hurried back his nurse looked at me as I looked at her and asked, how did he do when I left his room last night? She said Joshua took a turn for the worse and it didn't look good.

My eyes began to fill with tears I felt so bad, she patted me on the back and said it's not your fault I moved to be with him as quickly as I could. I apologized to him and said I would never leave him again and I meant it.

PRAISE

I openly rebuked Satan for trying to destroy what God was doing. I was thankful God was keeping him for us and didn't allow the harm to over shadow him or take him.

At that moment I knew I wouldn't allow him to be by himself for more than 15 minutes at a time without having family or a friend be with him. Whether I needed a break or it was time to eat, or to have the ability to go down to the Chapel to pray. Joshua would have someone with him continually.

I shared the news with everyone when they had come to visit him and everyone took turns to stay and visit with him while he was in the Intensive Care Unit this was a big help and a relief. God was working to reassure and to instill our faith so we would continue to believe in him.

We were going into the 72 hour mark and the big news for the mourning was Joshua had his catheter removed. Joshua had a movement and it was tested for signs of blood in his urine and his bowels and the test came back negative and that was great news for us.

X-rays showed just one cracked rib and the drain tube for his left lung was planned to be removed before the afternoon. As time had past fast and Joshua had his tube removed, there weren't any complications each of us sharing the excitement. Even the bruising from his head to his chest was changing it was fading. This was great what a wonderful way to start off the day.

I believe that God was moving mightily. God knew that we were uptight that Joshua had a difficult night and filled us with good news all the day and the night.

There were many rumors flying in our small town but the one thing is for sure no one could deny that Joshua was a Miracle Child almost everyone had heard his story by now.

Joshua's body was changing greatly and all of us were witnessing the transformation including the doctor's and staff.

Joshua's dad walked in holding a music box the tune it played was "Amazing Grace" it wasn't coincidence. He didn't know that I had requested music like this. I thanked him and said you know that I sang to Joshua this song upon arriving at the hospital of day one. He didn't know that until now.

I've found that God's mercy is extended to anyone that reaches out to him through the words and hearing this "Amazing Grace" song. It wasn't meant just for Joshua it was to all of us.

Joshua's dad "Scott" was hurting over this too, God was moving and meeting the need to help both of us heal.

A Legacy of Faith in 55 Days

God was having his will and way from the very beginning it was amazing. I know that in our experience it has changed everything about me my priorities and definitely my way of living and thinking even with Joshua's dad. We had never been able to talk agreeably until now, something was definitely changing the situation and at the time neither one of us realized what it was. Christianity

I will always take a stand and believe in what God has done for us. No matter what, and know that he has our best interest at hand at all times even when were not seeing it the way he gives it.

And I pray that I will never act or be that foolishly as I did in times past to be corrected and changed daily. Amen

In times past my appearance was full of pride, arrogance, and the evil way and that is what God hates. And no matter how much money I had or the things that I bought I was never satisfied I had a continual void until now.

Jesus was showing me so much more than I had expected and I felt a genuine connection. The joy and peace that only God can give surpasses our comprehension and understanding.

Almost everyone in my family smoked cigarettes and when you were given the chance you would have to walk 3,000 square feet to have one. I hadn't been delivered from this habit yet, but as others would leave Joshua's room often to have one I wouldn't being the one to continually stay with him. It took a lot of time to get to the designated area and then I would hurry back and have that what if? In the back of my mind at all times!

I didn't want to hear what everyone had been doing before coming up; it was the least of what was going on in my mind. I wanted our conversation to be about Joshua at all times, and to lift one another up in this trying time.

I couldn't help but think of my brother's death in May 1994, he was only 24 years old and all of us grieved. The circle of unity that once was shared had now been broke and none of us turned to God for help. I'm sure Jesus grieved he was right there waiting to reach out to all of us. We separated among ourselves and became bitter on the inside, and lost without hope. If only we would have called out. Ecclesiastes 7:26 (KJV)

At the funeral we had a preacher come and tell us my brother had came to him about a week prior and asked if he would pray with him, he wanted to dedicate his life to the Lord and he happily accepted.

If we hadn't known this we wouldn't have been able to rejoice but we know without a doubt he made it to heaven. God gives you assurance when it's in his hands.

This preacher drove a distance because he knew this would leave a lasting impression with all of us to remember.

Jelana Hobbs

As it did with the way Jesus had moved with Joshua. It wasn't coincidence.

I hadn't shared with anyone my repentance or asking of forgiveness other than Joshua. I knew they wouldn't understand I felt they would say it was because of the circumstance. Were Joshua and I sharing the same feelings. Yes, I believe we did.

HOPE

Jelana Hobbs

I chose to remain silent and not say anything I knew what I was feeling was very real on the inside. My spirit was being renewed continually.

This was a great day and yet, I wanted more. I asked for a sign as I did before. This was a trying time and the way I had prayed, I expected things to turn around immediately how selfish we can be.

It doesn't always work that way, however if we just hold on Jesus will see it through we have to believe, patiently wait, and hold onto our request by faith.

Donna was one of the visitors and we had the opportunity to go downstairs/outside. My mom stayed with Joshua as we left to take a break. As we found a place to sit and I was looking around there were three birds on a wire line perching right in front of me. They were just feet away. I watched in amazement and then I told Donna Joshua was going to be alright.

She asked how I knew. I said when I asked for a sign, what did I see? She said three rabbits, as I agreed. The rabbits can't be here due to the traffic, but the birds can because they can fly away and she said your right. We hurriedly walked back not wanting to take a lot of time, yet that was given to me at the right time. Biblically signs and wonders are given continually.

I believe our God created everything, and I believe he can use his creations as little extra's to encourage and get through to us along our journeys.

He did in many illustrations throughout the Holy Bible and remembering everything is God given even super naturally.

God takes the time to show and teach each one of us so that we have a better understanding of how mysteriously he works and how great he really is. As scripture says he will never leave us or forsake us – whosoever will.

I know that all of us have angels that watch over and keep us I wander in this situation how many more was sent to stay and be with us?

Angels have the ability to do all kinds of wonderful things, the things that you wouldn't normally see. And not just once but however many times that is needed to prove God is listening and he loves and cares for you.

As it reads in Deuteronomy 7:22 And the Lord showed signs and wonders, great and sore...

God sends all of us signs, it's up to us to choose whether they are given by him. I hurried back to share the visual with the others.

A Legacy of Faith in 55 Days

I know that the Holy Spirit was guiding me that's why I was of a sound mind and able to carry on.

At all times being Thankful for every second, minute, and hour meant so much. And not just to me, but to all of us.

In the beginning I felt that God wouldn't use me for his work the way he was Joshua. But he was every step of the way I didn't realize it. Jesus intervention is truth and light and has given me life, to believe and trust in him with everything.

There had been many times previously that God had tried to get my attention and I disobeyed and turned away, thinking there wouldn't be a payday, and that I had plenty of time.

I know each one of us is dealt with individually and that there will be a greater price that some of us have to be willing to pay as I did.

I am nothing without him, God is my rock and my fortress my very present help in trouble.(Proverbs) And what he gives cannot be compared to anything given.

A continual joy and peace and the sword as his word how precious it is to have the ability to use it at all times.

Young or old all have the ability to receive. God gave me the right and acceptable words to speak to those who didn't believe as needed.

John 3:16 For God so loved the world, that he gave his only son, that whosoever believeth in him should not perish, but have everlasting life.

When our hearts are open and we speak the truth, with all sincerity he hears us even as a sinner. I had been given another chance to make things right.

Ever since I was a child, the seed of belief had been planted and a one time Christian had stayed with me.

I had been told as a child by a priest, evangelist, and missionary at different times that I had a high calling on my life. I didn't know my purpose or Gods plan for me then, but I do now. I wasn't committed then, but I am now!

This was the beginning of all of the signs that would be given.

We returned to share with others one of my signs that had been given, one by one how the birds flew right in front of me. If I'd reached out I could've probably touched one of them.

I reached over to hold Joshua's hand, I said "I feel better;" I missed you." it felt good to touch him; by feeling him I had energy and felt the warmth of love thru his hand.

As Joshua's mom he knew that I loved him and loved taking care of him but throughout his growing up years, I wasn't affectionate with him not in the way I was now.

I needed him; I needed to be with him continually, I loved him so much. I wanted to take care of him. I felt that as long as I encouraged and held onto him he wouldn't leave me, we would fight back and see this all of the way through. I wasn't taking any chances; he was my life I couldn't live without him and he knew that and God did too. Everything was in Gods timing and not mine.

I thanked him for being there for me and that he was having a great day.

Time had past and visiting hours were over, everyone hugging and kissing saying there good-byes. It felt good to share the load, being careful not to overload. It was close to 6:30p. m. Time for the staff and for me a little quiet time.

I had the opportunity to go back and shower, brush my teeth and take a 15 minute nap. It felt great, I was refreshed, and I didn't have a lot time after waiting for others that had been in line.

I had to hurry it would soon be time to go back again. I didn't want him to think that I left him.

I had made arrangements with Donna earlier for the mail coming to the house and give her my checkbook to pay the bills. This was not something that I needed to worry about and I didn't. She took over immediately and without any complications, what a relief.

Whatever I asked of her she would do willingly. I would soon have daily request and it didn't seem to bother her and not just in the beginning she's always been like that, very giving and never asking for anything.

I know and believe in my heart God will send people in your path to be beside you in every aspect, she was everyday. Whatever you need she would be right there with it, even if it took many hours to get it. She too was working for God and she didn't realize it.

I had a few minutes before I would be allowed to go back, I sat and waited as other parents had done the same thing. I had the opportunity to talk to a man who was a preacher and his son had flipped in a four-wheeler and he wasn't wearing a helmet and it landed on him causing a tumor, which had been surgically removed and had some complications and he was worried. Yet, we both knew and believed in God's mercies. As he asked what happened to Joshua I briefly explained our circumstance and how God had given me the opportunity to witness a miracle continually in the making.

A Legacy of Faith in 55 Days

The doors flew open and it was time to go back, he said he was glad that he had the opportunity to talk to me and then I asked if he would like to pray and he agreed 1Cor. l: 3, 4.

As we finished our prayer he asked where I worked. And I asked why do you ask? He said that I had been given a strong testimony but I didn't look the part. I smiled and said your right, what's in the past is past I am a new person now.

The Lords just starting to change everything about me, I know it will take some time. This isn't about me but how God used Joshua to get me to change priorities, it works and I'm happy.

He said when God is ready for you to do your part you'll know, it will hit you like a ton of bricks and it most definitely did.

I wouldn't be content until I finished what he had given.

As I walked back eagerly to be with Joshua it was almost 8:30 p.m. and as I entered there he lay so peacefully. I had picked up a study guide earlier that day while I was in the chapel to pray. I felt compelled to read I just wasn't sure where to begin. I told Joshua in giving my life back to the Lord; I wasn't sure where I was to begin.

As I opened up this little study guide and asked the Lord where or what would he like me to read? Please Lord, show me. I was then guided to a story and it had referred to Psalm 27:5KJV For in the time of trouble he shall hide me in his pavilion: in the secret of his tabernacle shall he hide me; he shall set me up upon a rock. I believed God had Joshua in the heavens and he was safe resting in the Almighty hands he was protected.

I would tell Joshua that he was with God, man could touch him but they couldn't hurt him.

Little did I realize that from the very beginning in given this wisdom and words it would sustain us through the end.

I had spoken unusually different and didn't comprehend the complete interpretation yet, God already knew. I know from others that the way I spoke amused them too.

The evening passed and everything went great, it was mourning and technicians came into take ex-rays. I always stayed with Joshua to insure him everything was alright. More than anything else I needed to be reassured to.

BELIEVE

A Legacy of Faith in 55 Days

It was day four, we were feeling confident, and we felt everything was going great. I would continue to tell everyone that I talked to, he's going to be alright because he's in Gods hands. And I know he truly was. Joshua needed extra rest today and many surgeons were still there on standby. Every second, minute, and hour spent was all part of God's wonderful plan. God really was having his will and his way.

Ex-rays showed that Joshua's collar-bone was broke and his right shoulder joint was out of place on day one, mysteriously day by day his collar bone went back together and his shoulder blade was back in place.

Although the doctors hadn't touched him, I give God all of the praise.

Many family and friends came to visit and be with us again, we were continually surrounded everyone being limited to visitation. Everyone continually being reminded how critical the situation and Joshua was allowed two visitors at a time, and no more than 10 minutes.

All of us had been praying for Joshua's recovery and return home.

There were many of Joshua's friends that had came up to visit with him, all of them having something to give and leave with him.

Joshua was loved so much by all of us and it was truly a heartfelt situation at all times.

Joshua's friends let me know that as soon as they heard what happened to him, there were many that ran to the nearest church, gathering around, on there knees, bowing down, and having prayer for him I was so touched. It was so moving to see the compassion and sincerity in there eyes, they too wanting him to be alright he meant so much to them. God was comforting and giving healing to all as he had me.

I was told that all of the churches in our community and surrounding counties were praying for us, and asking God for a healing and to renew our strength.

Our names were placed on the internet and we were being prayed for worldwide, there were many that I didn't know yet it meant so much.

To hear that through different voices was a relief; it let me know that I wasn't carrying the burden alone.

And that there was many that hadn't believed that now believed through all of this. This was great news and very uplifting.

God chose certain ones to come to the hospital to see Joshua and his recovery, they will always remember and know that a miracle had taken place with one, and they will hold it dear to there heart wherever they go.

I thanked Joshua's friends for coming up even though I didn't get to talk to any of them much. I could see in there eyes they too was hurting and needed encouragement.

It was truly inspirational to see all of our spirits lifting one another up throughout all of this. When I had quiet moments with Joshua I would tell him that he had some great friends and that I had underestimated him. I was sorry for doubting who he had picked for his friends.

I asked him to be patient and he would see a new me, I promised that I would try not to be so quisitive of everything that he said or did. That I believed in him.

It was Sunday and the weekend would soon be over. Everyone had gone and my emotions were starting to take over. I was sitting in Joshua's room with Joshua and I began to cry, Joshua began to move around in his bed, awakened by the sound. As I watched in amazement Joshua's legs and feet began to move up and down rapidly and his heartbeat began to race.

I said Joshua your not on your bicycle you've been in a slight accident calm down its going to be alright, something was happening.

Joshua's monitors started to sound and the nurses came in, his doctor following right behind them they administered a drug to calm him.

Joshua's experience was very traumatic; I had to tell him the extent of the accident. He had to hear it from me it would help him in his recovery.

They said he was here because of me. I wasn't allowed to show or express any emotion that would upset him. I wiped my eyes and nodded my head and agreed to do what was asked of me.

I took a deep breath, and said I will tell him, and his doctor stood right there until I did. From that moment on I spoke the truth to Joshua at all times! I believed that God was preparing me for what was to come, and that we would go through this together, I said whatever it takes I will do.

It was a moment of strength from one to another all for Joshua's sake.

I told him the accident was really bad and that he had been life-lined or flown by helicopter to the hospital and that he was in the critical care unit and that I had been with him from the beginning and I wasn't leaving. I hadn't shown any emotion because I didn't want him to be afraid.

Remembering the story about the mother who hadn't given up on her son and it was through prayer and strong crying that allowed her extra years. I believed that we were given that opportunity too. God showing us every second what he was doing.

A Legacy of Faith in 55 Days

I had to tune out all of the negativity if I was going to live and speak of all of the good. It was left for me to do, it wasn't by choice I had to do it. It was a vow made to be kept to the end and God would see to it that I did.

Joshua and I was given quiet time, oh how I cherished that time!

I had shared with him the plan was to extubate him in the mourning, and that it would allow him to talk and breathe again on his own. It would be a big day and he needed to get as much sleep as he could.

I always shared with Joshua the care plan that had been discussed for him all the way to the end.

I believe God already had Joshua in his hands; this time was very much needed and I remember seeing a glow around Joshua it stayed with him.

I was asked to leave for a short time, it was necessary. I was able to a lot in such a little time while others were with him to prep him for the evening hours.

In two hours I showered, laundry, brushed my teeth, read the Bible, went to the Chapel to pray, and walked outside to meditate. I had the ability to talk to others and witness the Lord's miracles that had taken place.

Time had past and it was time to go back, I would enter in Joshua's room happy to see him again and prepared to go through whatever was necessary to complete the next 24 hour stay. I prayed with him continually, compassing around his bed, I asked for him to be repaired from his head to his feet, every inch of him I pleaded.

As Joshua lay asleep, I felt it needed for me to sleep. For a little while if you can in a hospital room. As I walked a few steps away from him and pulling two chairs together to form a cot, I had tried to nestle but was very cold and restless. I went and asked for some extra blankets and immediately returned to his room. I prepared a place to rest my head and being very Thankful for God's presence, comfort, and healing it was amazing.

Night had came through without any complications, and I believe it was because God was showing his love and mercies. Joshua wouldn't leave me.

God worked through Joshua to get to all of us as he did his only son on Calvary, his name is Jesus Christ. We were to have hope and believe in him.

Family members came up to support us and encourage us as we planned and prepared for the extubation process. I was nervous and uptight; I felt that it was too soon. I couldn't understand why they were rushing the healing process; everything that Joshua had been through will take some time, and I did ask why?

All of us gathered together to pray around him as he was resting in God's hands.

There were many asked by staff to wait in the waiting room, I was allowed to stay outside of his room.

I knelt down on my knees and began to pray as they were in Joshua's room working on him.

There was some commotion and they hurriedly moved to give Joshua back what they tried to take, I was concerned. Minutes pass, yet it seems like hours when it's got a hold on you.

Joshua's doctor walked out and spoke with me on the side, and said he's not ready he will need more time. My eyes held back the tears that wanted to flow; I wanted to be with him and had asked to go.

As I walked in moving closely towards him, I said I'm sorry Joshua I'm really trying. I was limited to what I could say and do and felt like I couldn't protect him. I said I knew that you weren't ready they wouldn't listen to me I'm so proud of you.

Even though they had to reinsert the tube he had proved to them what he was capable of doing and how God was moving. The procedure would be attempted again but at a much later date. I said your ok and that's great.

I went to tell family and they came back to see him. All of us were hurting and prayed again that Joshua be protected and made whole, he already was we just didn't know.

I had prayed that whatever impurities Joshua had, that it would pass through me and it did. I wanted to feel what he was feeling and if something was bothering or hurting him then I could tell staff my concern. There were countless tests on Joshua and sharing the same experiences was truly amazing.

Joshua had blood in his urine, I did too when mine passed his did too. I had a hysterectomy so I knew it wasn't coincidence. God was up to something. On many different occasions whatever he had experienced I did too and this was just the beginning. Joshua's toes were in a curled position for two days with blisters on his feet, my toes did the same thing and I wasn't able to wear a shoe. It was the same foot, and after praying for Joshua's toes straightened mine did to. There were numerous tests given, even by therapist. And they never received the same result twice after each report no matter how hard they may have tried.(my, my). Joshua was miracle in the making everyday and to watch it was breath taking.

RECOVERY

There were traces of bruising on his face and arms, all of Joshua's bruising had gone by the fifth day; He looked great! To watch him was encouraging to each of us. Joshua visually was healing rapidly; it didn't mean that precautions weren't necessary. I believe Joshua still needed the same care of someone that had visually more injuries. It was difficult to convince those with a degree of what I thought he needed. In God's hands not man.

Joshua and I had a strong bond between one another; the love we shared for one another would make your heart melt. We had been through hardships together and I told him that I was going to need a lot of help in this situation.

I believe that super-naturally we was given the ability to communicate with one another and every prayer was answered according to God's will, it is up to each of us to seek his will and way.

Many of the doctors and nurses were in amazement watching Joshua's recovery. No one could take the credit for what God had done and was doing from the beginning to the end. God breathed life back into him.

Many of us are used in ways that are beyond our comprehension, God knows each of us and our weakness and strengths. As we grow in the Lord we will see the blessings after we have faced a problem, because it's how we react to the problem that will determine what we reap. It will determine if we truly have a continual joy and peace.

The clock read 3:00 a.m. on the sixth day and I decided to decorate Joshua's hospital room. I started to tape the cards that he had received on a glass window built into the wall.

Joshua started to move around in his bed and immediately he had my attention. He opened his eyes, and turned his head and looked to see what I was doing.

I looked at him eye to eye and smiled and said it's just me Joshua; I was decorating your room. I said I'm sorry Joshua I didn't mean to wake you. I was so happy to see him awake and do this, I said were going to be here for a little while and I wanted add some color to your room. I wanted you to see what your friends and family had left for you.

Joshua's numbers started to rise and his nurse came in to check on him, and seem surprised when she had seen me standing and decorating his room.

I apologized as I moved towards Joshua saying relax, relax in a softening voice and then I sang to him Amazing Grace. Joshua immediately fell asleep and the nurse left the room.

I was so thankful that God moves so quickly and that I wasn't asked to leave because I had interrupted his sleep.

I left everything lying and planned to finish in the mourning, not wanting to take another chance with it.

God is so patient it took repeating things over and over (a consistent repetition) to comprehend just a little of what had been given. As he teaches throughout scripture, when were in the beginning stages of the learning process we wont act the way its been given to us, it's only through repetition that we receive the full meaning and have understanding.

As the day progressed I had shared with my sister and brother-in-law that I was hungry and that I had wanted to grab a bite to eat. Many had thought that I had been eating since we had been there but I hadn't. I didn't want anyone to worry about me it was all about Joshua. Food does give your body strength and I was feeling weak. As we went to the cafeteria I had picked out the foods that Joshua liked to eat. I believed that God would allow the food that I had eaten to be received by Joshua for nourishment.

Our belief being intertwined!

As we walked back to Joshua's room, we stopped again in the Chapel to pray for him. I felt relieved and knew that one could never seek to much of him a comforter, a healer, and a carpenter just to name a few.

Upon returning to Joshua's room I was informed that one of the Ivies that Joshua had would be removed. It had been giving him potassium but they wanted him to have real food. I smiled and agreed to the procedure. Joshua was given a food tube that was inserted into his nose and go directly to the stomach for nourishment.

When one has a loved one being cared for by professionals and you're given the opportunity to see everything medically being removed day by day. And your loved one is doing great, daily it renews ones spirit and mind when you're a Christian and know that it's coming from God. This was another sign given that everything would be ok. Joshua's doctor had said he was in the clear and that was a relief as everyone was leaving.

It was getting late and everyone had said there good-byes and left. I knew it would soon be time for me to prepare myself for the evening hours.

As the evening progressed and I was asked to leave, it being part of the routine. I wanted to stay yet I knew they had things they had to do for him. I would leave after having prayer and say to him don't you do anything, I'll be back soon.

Many families started to look for me when I took a break, those that I had met throughout the hallways. I was asked consistently to come pray with them or for there loved ones. And I did willingly; I knew what had been done for me.

It was a constant reminder for me that there are families daily that are affected by a tragedy and that many of them don't have family or friends to encourage them. Some had said they had lost hope and were giving up, and didn't have the faith yet I was asked to pray. I had to help them in every possible way.

FEAR

A Legacy of Faith in 55 Days

It may have been a test for me, I knew in faith I wasn't lacking. I tried to have some quiet time, I found myself praying for others need when I was given peaceful time. I couldn't remember all the specifics but when I took them to God, he knew all of the details of each one.

Before I knew it, it was time to head back. I was trusting in God and everything was alright. We had a smooth evening and that's a relief when you've been on edge literally for almost a week.

This was day seven and family had been consistent on coming up, everyone was eager to hear the good reports of each day.

Some had started to twist the truth, I had made the devil made and he was going to use and do whatever it took to turn our victory into negativity.

I believe he can only have what you give him and I wasn't going to allow him to have anymore than he already took.

Joshua had a monitor placed above him that read many numbers. We had been given a good report daily a miracle in the making. Some should've reminded themselves of that continually until they believed in it.

Many started to watch the monitor more than watching or talking to Joshua. After I perceived what others were consistently doing I repositioned the monitor. No one would be able to see the machine unless it was the doctor or me, because I stood in front of it blocking the view. I didn't want to be a part of a conversation that was tearing down and not lifting up.

Don't focus on that screen look at what God had been doing, I would repeat.

Some of us have a higher calling than others because God knows how each one will react and handle a difficult situation. It was God, Joshua, and me

I believed in us three a circle of unity.

I found myself keeping distant; I wasn't going to be a part of any negative conversation or setting. I was dealing with enough and didn't need anymore interference.

I had Donna and Chris backing me, they understood and loved Joshua as I did. Not murmuring or complaining about anything, that was a big help to me.

This was a trying day, Joshua's doctor had asked if she could talk to me privately and I agreed. Donna stayed with Joshua until I could return. As I walked in her room she said you know Joshua wouldn't have been here if he hadn't been life-lined. I looked at her and was amazed at what she had said and the way she had said it, I said no that's not true. All of you had already given up on him and was preparing me for the worse when I walked through those doors. God gets the credit, you can't take credit for what he's done.

She said God had already given me one miracle, I shouldn't expect another. I shook my head, and said God doesn't limit us to how many miracles we can have. I asked are you done. She said yes, and I left her room.

I had tears welling up and I felt crushed inside, I took a trip downstairs and went outside.

I found a spot away from the other visitors and allowed myself to express the hurt I was feeling. A beautiful garden is where I lifted my hands towards the skies as I cried, I asked the Lord to please help me, I know you understand.

He knew what I would be facing today and he was there with me every step of the way nothing is hid from him.

God sent the angels down I was immediately strengthened, calmed and renewed in my spirit. I was warmed by the Sun and had energy flowing through me. I walked back to Joshua's room and accepting the challenges that I would have to face.

Family had asked what the doctor had said, and I briefly stated that Joshua had a long recovery ahead of him and ended the conversation. They had decided to take a break and that allowed me a few moments with him privately.

As family left the room I was as close to Joshua as I could, I said I love you Joshua, and I know that you love me. I sang to him and played some music for him as long as I was allowed to. I messaged and kissed his feet, I said I need you to get better for me o.k. I know that God is doing so much for us; he has been working on and healing me too.

As a nurse walked in and asked what I was doing, I said I cherish him and I'm just showing him how much more he means to me by kissing his feet. She smiled and didn't say anything as she exited the room.

I had met a lot of moms working in the Intensive Care Unit, I'm sure they would have done the same thing that I was doing if it was one of there children or would they?

I soon learned that not everyone has a connection with there child and not everyone will seek Jesus Christ intervention. It was a heartfelt experience and I was continually moved by it.
Jesus sustained us throughout our stay, I wouldn't have been able to say and do what I did without him.

John 14:18 – I will not leave you comfortless: I will come to you. Jesus was there for us through everything.

PURPOSE

Joshua had been my reason to live for the longest time what would I do without him? I couldn't allow myself to think on those terms, we had already been given so much.

I had just shared with Joshua's doctor were not limited on how many miracles we can have, as moments passing how was I really reacting after saying that?

I started talking myself into a good mood, not being moved by the circumstance.

Joshua continued to rest quite peacefully and was heavily medicated. However, Joshua responded to certain ones especially me and I believe that is how God wanted it to be.

I've never coped well with Joshua being sick or hurting anywhere, and after fourteen years I wasn't about to start now.

Everyone had returned from there break and most of us gathered around him and prayed again with him.

Sometimes the hours seemed so long, and at other times it went by so fast. I wasn't sure how long it would take, the length of our stay, I was mind set and willing to do whatever was asked.

The beginning stages of preparation, a journey with a life long acceptance.

I give God the praise and the glory forever more with joy.

I was glad that my mom had the opportunity to witness these marvelous works; it strengthened her faith and belief again as it had many.

During the day there is a lot of commotion, and for the most part Joshua was kept awake. Visiting hours were soon over and some had said they would come up the next day.

Of the evening hours it was time to rest, having minimal distractions. When you have to go around the clock it can become tiring, God gives you extra to stay with it.

As one waits for the mourning hours to come praying to have what will be needful throughout our stay.

You can be startled by the sounds of the heavy equipment moving around in the early mourning hours. I would tell Joshua what it was so the sound wouldn't scare him. I knew that they would soon come to take ex-rays of Joshua again.

Every time someone planned to work with him or came into his room I would tell him who they were and what they were doing.

I stayed and prayed with him letting him know that it was time, and I was then asked to leave. I reassured him that I was around the corner and I would return in 2 hours. To be good and not to do anything until I returned, It felt good smiling from ear to ear.

I lacked trust; I had to believe and lean into God's understanding and not men. We were going through this together, no one knew or loved Joshua the way I did, I thought.

I found that Gods love was stronger than mine. It was through Gods great love for each of us that carried us through the entirety of all circumstance.

Our entire experience was because God knew how many lives would be helped and changed throughout our ordeal. We had wonderful things happening with us daily. And God didn't change his mind about anything that he had given, he had given to all of us right the first time.

Joshua was doing great! Two hours had passed and I had the opportunity to return to his room. I was always eager to see him and talk with him to witness his response and encourage him.

Joshua had a normal breathing pattern, and he had the ability to move his feet and hand to the touch. As I sat with him his doctor had came in and asked Joshua to open his eyes and he did. I would say how pretty his green eyes were and how proud of him I was, he was doing so much oh I loved him.

Joshua's right eye seemed a bit lazy, his response was truly amazing. The doctor's had asked him to swallow and they weren't expecting him to be able to, but he did. And this had surprised me too.

God really was having his will and his way and God allowed us to be witnesses of this transfiguration.

Everything that Joshua was doing was Big News for me, I had taken our lives for granted for the longest time and God knew.

I never thought that I would be a parent that would have pray and ask for the things that we had been blessed with for fourteen years.

For the first time having genuine compassion and understanding for those moms and caregivers that never has known what it was like to have a perfect child.

Realizing that you're not seeking pity, but you need encouragement to help you and your child find a way to get through this?

Joshua was able to swallow and open his eyes; he moved his hands and his feet, he wasn't able to speak but in time he would. I was completely renewed within, with everything that had been asked of him and he was doing. I couldn't wait until visitation, I was eager to share with others the good news of what Joshua had been doing.

The doctor let me know they had planned to wean him off of two narcotics which were fentnyl and morphine. I knew that Joshua had been doing really well, but was it too soon? I was questioning there expertise, only time would tell.

I needed an explanation to understand the necessity, and they gave it to me.

I didn't like the drug fentnyl because it paralyzed him; Joshua could see, and hear what was around him, but couldn't physically react with this drug. It was difficult to watch him be restrained to any expression that he was trying to give.

Joshua was disoriented when he awoke and in varying instance he was frightened.

As his mom it saddened me to see Joshua move, he became quickly agitated and his heart would begin to race, he would become red in the face.

It was then that I wanted him to receive the medicine.

Although he had been fighting back with everything in him, everyday was difficult for him.

I prayed continually desiring to do whatever I could to comfort him,

I sang to him, held his had and caressed his face trying to calm him.

In moments he would calm and began to relax, but the situation was to critical to take any chances.

Joshua had restraints and was given fentnyl to keep him from hurting himself. It was impossible for him to have any mobility while being ministered fentnyl and morphine at the same time.

I had to remind myself that everything was in God's hands and that whatever we faced it would be of necessity. I had prayed that what I would see and go through wouldn't be shared with the others when it was difficult.

The seed of faith had been planted for many but they weren't ready to face the same challenges and obstacles that Joshua and I had to face.

When you continually seek God he will give you the answers to your questions so you will understand it.

I had said if I could trade him spots I would, the scripture would've been void if that had happened. I had an experience with the Lord as a young girl and as an adult I remember at times being strong in faith but Joshua wasn't or was he and I didn't know it. It was too early to tell it had to be God's way or no way. Joshua was ready but I wasn't.

They had said that if Joshua is on either narcotic for more than two weeks it will become an addiction for him. And that it would cause serious problems later on.

I reminded Joshua's doctor and nurse that any information in regards to Joshua's medical condition or records was to be discussed with me directly.

I had requested that from the very beginning, it wasn't necessary for them to give medical information to those that hadn't been a part of our daily living.

I didn't want any information taken out of text as it had been done in times past. Everyone had agreed upon my decision. After all I was Joshua's mom.

Upon receiving that information, I accepted the process that would be needed to start the weaned process. I asked for a quiet moment with Joshua and shared the news with him.

I said I know that you had been against drugs for the longest time, and I don't want you dependant on anything. Trust me on this I feel it's the right thing to do.

My mom was the first one to arrive; I greeted her with a smile. I was so excited to share with her the good news, of how well Joshua was doing. She was a witness in seeing his speedily recovery as she was with us in his room.

This was one of the best things that could've happened between my mom and me, for the first time she was there for me trying to share the load and understand how I was feeling.

In times past we had spent so much time arguing and apart from one another, we had a difficult time disagreeing agreeably.

I had built many years of resentment towards her for many hurtful things said and done throughout my childhood days, and young adult years. Often I had walked away hurt because she hadn't tried to understand what I was saying. You feel separated, and you feel like if you can't talk to your parents then no one else will understand either.

Every moment of each day I was learning to trust God. I was in the beginning stages, yet I knew that God had never left me, or disappointed me in anyway. I never felt alone I knew he was with me.

With my family it would take a little while longer and a lot of convincing for me to even want to open up or share with them like I had shared with God.

RESENTMENT

Everything you learn as a child at home whether its right or wrong will affect the way you are, and who you are as an adult.

My mom hadn't reacted towards me the way I thought a mother and child should be.

There had been many times that I really needed her and her comfort and cried out to her only to be turned away and feel abandoned.

I had been a rebellious child many times, I was right and everyone else was wrong I thought.

I hadn't ever been satisfied in my life until now; we were faced with a crisis some couldn't understand. God was there the entire time extending his hand.

I had used being younger as a child, sister, friend etc as an excuse to have things go my way or no way. If someone had offended me I wasn't going to be the one to apologize, why should I? They were the one that was in the wrong. I found the answer in scripture to correct my thought process Read I Corinthians 6: 5-7

I hoped I hadn't expressed that same pattern with Joshua as I had shared with my mom in the past.

God was moving and I knew it because all of those feelings of resentment that I had had for her was gone. I had been forgiven and I had to forgive and I did. I hadn't felt content or satisfied in my life, until now.

I had forgiven her but my feelings and expressions for a connection weren't readily available for me to give to her. God was working with me continuously; I had developed a personality and a lifestyle that I had lived for many years. I had a desire to change and conform but I wasn't where I needed to be over night. It is a continual and daily process that takes time.

Our experience was so inspiring, the way God was moving was incredible. It was his will and his way everyday and not ours to say.

I appreciated having my mom there; it gave me the opportunity to share a good report and to have a few moments away from Joshua. I had to work at building a relationship with her that I had never had. Trust and confidence were lacking but I was trying with all of my heart.

I enjoyed having the opportunity to be strengthened and renewed in my spirit daily.

It's important for every believer and Christian to have moments set aside to hear Gods instruction, to know when he wants to speak with you. In most instances God chooses to do it privately that way there's no interference or distractions.

When I took a break I always made it a point to stop in the Chapel to pray and to give Thanks for all of the extras that had been given for each hour and day. It also was teaching me to depend and trust in God completely and to seek him with everything. Isaiah 26:3(KJV) Thou wilt keep him in perfect peace whose mind is stayed upon thee: because he trusteth in thee.

God's timing is everything and I didn't stay away from Joshua for very long at any given time. I moved quickly in everything that I did and as soon as I finished praying I immediately returned to Joshua's room.

Moments seem like an eternity when you're placed in a position like I was. I couldn't and wouldn't take anything that had been given for granted, everything had meant so much.

This was the first time in my life that I had joy and I wanted to share it with everyone.

Some had even thought that I was in shock and that it hadn't hit me yet. What they couldn't comprehend was God had already stepped in and had both Joshua and I in the palm of his hands.

My mom had left to take a break and that gave Joshua and I a few minutes with one another again. I was so energized I know that he could hear the excitement in my voice as I moved close to him.

As I watch Joshua lying there and his numbers started to rise, I said its o.k. Joshua I'm here you're in God's hands your going to be alright.

I became nervous as I watched Joshua starting to move and what he was doing.

Joshua opened his eyes, lifted his head, arched his back, extended his arms, fisted his hands and his legs and feet was going up and down as he was in a riding motion.

I began to panic and I felt overwhelmed inside, I watched as his heart rate really started to rise and he was having a difficult time breathing, his monitors started to sound and I said Joshua you're not on you're bicycle anymore you've been hit and you're in the Intensive Care Unit at Methodist Hospital, we've been here one week now please Joshua don't do this.

Joshua please calm down, you're going to hurt yourself. I asked for help as Joshua lied there I felt so helpless. Joshua immediately started to calm and I felt relieved.

I never wanted to see another episode like this one; it was really hard on me. As the doctor's came in and seen how quickly Joshua had started to relax, I was singing to him Amazing Grace softly and I appeared relaxed and calm they had left without administering Fentnyl to him. I wanted to believe it was part of the weaning process.

WEAK

I didn't want him dependant on any medication, I wanted to see him off of this.

It had been less than 10 minutes and Joshua opened his eyes again, lifted his head, leaned over to the right of his bead, he grabbed the bed rail, lifted up his legs, moved them over the rail, and was trying to get out of his bed.

I screamed and yelled for the doctor to help him and I was trying to keep him from hurting his self without force and to keep him from exiting the bed, I was so scared. I didn't realize at the time what was really going on with him, and what he was trying to tell me, until now.

The doctor and the nurses came in and quickly administered fentnyl to him to paralyze him and morphine to calm him even more.

I couldn't help from cry this wasn't a good sign. I thought my knees would give out; it took everything in me to continue standing up. I was asked if I was alright, I said yes as long as he is and left it at that.

I couldn't help from ask God why? I believed Joshua was in Gods hands from the very beginning and I knew that no one could hurt him, he was protected. This is real because we could see and be with him.

As I prayed I immediately received an answer, it was a distinct bold voice that I understood and he said **this is the last thing that Joshua remembers which was riding his bike.**

It completely took me by surprise; I couldn't grasp the entire meaning.

All that we had been given Joshua was coming home with family and I wasn't he? I am so glad that I was given this experience and message; in the beginning because it has helped me in healing. It has kept me from being tormented and torn about the experiences that we would have to face together throughout our visit.

Time had past and Joshua was real relaxed, I liked seeing him sleep so peacefully. It was good for me, I wasn't sure how much he would remember but when the time was right I would share it with him.

I held the Upper Room in my hand (a pocket size Study Guide) continually whenever and wherever I went, it went with me.

I was being prepared to learn to carry a Bible and didn't realize it at the time. I hadn't read the Holy Bible in a long time; I was void of understanding of what the scripture read. It was through this little guide that would direct my path daily. It gave examples of people today facing tragedy and difficulty and then it gave scripture that you could compare to those who had faced the same thing in the Biblical days. And those who turned to God for help received victory and those who didn't failed. I loved sharing with Joshua daily these stories of glory. I didn't understand the full capacity of each, God seen that I was seeking and he was teaching me.

(KJV) Isaiah 57:15 For thus saith the high and lofty One that inhabiteth eternity, whose name is Holy; I dwell in the high and holy place with him also that is of a contrite and humble spirit, to revive the spirit of the humble, and to revive the spirit of the contrite ones.

When I was given this scripture I didn't understand what it meant.

God showed me through his great love healing and a preparation for what was to come.

I had a humble experience, I was brought to my knees before the Lord, it was through this experience that opened my eyes and caused me to hear and obey his voice for the first time in my life. And I understood why

God was with us and he seen everything, it was he who healed my wounds and broken heart. I appeared to be strong, on the inside I was hurting really bad no one knew but God.

I learned that God was creating in me a new person and that he had given me a knew heart to know him, that is why I continued to fight back and had no thought of Joshua and I giving up.

I had said that I was taking Joshua home the following Tuesday, I hadn't asked God what his plans were for us. And anyone that serves the Lord knows that we shouldn't say or do anything without seeking his will for it first.

James 4:15 (KJV) For that ye ought to say, If the Lord will, we shall live, and do this or that.

Several hours had past and each time Joshua was ministered medicine it was lessoned. I was relieved to see Joshua excepting the decrease in medication so well. It encouraged each one of us to hold on and to continue in God's wisdom and deliverance.

All of us had seen and believed that God had intervened with Joshua, and that he was truly a miracle in the making daily. We had been so selfish in our ways, yet God looked past that and gave back to us more than we could ask.

God had extended his mercy and compassion to each one of us, some may have not even known. There is nothing coincidence about what God does, and when you know him and trust him it's not luck, its God's way of showing his love.

I adored Joshua their wasn't anything that I wouldn't do for him. I loved him so much; he was my life for the longest time. I was willing to change everything;

PRIORITY

I've realized in this time of his recovery my willingness to change was for the Lord and not for Joshua; I was trying to prove myself worthy enough to receive God's healing for him. And to do what was asked of me because I had ran and failed from God in times past and I knew that he had enough.

This was my last chance all that you ask of me I will do, I said repeatedly.

Not realizing the sacrifice that would be made to leave a Legacy of Faith.

I found the scripture that backed what I had been feeling it's in (KJV) Matthew 10:37&38 – He that loveth father or mother more than me is not worthy of me: and he that loveth son or daughter more than me is not worthy of me.

God has to be your # 1 priority he won't take back seat with you, or compete for your fellowship and unity with him. It's a willful choice that each of us will make, but in choosing him he won't disappoint you or leave you when everyone else does.

(38) And he that taketh not his cross, and followeth after me, is not worthy of me.

No one is to be put before the Lord, no matter how close you are to them.

Everyone should be willing to offer there life for the example and sacrifice Jesus Christ did for each of us and he didn't even know us.

When you carefully read scripture in reference to his Crucifix, you should be filled with tears and sorrow it should be a heartfelt and humble experience and leave you feeling forever grateful and to know that you owe, you owe, you owe and what he done you should to if its asked of you.

As my mom had returned from break, I had shared with her what Joshua had just done and she was so excited. Maybe she hadn't grasped what I was seeking from her; a hug would've been nice.

I smiled back at her holding my tears back; I was so overwhelmed I had to go outside. She stayed with Joshua and as I was leaving, I heard her ask him to show Mamaw what he had just done for me. She hadn't seen what I had just seen, and this was the last thing that he needed to be doing. Didn't she realize how dangerous that could be for him? She was reacting as if she needed proof, God had already revealed his works to each of us what he had given was enough for all of us.

I knew that Joshua was at complete rest and that put me at ease as I was leaving. Please Lord protect and watch over him, I can't.

This was not the time or the place to confront issues of others behaviors, while Joshua was still in the Intensive Care Unit. I had planned on doing at a later time; I found that's not what the Lord allows. If someone has hurt you by word or action it doesn't affect them the way it does you, it's better to take to God and allow him to work it out for you.

I had learned from the very beginning to ignore others conversations and opinions, hurtful acts and deeds in receiving and expected end and victory in all of this.

God deserves the praise and the glory for everything, it was his intervention that gave to us exceedingly, abundantly, all that we could ask. It wasn't given by any woman or man.

I had said I trusted, but I was continually repeating my request just in case he hadn't heard me. I didn't want anything to go wrong, I was holding on!

Even if no one else could understand the three of us God, Joshua, and me could keep the prayer wheel going and seeing the faith with others growing strong.

I went to the Chapel to pray lifting my arms towards heaven, saying Lord God I will do anything that you ask of me, please Lord don't take him from me, I pleaded.

As I sat and cried trying to understand I had asked our Lord to mend and repair every inch of him. I had asked why I had to see what Joshua had just done, it hurt me so bad? I wasn't ready for that, I know that I've been bad but he shouldn't be the one that has to go through that.

I stayed and waited until I was showered with peace again. My burden was heavy and I didn't take anything lightly.

I thanked God for giving me comfort as I found myself pulling myself up from the floor. I left the Chapel and went outside for a few minutes and I was always looking for a sign.

I had asked the Lord to give me a sign, and it would be one that I would know and understand and he did.

I had sat quietly away from all of the others that surrounded the place waiting to hear the voice of the Lord.

As I sat and watched patiently there were three birds that came by and moved around about my feet. I was quiet and relieved because I knew that God had seen and heard me weeping and that he was right there with me.

I thanked the Lord repeatedly for what he had done and what he was doing. I proceeded to walk back happily ready to except our challenges because I knew we weren't going through anything alone.

HELP

As I was about to walk in the entrance doors, I felt extreme warmth from the sun. I looked to see what direction the sun was shining from because it was so inviting, I've never been good with directions so I couldn't tell you.

Upon entering the 8th Floor the sun blinded me as I was exiting from the elevator doors, I was excited yet I wondered why.

I believe that Gods word is light and in him is life as scripture reads.

And for me the sun is representation of Gods creation, and that no matter how dark things may appear if you trust in him he will give and show you his light continually and will never leave you, we will have light even in the darkest of our days.

Man has taken credit for most of Gods creations, but there are three things that they can't take credit for. The Sun, Moon, and the Stars all represent light were not able to reach out and touch either of them with our bare hands.

I felt continual protection and I knew that God was with us.

Upon entering Joshua's room, my mom let me know that Joshua had showed her. His last remembrance was the bicycle seen.

I looked at her and she smiled, for she wanted to see the things that I had seen. God had used Joshua to give her peace within, she to was holding onto him. I felt for her and didn't say anything.

I walked up to Joshua's head and leaned over and kissed him. I told him that I knew the angels were working on him inside out. We had to believe to get through this, Joshua's curtains had been closed but there were strong beams of sunlight that had entered his room. I walked over to the windows and opened the blinds. The sun was shining in so bright, I moved to the side to let the rays shine on him, while he lay in his bed.

I told Joshua that God was sending his energy through and that our Lord was healing every inch of him.

Some of the staff walked in and had questioned what I was doing. I told them that God was having his way, and that Joshua was feeling his presence. I wanted Joshua to know how beautiful he was and the shining light was I had to share it with him. The warmth of the light was a continual reminder of God's presence.

My mom sat quietly and didn't say anything; she couldn't comprehend what I was saying. I'm sure our actions baffled many. I know in her heart she was grieving and it wasn't just for Joshua it was for me too that's what mothers sometimes do.

I accepted everyone's feelings that they may have had, and believed any and all of the negativity would come to pass even with some of the staff. God had been so merciful and heard our prayer I couldn't explain in the depth that God was giving it to anyone, I don't think one can understand unless you had a super- natural experience like the one we had been given.

Lord God he is in your hands, I trust in you to take care of him I said. God was taking care of me to there is nothing that could've given me the continual peace as he did.

As the day progressed family and friends continued to come up and visit us. I always gave a good report, having a deep desire for everyone to continue to think and act positive wanting or asking of nothing more. Everyday I would let someone know Joshua's continual progress and what the plans were for his immediate recovery. I left out some of the information feeling it was necessary to leave them feeling positive and not negative. There were many children involved and I didn't want to be a stumbling block to any of them.

I was being watched closely by many and it didn't bother me. I knew that God was with Joshua and I and everything would be alright.

You have to have God no one would've able to endure what we did. I was truly praying and seeking everyday 24/7, whatever it takes. I had the desire and was given the perseverance and understanding daily.

Time went by so fast it was getting late and everyone started to leave, I had began learning the process of what Joshua's daily care routine had consisted of and didn't think to much of it at the time. I had been writing it in this blue notebook that had been given.

I soon had the opportunity to walk those that had visited downstairs as the staff had an appointed time to work with Joshua privately. Donna and Chris stayed with me as we went and found a place to sit and allow me to feed the birds.

I had made it a practice every mourning and evening to go out and feed the birds; I was reminded of two things (1) birds don't worry about the food their going to eat, God provides for everything. (2) That when you die you fly away and you don't have a care about anything. At the time my second thought I hadn't taken it to heart it couldn't have been about us we were on the road to recovery, weren't we?

I didn't share my thought at the time with Donna or Chris; I felt it was given to me privately. They had to leave and we said our goodbyes with knowing that I would see them again the following day.

I made it a point to see how long it would take for me to return to Joshua. In just seven minutes flat I was on the 8th Floor, it felt great to know how long it would take to get to him not wanting to be away to long.

PRAYER

A Legacy of Faith in 55 Days

As time allowed and I had the chance God was using me to help others heal. I went to visit with many children that were on our floor. Praying with parents, sisters, brothers, uncles, and other relatives for the recovery of there loved ones. I know that when you seek for others, God will meet your needs.

There were many who said they were amazed at the faith, courage, and strength that I had shown. I had simply said it wasn't me I'm not doing anything it is God that has taken hold of the situation, and I believe in him. I know that everything is going to be alright. It is he that makes me feel and act this way, the Holy Spirit that dwells inside of us he is with me in everything as many of us prayed.

I had met so many people throughout our stay; it was God's amazing grace that kept me standing and gave me the right words to say.

I had said I planned on taking Joshua home the following Tuesday, I did regret saying that I vowed not to do that again. I had to seek Gods will about everything it was a necessity. I had wanted so bad to walk out of those hospital doors with Joshua and turn and tell everyone to never underestimate God's healing hand. I can still look at everyone and say never underestimate God's healing hand.

As I had spoken numerous times and I had used my hands in conversation I didn't realize how much of a distraction they had become. I had been given a new set of eyes and realized that they were of the worldly nature; many people were starting to cut the topic of Joshua being the miracle boy to how many diamonds that I was wearing on my hands. And at the time I had extensive nail art that consisted of 14kt gold charms pierced thru each of my nails except for my thumbs. It hurt and made me mad how they could even think of making a conversation about my hands when Joshua (my baby) was struggling for life in the intensive care unit.

I later realized in reading God's scripture that people will not sympathize or care for you the way God cares. And that people will say and be critical even when you're faced with a difficult and trying situation. Even then God will carry you if you let him.

It didn't take me very many conversations like that to realize that I had to remove them and make a decision never to wear them again. I didn't want to bring any negative attention to myself or bring shame to the great I am.

I had been given a tremendous testimony but I hadn't had a complete transformation, but this was the beginning and I was willing.

I said the jewelry I wore didn't mean anything to me! It didn't seem to convince anyone on the other end. I had idolized diamonds and gold in the past, immediately I didn't have interest in them anymore. I no longer looked at how much they were worth because they won't help you in the day of wrath.

I had made a plan to remove them the following day when Donna and Chris had came to visit me. Replacement cost was estimated at $75,000.00. It was the first time in my life that it wasn't significant to me anymore.

There would be one that I would continue to wear, and not have the conviction as I had with the others. It's one that I still wear and it was given to me by my son Joshua.

There had been some discussion over this ring before Joshua ever bought it. Joshua had insisted on spending part of his birthday money on getting this ring for me and I disputed it with him against it. He was only 10 why would he want to spend his money on me? Joshua's eyes started to fill with tears and immediately my heart sank, I couldn't do that to him. I grabbed him and hugged him and said if that's what you want to do, I didn't realize it meant that much to you, I love you and I'm very sorry in hurting you.

He had already picked it out and needed me to consent to the cashier as I did; his smile was big as he gave it to me. I cried it was given with a pure heart and it meant so much. I hugged him again and said now you have to promise me that you won't spend anymore money on me, and he agreed.

I was as happy to receive it as he was to give it because he was showing me how much I meant to him. That he was always thinking of me.

I couldn't wait to take it to the jeweler's the following day to have it sized down to a 3. Joshua accompanied me, I asked Joshua if I could put a diamond in it and he smiled gleaming. I watched Joshua tell them that he had gotten it for me as they commended him on his thoughtfulness that was a great quality that Joshua had showed to many including me.

The jeweler said they would have it ready in three days; the hardest thing for me would be to patiently wait.

Three days past and I received the call to pick it up, as I picked it up and I immediately placed it on my finger.

Anxiously waiting to pick Joshua up from school to show him that I was wearing the ring he got me.

Joshua had seen that I was wearing the ring and said now when you look down at your hands you will know that one came from me.

I had started to cry and Joshua asked why? I said Joshua it is you that is in my heart you mean everything to me, I told him his ring was greater than the other ones and that was something he couldn't understand/ not in price keep in mind he's only 10.

MEMORIES

He smiled and hugged me I loved him so much and was so thankful to have him for a son. I never thought our lifetime together would be shortened of those kinds of memories. Parents and children remember what they've been given to one another for a special remembrance.

We had made it through another evening and everything appeared to be going quite smoothly.

We had to separate for a short time but this gave me the opportunity to write. I had taken notes previously to help me when I sat down to write in the journal.

I wrote everything that was taking place with Joshua; I listed the doctor's, nurses, and therapist names. I even started to write Joshua's care plan and jotted down those who appeared to be mishandling him. And I insisted on his medicine to be given with a consistency.

I had made my own record of Joshua's care plan and the many changes that were taking place daily. This kept everything in order and minimized the confusion with various staff and the shift change.

I wanted to help as much as I could and I felt that this might be a great solution. I wanted them to know how much Joshua meant to me and I wasn't leaving without him.

The staff had started to ask for my assistance in caring for Joshua's medical needs, I was excited. It was an answered prayer because I needed to feel like I was helping him and was willing to do anything that would help speed up his recovery.

I had began by slowly removing tape that was affixed to him, it held gauze in place for the many burns that he had received. Carefully removing each one not wanting to hurt him and at the same time feeling like I was having a difficult time breathing. I cleaned each one with sterile water and then I applied a Sulfadiazin cream. I then placed sterile pads and gauze back on and re-taped the area for him to help protect the area against any infection.

In my heart I was saying Lord if I'm willing to do all that you ask of me, Lord I'm not going to have to let go of him am I? Without receiving a response I believed in my heart that God wouldn't ask that of me, would he?

Look at how quickly he's recovering this is great news this is what you're doing Lord. God had made Joshua whole and was breathing life into him. I wouldn't openly say anything negative because I wasn't the one to take claim or be blamed for any negative situation.

Joshua was a continual reminder daily of God's great mercies and his love.

I believe that Joshua had been compassed with angels from the very beginning and that God was showing his great work to all of us.

The initial process to complete everything in the chart, which including bathing and changing his sheets took approximately two hours. I didn't mind it helped to pass time. Joshua even were (TED hose) to help keep circulation in his legs and feet going.

Our 9th day at the hospital and many of Joshua's tubes and monitors had diminished. Joshua no longer had need of the many things that had been in his room in the beginning. I was so thankful it was God giving us a miracle in the making and everyone got to witness it.

Joshua seemed to be more agitated than he had been and I was concerned because he had a big day coming up again. I was nervous there were many things that I had felt that we were sharing together, and it wasn't up to me to share those experiences with anyone. I believe in my heart it was a test from God of trust in the very beginning that was needful to carry out what God had given us.

I knew that our love was intertwined and that Joshua wouldn't hurt me by leaving me, I needed him, and when God is moving it's in his time and not man's to say when.

I told Joshua that I had planned on taking a break and that I was going to the Chapel to pray, to be good and not to do anything until I got back.

I had to continually and fervently pray whether I was in the Chapel or standing in the hallways. It was very needful to get rid of the fear and anxiousness, and to have the calm that God had given and been so good to us to keep in remembrance.

As I had entered the Chapel to pray and I knelt down on my knees, I looked at this stained glass again it reminded me that our situation was out of my hands, and that I would have to completely trust in God to receive an expected end.

I thanked our Lord daily for being so good to us and we hadn't had to face the struggles of other families had faced; it wasn't the right timing yet.

I prayed aloud and said Lord you gave him to me and now I'm giving him back to you.

I know that you're taking really good care of him for me, I wouldn't give him to anyone else but you, I know that you know how much I love him.

I know that everything is going to be alright, right?

I had streams of tears rolling down I hadn't thought about giving him back, but I knew Joshua wouldn't have been with us 9 days later if God hadn't have breathed life back into him on the first day.

GUIDANCE

A Legacy of Faith in 55 Days

It was God that was taking care of Joshua; it wasn't I or anyone else that could take that credit at the hospital. God allowed us to be partakers of his plan, but it wasn't for anyone of us to take credit for what he'd done and I made sure that none of us did.

The Holy Spirit was continually guiding and directing my footsteps in every way. I had planned to stick it out no matter what the circumstance, or who I would have to stand up against.

Always being thankful for what God had done and what he was continuing to do. Although I was a beginner in the Lord, all of those things that I had been taught when I had lived with my Grandmother as a young girl were being renewed in my spirit again.

It hadn't been taught in vain and the word of the Lord wasn't void or without understanding. All of my teachings was coming back to me so openly and vividly.

As I ended my prayer and felt God's love compass me, I felt I was ready to go back and face anything. I reminded myself that I was nothing without God and he needed to be my everything, and not when it was convenient but he had to be my priority for the rest of my days.

I had left the Chapel to return to Joshua's room and I had seen the Emergency Room doctor that had made heavy decisions on our first day. This doctor had gave up on him and had instructed others to prepare me to say good-bye to Joshua.

I had walked to catch up with him and share our glorious news, when he realized who I was he speedily walked across the floors. I knew that I wouldn't be able to talk to him face to face because he was trying to avoid any confrontation; he was approaching the elevator doors, walking in a fast pace.

I addressed him with a loud voice and said have you heard the news? He looked at me and turned away, I proceeded to walk faster and I became louder and he stopped and stood he was approximately 50 to 75 feet away. I said Joshua is doing great he's in the Intensive Care Unit on the 8th Floor you should go see him if you have the chance and I smiled as I walked away.

He turned away not saying anything, and I didn't think he understood what I was saying. He may have even thought I would be mad at him for making that kind of judgment call, but God was in it and that changed it all.

I wanted to prove to him that God's not dead, he's still alive and he hears our pleas and is so merciful to intervene when needed. Maybe this doctor needed a good report from the Lord, maybe he had been programmed to see so much trauma and negativity that he had a hard time thinking positive.

I had stayed away a little longer in hopes that Joshua would calm and get plenty of rest that was needed for him the following day.

I couldn't wait to hurry back to Joshua and share the news with him; after all he was a miracle in the making daily. I was so grateful to have this extra time. As I entered his room Joshua had a continual glow and was resting peacefully, like he had an angel lying there with him and that is what I was witnessing. I had asked others if they could see anything different about him, but no one else could see what I was seeing.

I didn't say too much I know that it was a gift given and it was one of God's little extras. I was appreciative of everything that had been given.

As the evening progressed, I sat back quietly in a chair allowing him the much needed rest. It was so loud and he needed no distractions for the following day. I had asked the staff nurse if I could close the double-doors to his room, to keep the sounds at a minimal coming in his room. She agreed, and I closed them but allowed enough room for anyone to come in and out of his room without moving the double-glass doors back and forth.

It was hard for me not to touch him to show him continual affection, but I was told by his nurse Stephanie that it was a necessity to minimize the touching because he had been so agitated. I needed him to know that I was right there with him but I didn't want to do anything that would cause a set-back for him. I patiently waited, and watched in the corner as the mourning hours came and was so excited that Joshua was doing so well.

The extent of his injuries would never be known. It wasn't meant for any of us to know. God's way is best in everything!

Joshua's body had endured a great deal of trauma, but God had kept it all in tact and extended his life span regardless of the circumstance.

The plan was to extubate Joshua again, Joshua's doctor had discussed other options if in this attempt they didn't succeed. Deep within I felt confident and was ready for them to proceed as planned. I asked for a moment with Joshua as I prayed for his immediate recovery and asked for this to be a permanent solution, that I couldn't handle any experimenting with his condition.

In my heart I knew that it was right and I told Joshua I would be right outside of his room praying for him, until they finished with the procedure.

FAITH

There were many that had entered his room, and I knelt right outside continually praying to give us victory in this. Within ten minutes they were done and Joshua was breathing on his own, without the assistance of oxygen or a breathing machine. Joshua's doctor came out and said that she was impressed and I was told that she doesn't say that aloud to anyone, I was so ecstatic. I couldn't wait to see him as I pulled myself up from the floor; I had prayed consistently willing to do whatever it takes. I was so excited, another answered prayer. I eagerly entered and went towards Joshua's head, I gave him a peck and said you're doing great and I give God the praise in a very calming voice. I didn't want Joshua to loose his breath from me showing too much excitement. I love you so much and I'm so proud of you I exclaimed.

Never underestimate what God can do when you truly put all of your worries and doubts in his hands.

I was sharing the joy with everyone in the room many of the staff stayed around a few more minutes to make sure he was safe before leaving him. I had told Joshua I was going to get family they had been patiently waiting to hear the news in the waiting room.

I hurried to get them and shared with them his success, but I had also shared with them the importance of remaining calm when they seen him because he would feel and express what they were feeling.

I didn't want Joshua to get too excited for fear of him loosing his breath. My faith in God to sustain him showed little, but God showed each of us his mighty power and kept our testimony firm. Not just in his word but with his presentation that he gave us.

All of it was God given, what a glory to witness every event.

As many of the family had gone back to see him all of us expressing our gratitude and taking a moment to give thanks and to give praise for what God was doing.

Everyone had felt comfortable with Joshua's speedily recovery and some went to take a break Donna and Chris had stayed with us. There were very

I heard the Lord's voice say show me your willingness to change! I asked how I can. Immediately I was instructed to remove my jewelry and I knew now was the time to remove all that I could; I had said I would and I did.

I placed all of my rings and bracelets in cellophane baggy and handed it to my sister Donna to take home and put away. I still wore several necklaces without conviction, and because no one could see them behind my shirt. At the time I had felt confident in doing what had been asked. I hadn't given it all but eventually I would in God's timing.

I felt relieved knowing that I wouldn't be distracting from the testimony that God had given.

I'm sure it was a shock to them and family, even to Joshua because no one had ever seen me go without it. It wasn't a temporary decision it was permanently based, I had a life changing experience and nothing said could take that away from me.

The day had past and it was soon time to leave Joshua for a couple of hours with staff. As I left I would always caress his hand, kiss his head, pray with him and say don't do anything until I got back. He meant so much to me, I was there for him and I believe he knew that. He was already working to full-fill God's plan and I didn't know the extent of it at the time.

I know that God had seen the sincerity with me for the first time in my life, and I was willing to say and do whatever it takes to win favor and delight in his eyes.

I continued to witness and walk by faith feeling strengthened every moment of each day. Expressing my tears, and showing my fear to the Lord only. A desire to lift up others was helping me heal.

There were so many that had specific request, each with great needs. I couldn't understand why so many were coming to me, could they see God's compassion in me, and did they see his light in me and feel confident to confide in me?

I believe everything happens for a reason and although I was a newborn babe in Christ, I was told that there was something about me.

I had requested specifically for a certain preacher to come up, one in whom I believed and trusted. Joshua and I had frequented his church many times in the past.

There were miracles that had taken place in our family that we had witnessed and knew that he was a man of God and that at this church is where we belonged and felt at home.

I knew that it was very needful to call upon others that no one could carry a burden like this alone. I had been waiting patiently everyday for his visitation.

I knew that if this preacher had gotten this request he and his wife would've come up with others and would've helped strengthen us.

This was one request that had not been met, and later I would have the reasoning and the understanding behind it. Not by any man but by our Lord God that makes all of the difference.

Even though others may go the rest of there life not knowing, God showed me and that would sustain me from the beginning all the way to the end.

I was reading as much as I could, these little guides were very uplifting. And I could relate to a lot of the passages just by seeing there were others that had already faced what we were faced with.

BLESSED

A Legacy of Faith in 55 Days

It was soon time to head back to Joshua's room, visiting hours were over but parents were aloud to stay and visit with there child as long as they wanted.

I shared each story with Joshua thinking they were for him, not realizing how much they were helping me.

I was so blessed to have the opportunity to stay with him; I wasn't in a position like others that had other obligations with children at home or a job that limited you to how much time you were aloud off. That was enough to be thankful for, for the rest of my days on top of what God had already done for us.

I may have appeared strong but I was very weak the Lord had placed me in this plan of his and that's why we were given this extra time.

I told Joshua that I wasn't as strong as what he had thought I was, but I did believe and trust in God that he would get us through this. And I had remembered that we will never face more than what we can handle, and I'm glad that I received that in these early stages of his recovery.

I made sure that Joshua received everything that would keep consistent of his plan; I had even monitored how long he was on one side and to assist staff in repositioning him as needed to keep him comfortable.

I continued to attend to Joshua's wounds as needed as charted three times a day/ mourning, noon, and night. I moved as gently as a bird's wing not to hurt or agitate him. Joshua watched and seemed so content over every adjustment made. It was a blessing just to see his beautiful green eyes; we should never take anything for granted.

Joshua had blood work, respiratory treatments, and ex-rays done mourning, noon, and night. Joshua had physical therapy given twice daily. It didn't matter when they wanted to do a test it was given at any time upon the doctor's request. God had sustained Joshua throughout the entire ordeal and God gave me the ability to withstand as a young mother to watch her child go through all of this.

I hadn't even asked God what he wanted; it had been what we had wanted from the very beginning. I hadn't asked Joshua what he wanted; I felt that he would want what I wanted.

I loved watching Joshua sleep so peacefully, I would stay awake and dose off on occasion. I watched every move that Joshua made; anyone who entered the room would cause Joshua to move and start to sound. I would assure him that everything was alright and that I was right there with him.

Joshua had made it through another day, a time of celebration for starting day 10. Joshua was being weaned slowly off of the fentnyl and the morphine and he was doing great, it was critical that he not have either one for more than two weeks.

The nurses had came in and changed his sheets, while they were moving him from side to side Joshua said Owww. I was so excited to hear his voice, yet I wanted to know where he was hurting, he said it again. I asked again and looked at the nurse that was assisting him, I smiled and yet wanted to cry at the same time because I didn't know where he was hurting or what was bothering him then I couldn't help him. She said she would report it to his doctor as soon as she arrived.

This was a new thing that Joshua was doing; it was very encouraging to start out the day with hearing these words coming from him. All of Joshua's bruising on his arms and chest were completely gone, compared to other patients it should've taken weeks or months to see this much in his recovery happen so quickly it was amazing.

I sang to Joshua Amazing Grace and when I was lost for words I just hymned a song for him. There was very little equipment left in his room, something was being removed everyday.

There would be many that would come to visit us and it was great to share those extras that God had given to show his love that he had for us.

Joshua's therapist had come in to work with him and I had shared the oww expression that Joshua had made earlier. She thought that was great as she proceeded with the therapy. I watched Joshua very carefully; if Joshua moved or flinched I would ask her not to continue, or to be careful as she was doing it. Joshua made facial expressions from time to time, and that made me feel like maybe it was too much. If he appeared to become more agitated she would wrap it up, and wait for later to repeat the therapy.

The therapist had left and I soon exited to take a small break, Joshua was resting and I had quickly realized that when you go 24/7 it starts to ware on you just a little bit. I wasn't sure how long I was gone, because timing is different when your feeling drained. I found myself avoiding many having the need to have a little peace and tranquility. I took deep breaths as I sat outside loving the warmth of the sun shining down. I quickly hurried back to his room, even though I didn't feel like I was moving very fast.

As I entered Joshua's room his nurse came in and said while you were away he soiled his sheets, I asked if I could help her change them and she agreed. I had always taken care of Joshua and this allowed me to feel like I was contributing to something to help him in his recovery not just doctors and the medical staff to take care of him. I had seen that if you moved to quickly it would agitate him. I had nothing but time, I would stay with Joshua through everything.

I quickly realized that in changing those sheets, the small threads would catch in the crease of my nail tips, and when I would pull away it really hurt.

I never said anything because I wasn't about to pass up a golden opportunity, that is to still feel like Joshua's mom.

CHANGED

However, I made a mental note that as soon as we moved from the 8th Floor I would take the time to remove those nails from being a hindrance in any moving technique that would be needful to help Joshua.

Joshua and I had shared experiences daily at the same time, test showed we both had extra protein in our systems, I had pain and shortness of breath, Joshua showed variations in his breathing patterns and we had done it at the same time, I experienced a shooting sensation of pins and needles running through my left elbow Joshua's left elbow had previously had infection the same arm that they had planned to pin and every time you touched this arm Joshua would flinch. My throat was extremely irritated, and hurt really bad. In comparison Joshua's throat and mine had looked the same and I know that his caused him pain.

In doing this it gave me a sense/understanding of what he was feeling and it had been an answered prayer request that I had given. I wanted to know what he was feeling, little did I realize how much this would help me later, and it would keep me from making any selfish decisions for the future.

I believe that in having this experience it was teaching me to be specific with each prayer request that needed to be met and that we can have an experience with a heavenly and spiritual being as well as earthly people and things.

God knows what is needful to keep what he has given in continual remembrance and to keep it in truth.

There is nothing that could be added to or taken away from what he has given, not in the way God gave it.

I was told that once we got to the 6th Floor (Rehabilitation Unit) we would be out the door, I was so happy this gave me hope to press forward.

As family and friends had arrived and we shared the news, much family had consistently asked if I needed to rest or if I wanted a nap. The amazing thing was that I didn't feel sleepy or want to snooze.

I'm soon reminded of the biblical story in 1KINGS 19 (KJV). Elijah was chosen by God to prophecy before the people to prepare them before anything would happen. Elijah didn't want to be the one to do it, but God had chosen him to do it.

Elijah had a long journey ahead of him and was given a cake and a cruse of water twice in one night by an angel, but because it was heavenly sent it would be enough to last him in strength for forty days and forty nights. That was only because he believed in God, and had placed his trust in God.

A Legacy of Faith in 55 Days

I was given the same ability as a great prophet in the biblical days and provisions and preparation to carry it through. The increments of sleep that I had received was enough to keep me going, I didn't feel the need to have more sleep.

I had thus endured by believing and placing my trust in God to get us through. I was seeking God's way and not my way daily. We had a long journey ahead of us in our hospital visit; God knew the plan and had seen the complete picture before giving it to any of us. We hadn't seen the end because we hadn't been prepared to receive it the way God would give it.

I hadn't questioned my part in all of this, yet I had continually said whatever you ask I will do. Later, I would understand why the necessity of choosing me to help full-fill this legacy. All along thinking I'm not able to do it and I don't have the degree to back it, but when God's in it that's all you need, he will qualify you to do all that he's called you to do.

I was in tune with everything that Joshua had done, or was doing. Joshua had acquired his own body scent, and everywhere I was I could smell him.

Whether I was with him or away from him his scent was with me.

I enjoyed visiting with family and friends, yet it was tiring to entertain them and take care of Joshua at the same time. But, God was with me and it was he who strengthened me.

We were in the beginning stages; I had no idea how strategic his care plan would be or what it would involve.

It would be hard for anyone to understand the demands of a caregiver unless you've had the opportunity to do it consistently. Doing it for a few hours, days, or a week doesn't qualify you to know the true meaning of a caregiver.

Any experience however gives you a better understanding of those who are on call, to know what it's like to go for 48 plus hours with little or no sleep. And to know that there are many of those who have made it a career as a caregiver to make a difference in people's lives. To succeed it's not a temporary position.

Visiting hours would soon be over; everyone was given the same opportunity to visit and spend time with him. It was important for them to see him and it encouraged them. Everyone took turns to talk with and comfort him for me.

Many would go home and have the luxury of sitting back and relaxing.

We would still be going, at the hospital there is little or no rest throughout the day or night for anyone.

As time progressed and everyone had left, I had remained with Joshua.

SUPER NATURAL

The nurse had came in and asked if I would like to give him a sponge bath.

I had said yes, with excitement.

This was one more thing that I had been given the opportunity to do. I loved having the opportunity to do something for him; I needed to feel needed too.

I would talk to him softly about the day he had and how I knew that he was resting in God's hands. And that having this experience had changed everything; there were no more games to be played. I was committed in leaving a testimony, now it would be known as a Legacy.

Joshua opened his eyes and stared at me, it was hope and I was gleaming. I sang to him and caressed his head and said I know that you know how much I love you. I'm not a singer but I had shared with him tunes that I had felt were God given and heavenly sent. To see his heart beat that was giving us extra minutes.

It was so important to keep that unity and the circle of faith going, we had to it had been meant for us to do.

I had soon finished and remained in his room, sitting back in the corner watching his every move. I had the opportunity to write some of his activities keeping consistent with the daily routines. Remembering the names of those I had spoken with and all that Joshua had gone through and what he was doing.

I had written the activities that I had been included in with helping the attending staff. The notes were also helpful when the administration of his medications had changed. It didn't seem like a lot at first but as the days progressed I would learn to do what his nurses were doing.

I had learned to know the difference between a good vain and a bad vain to draw blood, that's how observant I was. God's ways are amazing.

I wanted to share the bed with him, to lie beside him and hold him but that wasn't possible without bothering him. I had requested that in my prayer, little did I realize that eventually God would grant me that prayer request too.

I told Joshua that I was taking a break and that I would return soon. I gave him a kiss and exited his room. I was always amazed at the number of people that I met and the numerous opportunities to witness what God was doing. We have the golden opportunity to witness for him daily it's what we chose to do.

I believe that I was strengthened by my own words that I was saying, it was helpful to others but it was what I was feeling within. I believe if you think positive you will receive positive results, and if you admit and accept negativity or defeat that's what you will receive.

Often times I would be faced in a circumstance that I didn't have the answer, but I would refer those to seek the Lord and he would be able to answer there questions.

No matter what we were faced with I would say all is well, I would ask many of whom said they were Christians and believers to pray for Joshua's recovery as everyone had continually.

Our situation was not something that I took lightly. It was important to

Stay consistent with prayer and the word this was something that I had done repetitively from the very beginning.

I often wondered what God was thinking when he chose me, today it still baffles me.

As much as I wanted to get Joshua home, I knew that it wasn't my choice to make and that I would have to wait on the Lord.

I had continuously played music either by a select CD or a music box with the melody of "Amazing Grace" both was helping me tremendously. I hymned and praised all night long sometimes just to stay awake.

The evening hours seemed so long and at times I wasn't sure if I could go on. However, God was there and strengthened my every move and I will forever be so grateful for what he did.

Joshua's surroundings were quiet for a little while and that's unusual for a hospital. Throughout the night Joshua would awake and I would say I see those pretty green eyes and I'm right here with you ok. I would hold his hand and ask him to squeeze, to reassure me that he knew that I was with him and he would. He would then go back to sleep.

I asked very little of him, but I was so thankful for all that he had done because it encouraged me to move forward with him. I believe in my heart Joshua knew his part in God's wonderful plan, and God used Joshua to get me to do mine.

Later I had shared with Joshua's nurse what he had done and she insisted that he do that with her, but he didn't. It didn't bother me whether he showed them what he could do or not, I knew that God had given him to us and he was a miracle regardless of what he did or didn't do for anyone.

Many individuals sometimes act as if what God does isn't enough, but in my mind I knew that what God had done was more than enough and would last a lifetime.

SIGNS AND WONDERS

We had the opportunity to start with Joshua's care an hour earlier, before I was asked to leave. This gave Joshua more time to sleep. I was with Joshua through every ex-ray and test given with the exception of two, and this had been done when they had seen that I had left the room.

I learned very quickly not to share everything with staff or family in what Joshua was doing because with staff they had seemed to become aggressive with him. And with family they were questioning God's abilities with him. It was too much so I kept these things to myself as God's extras to his children.

I had to learn the conditions for the necessary steps to complete what God had given. And I had to listen carefully for the voice that was sound and didn't cause any fear or confusion.

I had started to develop a routine that is how I had done things previously to keep consistent. Many people started to learn where I would be, or what I would be doing at various times throughout the day to find me.

I believe that I was given this time to understand and have compassion on those that has been faced with trauma and tragedy and to have the opportunity to help those who otherwise wouldn't be helped.

I had developed certain characteristics and a lifestyle throughout the years that was addressed immediately to get me to the next level spiritually. As scripture reads as the clay is in the potter's hand, so ye are in my hand. God had fragments to work with and knew that I was completely scarred and shattered and yet God took me in and recreated a newness and likeness of him.

I couldn't explain or describe what was going on inside, however it was very exciting. I was showered with God's love and was shown his grace, and in that I had faith. I was so thankful for everything that had been given then and now, I will forever give my praise and be faithful.

This was the first time in my life that I understood and realized that in a matter of a second, lives can change forever. Never, ever take anyone or anything for granted including your salvation. It is of great importance to remember forever.

As the day progressed everything was going great, Joshua had continued being weaned off of certain narcotics and was having success in doing it.

Joshua's physical therapist had come in and worked with him, Joshua did therapy according to the scheduled plan. We had busy mornings Joshua and I but he seemed to be taking them in stride. I would do everything that I could when I was asked to assist and I did. As the therapist left I reached down and kissed his feet, he didn't like it but he did move his foot a few times and that uplifted me seeing his response. Family and friends had came up to visit I enjoyed showing others what he was doing.

Joshua's days were very well planned, even with all of the continual changes.

I continually asked God to show me what he wanted me to do; I had to find favor with him to have peace of mind. And it would show others that what he was doing for me he would do for them if they would seek him.

There were many times that I had been hesitant to leave his room, but I had to believe and trust that nothing would happen and that he would be alright until I returned.

I reminded myself that this was in God's hands, and that we had said God have your will and your way everyday and he did.

I had to feel this deep down in my heart, or else it wouldn't have had such an impact as it has.

Joshua had showed more movement during the night than in the day, I believe that he was getting his days in nights mixed up in just a short time.

I knew when he moved and heard the slightest sound coming from him. I made sure Joshua was always clean, no matter how many times we would have to change the sheets.

Joshua was given a suppository to regulate him, he hadn't had a movement in three days and that had raised concern. Within a few hours Joshua had responded and I was relieved because this procedure had agitated him.

I hadn't questioned the doctors then, in time I would. I realized from that moment on how many series of test and procedures they would do to him.

I know that the medical staff couldn't understand what was going on with Joshua, and there were some that wanted to explore with him. Joshua was in God's hands and it was evident that he was in a spiritual realm of things and that I was included in.

The Upper Room at the time had been so uplifting, although I couldn't interpret the scripture fully as it stated it gave me a since of calm. The passage for the day had been in Psalm 27:5 – For in the time of trouble he shall hide me in his pavilion: in the secret of his tabernacle shall he hide me; he shall set me upon a rock. Knowing that Joshua was with God would sustain me through it all.

I believe in an instance when we face judgment we are used instantly to help others, as an angel to our lord Jesus Christ Joshua was willing and did what was asked and immediately placed to fill this task.

I believe as we have all given special request whether in secret or aloud Joshua prayed for me before the accident that is why God had intervened. Joshua wanted to see me saved, and that when I faced judgment day I too would be used as an angel like him and the many others.

Time had past as it seemed as it had, I felt we had been there longer. I knew we hadn't but when you go continuously without sleep your mind will sometimes go in a slow mode.

I had the opportunity to watch others as they visited, I was given the ability to read there feelings and see them with compassion. I knew what to ask as we prayed and I was specific with some of the request that they had been thinking before they had said anything to me and some had conformed that it was amazing. God's work is great.

My brother (Jimmy) had made it up to see Joshua and I. It had been hard on him because he had been the one to drive, the day of the accident and he had seen as much as I. I had the opportunity to talk with him and I could see the pain in his eyes, I told him Joshua was going to be alright. He sighed with relief and he needed to hear this from me, he was having a really hard time and had a great deal of resentment towards the driver and explained to me what she had did. I didn't want to hear it, yet I sat patiently waiting for him to finish so I could speak. And I told him it was an accident, she didn't see him and she didn't mean to, we have to forgive to have healing.

I told him that I believed the angels had came down, and that they had mended and repaired every inch of him. And all of us had the opportunity to witness it. We prayed together he needed help and healing to deal with this too.

I shared with everyone how well Joshua was doing, even though test showed that Joshua had pneumonia setting in. This was very common with patients staying at the hospital. I didn't look at it the way others did I felt that God would get us through it as he had. Therapy treatments had been increased and Joshua appeared to be overcoming another challenge that had been given. He had adjusted so well, in such a short time they would say that everything was fine that he was healed, again another blessing that God had given.

Visiting hours were over and everyone was leaving, all of us gathered around him praying continually for Joshua's recovery. None of us were letting up, I had begged Joshua previously not to give up and he hadn't.

Joshua had done all that was asked of him and then some. God knows who will complete the work that he has for them not making any excuses.

On numerous occasions Joshua would open his eyes and the numbers on his monitor would start to rise. I would immediately tell him that he was at the hospital, and that he had been involved in an accident that he was doing great and that all of us were very proud of him. He would instantly calm and the numbers on the monitor read normal again, if he had done anything different I would have gotten help immediately because I had remembered what he had done previously. I softly sang little tunes to him reassuring myself and him that everything was going to be o.k.

I felt that it was best for him to have as much sleep as he could, because I was told that when we moved from the 8th Floor he wouldn't be allowed to rest anymore until we got home. Others doesn't have the connection or compassion to a child the way that child's parent does.

I had communication with Joshua; I heard his voice even though his lips didn't move. God gave this as he had others in the Biblical days. There were other things that were going on; I knew it was God's will and his way and there would be an explanation for it later.

We had many experiences that I can't describe, I know it was real and it would stay with me for the rest of my life.

As Joshua lay seemingly rested in his bed, I would step out of his room for a few minutes and talk with the attending staff. I would step back in to see that Joshua's legs and feet would be in between the rails, and his feet would be touching the ground and he would be sleeping sound.

Throughout our stay he would do this many more times.

How did he do this, without making a sound? I would ask the staff to help me reposition him; trying to figure out what was going on with him. Did Joshua want to leave then and I hadn't understood it at the time?

I would tell Joshua not to rush in his recovery that soon enough we would both walk out those hospital doors and tell everyone to never underestimate what God can do. I had felt confident enough that it was all part of God's plan, although I couldn't comprehend or explain every situation that would take place with us.

Joshua was doing great, and I felt that we would be home soon. Joshua had gone 11 and ½ hours without morphine, and almost 24 hours without the fentnyl. Joshua had adjusted better than expected, but when God is in it you're able to do more than anyone can comprehend. God doesn't limit us; we limit ourselves in what we ask of him.

I made sure that I took breaks after everyone had finished working with him, not leaving him unattended with anyone. Before I'd leave I always ask if they had planned to do anything else with Joshua that would reassure me he would be left to rest comfortably until I returned.

I never knew when I would leave, I had done showers, eating, praying, and breaking all at random.

TRIAL

A Legacy of Faith in 55 Days

I believe that we were united unto God by a circle of continual faith. And I put all of my trust in God that he would work it out. I was learning to focus on our new life, with a new set of eyes and not considering the old.

I had to prepare and accept God's plan for both of our lives and seek through God's plan all of those questions of why. Through him and his love would give me peace with each answer.

Everyone that I had come across had heard about my boy Joshua. I loved telling them how God so graciously gave him back to us. I kept my visitation short not to be away from Joshua for very long, but I loved to encourage and pray for others as so many had done for us.

As I would leave many would say they would look for me the following day and I would nod my head yes as I walked away. I was happy and walking with a melody in my heart.

I hurriedly walked back to Joshua's room to enter and see him be agitated. I softly but quickly spoke to him letting him know everything was alright. He started to calm but little did I realize that this would be another trial that we would have to overcome. We would be tested to stand strong in what we believed in, just as Jesus was tested by his words in faith in the biblical days.

God would sustain us to see an expected end this being our 12th evening.

Joshua's nurse for the night had continually come in every few minutes and moved him and it started to agitate him. She then began to start administering morphine and fentnyl the drugs that we had been working to wean him off of.

I had questioned her and said I didn't think Joshua had need of these because he had been doing great without them and she said she wasn't going to take that chance. And if they wanted to take him off of these medicines, it wasn't going to be on her shift. I was irritated with her decision but was limited on what I could say or do at that time.

I told Joshua not to worry that he was about to be moved and they were trying to cause a set back to keep him on the 8th Floor, but God would have his way and I left it at that. I started to sing to him and at the same time it helped to calm me. It seemed like it took forever for mourning to come and by then you would never known with all of the doses that she had given him that they had even tried to wean him off of anything.

I would have to leave it in God's hands. Shifts were about to change and I was really upset.

I went to the Chapel to pray; I entered and fell to my knees I asked my Lord if I had done something wrong as my eyes rolled with tears.

Joshua was to be moved and they wouldn't do it if he had a setback I exclaimed I can't do this without him.

Please Lord show them that you've got your hand in this and on him.

I need him Lord, I love him I exclaimed. Moments later I began to calm and had remembered that I had previously read in Lamentations that God had chose Joshua to be a high priest and have the attention of both young and old to leave a testimony. I had read this to Joshua and I knew that with Joshua's story he had reached the heart of many both young and old, what did all of this mean?

God had given us the ability to withstand another evening, to take another day even with all of the tests. I left the Chapel and stepped outside the birds were singing and the sun was shining what a delight. This was the day that the Lord hath made; we will rejoice and be glad it is. If we were going to be moved off of the 8th Floor Joshua couldn't be given any more morphine or fentnyl from this day forward. As I walked back not realizing how blessed we had been our prayers had been answered once again.

The day had been going as seemingly planned, consistent with scheduling and the therapists; Joshua made no indications of needing any additional medication, keeping consistent with the weaning process. Joshua hadn't had any difficulty with the pharmaceutical changes truly a praise report giving God all of the glory. To have the opportunity to witness God's grace is amazing, this was day 14 and everything was going great.

Family and friends came to visit and be with us again; continually lifting us it was so encouraging. I shared with some what staff had done throughout the night, I was still mad at what they had done even though Joshua had adjusted to the changes just fine, because God was in it that's why.

Joshua's doctor had came in and checked to see if Joshua had a gag reflex and he did, that was a good sign indicating that he wouldn't have need of surgery to place a tracheotomy tube to help his airways or to swallow. That was great news enough for a celebration.

God had showed all of us that he was in charge; all of us knew how critical Joshua's accident had been, keeping in mind that on the first day many had said that they had done all that they could for him.

God had allowed us to hold onto Joshua with good memories still in place not allowing anyone to strip that away from us.

To remember Joshua as he was before the accident, and not what the accident had done to him. We have a choice to see the positive and not the negative.

As the day progressed I was informed that they didn't have room for Joshua on the 6th Floor, but there was room for him on the 7th Floor he would be there for a period of five days

A Legacy of Faith in 55 Days

and then he would be transported to the 6th Floor Rehabilitation Unit. They had planned the transfer of him and if they didn't move him soon he would have to stay another weekend in the Intensive Care Unit.

This was exciting, if I agreed they would make arrangements for the transfer immediately.

I had quickly made this decision without seeking the Lord once again and we would face more difficulty throughout our hospital stay not realizing it at the time.

It was getting late and Chris, Donna and I took a break, as we entered the elevator it took us to the ground floor, the doors opened and we looked at one another remembering that originally we had started from the ground floor and that should always stay in our minds.

This was a sign and it would help remind us what God had done for us. Time had past and we had headed back, I believed that we were praying in agreement and that God would intercede.

Upon our return I had inquired about the wait, there wasn't anyone that could transfer him other than his nurse and I at the time they were short staffed, the paperwork had just been signed and now we were able to move.

Tracey had suggested changing the bandage on Joshua's left elbow before the transfer. I had agreed to assist her. Joshua was a little agitated when you moved his arm. Tracey had a pair of surgical scissors to remove the old bandage and cut the tape in the process she nipped him with her scissors close to his incision and he started to bleed.

I started to cry and she apologized, she said he will be alright. I knew that her apology was sincere and that helped take away my tears.

As we finished and I lay his arm down to rest, I had observed his knick and it appeared to be deep. I prayed that God would take away his pain and comfort him.

From the moment she had done this, the wound never bleed, it looked clean at all times and no one including me had to attend to this wound at anytime.

It closed and was completely gone within the next two days, something that couldn't be explained. The only thing that remained was a faint mark of where it once was. I give all of the praise to our Lord Jesus Christ.

Joshua's nurse Tracey had asked if I would help transport Joshua and I said yes, We had been waiting and it was getting late this was an answered prayer and something they could go back and share with others who couldn't come up and make it.

During Joshua's visit he never required the extensive care that everyone else had from the staff, God overshadowed him every step of the way and was allowing myself to do things that normally I wouldn't have been able to do.

Everything was packed and ready to go and before you knew it we were on our way to the 7th Floor, Joshua's chart was missing but they said they would send it to us immediately and that we could go ahead and leave without it, that is something that one should never agree to do and I say that from our experience.

We were on our way as I looked at Donna and Chris sharing the same gleam in their eyes as I had in mine. I knew how much Joshua meant to Donna and Chris he was like a son to them. They had catered to Joshua as I did; she had babysat him four to five nights a week for me. I know that there wasn't anything that she wouldn't do for him. I trusted her with everything.

We had arrived to the 7th Floor and his new room, it being the first room on the left side. Joshua was 1st priority of each floor the entire time. This was amusing to me, I couldn't explain why.

We quickly maneuvered to accommodate him and we decorated Joshua's new room with all of his cards, letters, decorations, flowers and stuffed animals to give him the same environment that he had been used to. I had adjusted Joshua's thermostat to keep it cool, just like his previous room. I believed that this helped keep Joshua's temperature down.

After we seen that he was settled, we had decided to get a bite to eat. We had done everything in a quick and timely fashion to get back to Joshua as soon as possible. Joshua was our focus the entire time and I made sure that regardless of whom I was with even Donna, that we didn't stay away for very long.

I did everything in a hurry. And she never complained the way I did things, she showed love and patience all of the time.

We quickly finished eating and visiting she knew that I was ready to head back.

The day had been long, but we had made it and it was worth the wait.

She made the effort to come back and tell Joshua that she would be back the following day and that she was really proud of him, that what he had done was very encouraging to all of us.

EMOTION

She had planned to come up and spend an evening for the upcoming weekend, to help take care of him upon our release that was requested of her. I couldn't be the only one that knew how to do all of the procedures, in case something happened to me, there needed to be someone to help him. I was relieved that she was willing to do it; it took a tremendous burden off of me to know that I didn't have to do everything. I looked forward to our visits every night that we had had.

We hugged and said our good-byes and I knew that I would see her again the following night.

This had been a big day, Joshua had been transferred from the Intensive Care unit to the Maternity Unit and for the first time we had some privacy, this was great. Words cannot express how thankful I was.

I had planned on having a great evening, and then Joshua had become agitated and I realized he hadn't been given his medicines yet. I wouldn't get a shower until after he was calmed, I was learning patience and what it was like to wait upon others for the first time.

I looked at the time and went and informed the nurse, she told me she couldn't give him anything until they had received his chart. I asked how long that would take trying to be patient. She said, when they have someone from the 8th Floor to bring it down, they will minister medicine to him.

It was getting late and Joshua wasn't doing so great, I asked the Lord what I could do and in a firm voice I was told that I could go and get the chart, and without asking any of the attending staff that is exactly what I did, I retrieved the records and I quickly handed it to the nurse to help him.

Upon reading his charts they administered medicine to him and he soon began to calm. I was relieved and relaxed as he did, Joshua hadn't showed any extensive agitation until now and this wasn't something that I had planned on having to adjust to we had did everything in rhythm previously and I still expected to receive the same treatment that we had been given in the Intensive Care Unit.

It was almost 10:00p.m. I wanted to take a long shower but realized that I wouldn't have a lot of time. Joshua's respiratory therapists would be coming in soon, and Joshua didn't like some of them, and through his actions and the way they had done things I didn't like them either.

I understood what Joshua was feeling.

As his mom it was natural for me to want to protect him from anyone or anything that would be harmful.

A Legacy of Faith in 55 Days

I prepared for the later part of the evening, it was the first time that I would have the opportunity to shower in his room and I was close enough to him to here his every move. Joshua was still in a regular hospital bed and our first evening was going pretty smoothly.

I had stayed awake having a lot of adrenalin and adjusting to the quietness of our new environment.

I introduced myself to all of the new staff continually, there were so many. I wanted them to know that I was there for Joshua and would be for everything. And whatever changes that he would have, it was necessary for me to be included.

Mourning had come and I felt great, Joshua looked beautiful as always, my little angel. I took a break not realizing what this day would bring or how tiring it would be. I greeted those throughout the hallways making my way to the Chapel to pray, I would start out all of our days with prayer first and reading.

This was very helpful and needful for our healing both spiritually and physically.

I hurried back and as I entered to be with Joshua he had seemed so irritated, I couldn't understand this, I asked what had upset him. He hadn't been like this, what was happening?

I quickly moved to attend to him praying, caressing, singing, and repositioning his pillows to make him comfortable. I hit the nurse call button and I was in a panic state. My heart was racing this was really hard for me to see him this way.

Joshua's nurse had came in and I had asked her to help me, Joshua was continually moving his legs and he was so rigid that when he would hit the rails it was a hard hit, no one told me that he was going to do this.

Joshua was breathing rapidly and moving differently. I was afraid!

I didn't want Joshua to hurt himself and asked what I could do to protect his legs. We had placed many pillows around his bed to protect his knees from the hit, it was early in the mourning and we were going to go through this all day.

She told me Joshua was posturing or storming and I asked what is causing it, we have to help him. She said that Joshua had sustained a major head injury and that he should really be on the 6th Floor they are equipped to handling this situation. Every patient will go through this when they have experienced an enclosed head injury she said.

I said that Joshua hadn't done this once in the I.C.U. and we had been there two weeks, it has to be something different other than what she was saying. I didn't want to hear or see any negativity Lord I know you see us, please

Help us I said.

She had said Joshua would need a Vail bed and I asked her what that was, she said it was a special bed designed to help patients like Joshua. That it had a net to keep Joshua retained in his bed and that it had a special padding to keep the patients from hurting themselves, Joshua wouldn't need restraints with this.

I requested one right then; a request doesn't work that way. It's a process, first the doctor has to authorize it, then it has to be approved through the insurance company, and then you have to wait for availability.

I asked what time would the doctor be in and was told it would be later in the afternoon, I was nervous and said but he needs one now. I would have to wait like everyone else she said and walked away.

This was a lot for me I hadn't thought about any of this, God had done so much for us he wouldn't allow us to suffer to leave a testimony, would he?

After all, God had breathed life back in to him he wouldn't allow anything to be hurtful for Joshua or me would he?

I had a lot of questions and thinking very heavily. I tried praying and asked God to help us; I wanted everything to be his way and for him to give me understanding. I give it all to you Lord; I can't do this without you I said.

Please Lord calm him down for me, I simply said. Within minutes Joshua began to relax and watching the transformation was truly amazing. As Joshua calmed I did to.

The time had gone by so fast it was already mid-afternoon, we had a very active mourning. Joshua's doctor (Ms. C) had came in and we had brief conversation with one another, I was upset and I know that she could see the hurt in my eyes, she showed compassion and that was one of the things that I liked about her, I had need of that at the time. She agreed with me and said she would make the necessary arrangements for Joshua to have a Vail bed, I was so happy. She had also said that they would be changing his medicines to regulate him. I thanked her repeatedly as she was leaving. I had been confined in Joshua's room all mourning, I was afraid to leave him because I was afraid he would hurt himself, yet I needed some time too.

I told Joshua I had tried to wait for others to come up, but I really needed a break from him. Part of me felt like I couldn't breathe and I to needed to be strengthened especially after experiencing what we did.

I went and asked a nurse if she would come in stay with him for a few minutes so I could take a break and she did. I may not have shown the anxiety that I was feeling, deep down I felt it taking over.

A Legacy of Faith in 55 Days

I left knowing that I would soon return.

God had something in store for me as soon as I would walk outside the revolving hospital doors.

I had walked to enter the garden lifting my hands towards the heavens, asking the Lord to show me what he was doing for Joshua.

I really feel that God had showed me the restrictions of Joshua's blood flow to his brain and that he was replenishing and making the way for Joshua to continue. As he had with his heart, breathing, and many other things it had all been God given from the very beginning.

It was important to remember all of the healing that Joshua had already received and what had been given. I had to be showered with his grace, so I could give back what he had given me to others who had experienced the same heartache.

God already knew what lay ahead; I didn't being made of the flesh. I had trusted that I would have what I had asked of him and that was to bring Joshua home with me. God had our best interest at hand all of the time.

I had hurried back not wanting to stay away to long; I didn't want the nurse to think that I was taking advantage of the situation. I wasn't ready to face this again, but didn't think before entering that there would be another alternative.

As I entered Joshua's room there was Donna and Chris that was with him, they had greeted me with a smile. I was so relieved to see them, I started to cry and Donna asked why. I exclaimed how difficult our mourning had been, detail for detail in how Joshua had reacted.

I told her that had been the first time that I had left him since 6:00 a.m. that mourning. I was deeply hurt and moved the way I had seen Joshua do. She hugged me and said everything is going to be alright, this was a time that I felt helpless and wanted to close my eyes to reopen them wishing everything would be different. Donna was there for me comforting me and encouraging me that we would get through this, no matter how it looked. I found in myself to believe as she did, knowing that we would.

There was such a closeness that I had for Joshua it was needful to see and go through this experience with him. This would give me the strength and the ability to make decisions that affected us in the future.

We stood around Joshua's bed chatting for a little bit, and then Donna had asked Chris to stay with Joshua so we could go walk for a little bit. Chris agreed to stay talking to Joshua like he always had.

Donna and I walked rapidly to get to the hospital grounds, and I again expressed myself, it had been a lot to hold in. It really felt good to vent and to know that I could trust her with the way I was feeling. She prayed in agreement with me and I know that the Lord heard our request, and that it didn't go void in anything.

I was glad that we didn't have a lot of visitors today, it was Thursday. It was already evening and Donna and Chris waited for Joshua to move to his special bed before they left, I was so relieved when they moved Joshua into this Vail bed. I hadn't had any peace all day. It was a relief to know that he couldn't hurt himself, especially with the bed rails.

I knew that we would have a lot of visitors the following day with facing the weekend; Joshua was doing great in the Vail bed. We had to encourage each one that came up and that had seen and visited with Joshua no matter what.

God had answered our prayer; this was the first time that I had looked upon others with compassion and love as God had done with us. This was the first time that I wanted to make things right with those that I had felt enemies with in my past life. God had forgiven me now I would have to learn and ask for forgiveness of each of those that I had offended. I was in the conditioning process, and was willing. I loved what Jesus was doing; it wasn't just for me but for all of us who believe.

I loved having the opportunity to witness to anyone who would listen; God had done so much for us from the first day. Jesus is the only that can set you free, it is through his grace and love that will also determine what your present, and future will be.

I had done all that had been asked with the care plans for the evening, and as the evening progressed and Joshua seemed to be resting, it had been a long day and I planned to take an extra long shower.

I couldn't wait, that was something that I had taken for granted and never realized how thankful that I would be to have the opportunity to take a shower in privacy and with the basic amenities.

I found myself not taking as long as planned, for fear that if Joshua needed me that I wouldn't be there for him. As with everything I hurried once again.

I felt relaxed afterwards and I came out of the bathroom, to find Joshua moving around and I told him I hadn't left him that I was right there singing to calm him.

He started to relax again, and I felt confident that we were going to have a good night.

I had let Joshua know that I was there for him at all times; I didn't want him to give up but to hold on no matter what.

As Joshua's mom God knew what I had need of and gave it to me the way it was needed.

ENDURANCE

I hymned Amazing Grace and soon he was back to sleep. I didn't mind that he slept so much; I felt that what he had been through it was helpful for him to have consistent sleep.

Joshua had to wear a monitor in the evening. It would sound if anyone entered the room. The therapist came in Joshua started to move around and make sound. This assured me that he knew when someone else was in the room with him at all times and I didn't have to do or say anything.

The therapists and I had exchanged some words and they too had been convinced and were a witness to Joshua's recovery.

As he had planned to leave I simply said "one should never underestimate what God can do" he agreed and had said that he sees and hears of miracles taking place everyday. He had seen Joshua for himself and I didn't have to say anything to him to convince him.

I suppose it's not uncommon in a hospital to see miracles happen, it's really not uncommon anywhere when you believe to receive victory.

I felt so blessed and content to be given a second chance and all of these extras with him.

It was getting late it was around 12:45a.m. I had prayer with Joshua and began to feel content again as I had numerous times before.

I had always asked for Joshua's recovery and had asked to feel God's continual grace, and that we would have the ability and strength to handle each circumstance that we would face together.

I had thanked the Lord for a good night sleep as I thought both of us would receive.

I had been given a cot, and I made my bed and thought this is great I will catch up on my rest now that I'm able to sleep next to him.

I had spoke with Joshua's nurse Debbie and said if you need me, wake me and she agreed.

I was so tired and thought after this night I would be well rested and be able to face what would come next.

I gave Joshua a kiss and said good-night letting him know that I was a foot a way, sleeping in a cot. I had asked the Lord not to let me sleep through anything, that whatever he needed he would know that I was right there for him.

I had lain down and within approximately 25 minutes, I was awaked by his nurse it was 1:05 a.m.

A Legacy of Faith in 55 Days

She said that Joshua had pulled his food tube out from his nose and it had caused a nose bleed. I quickly arose to assist the nurse and him and spoke softly to calm him, he was so upset. There was a lot of blood on his sheets and he was again having difficult time breathing and continually saying oww. She immediately requested ex-rays to insure no fluid settled in his lungs.

I had to stay calm at all times or else I wouldn't have the opportunity to assist with anything.

I believe that the way I had moved and knowing how to move him that God was working through my hands to show me that he had been in it the entire time.

I had to focus on God's will and his plan or else I wouldn't be able to get through all of this.

I had fixed some bath water to clean him up, and as I turned him on his side, Joshua was still saying oww I had seen a metal plate in bedded in his hair, close to the scalp.

I said oh Joshua I see what is hurting you now, and grabbed some scissors and cut it out. They had forgotten to take it out; it had been part of the procedure when he had been first admitted to the Intensive Care Unit.

It had been in the back of his head for almost three weeks and no one knew.

Joshua's hair was really matted and prior to the accident he had been growing it out. Some had suggested shaving his head but I wouldn't even consider it. I had made a solution of warm water, conditioner, and baby oil applying it to his head with a wash cloth. I carefully used a large pick to comb his head and all of the tangles were easily removed

Joshua was Debbie's first difficult patient and she was having a hard time trying to assist him, she worked in pediatrics not in this. And she thanked me for knowing what to do.

We hadn't been off of the 8th Floor for very long but it seemed like a lot of things had started to go wrong.

Had Joshua been moved to soon? This is what we had asked for and prayed for, was it in God's timing or ours? I had felt guilty for hurrying Joshua's recovery process, as much as I wanted to be on the 6th Floor and then out the door. I didn't want Joshua to have to suffer for any of us.

Joshua and I had a genuine love for one another and this was a humbling experience for me to see him go through this, I felt like I couldn't do enough for him no matter how hard I tried.

I had to trust in the Lord, and believe everything was going to be alright. I believe Joshua knew what was going on and the reason that we had to go through this.

Debbie had started an Ivie for Joshua and I believed that maybe Joshua had this reaction to encourage me that soon he would be eating on his own. God knew what was happening. Shortly afterwards he was quieted for the evening but remained awake looking at me. I was so blessed to have this time with him.

I had moved quickly to comfort and accommodate him, time had past and soon he was resting comfortably again. I was shook up after seeing so much blood come from him, was it just a nose bleed? This was something that I would take to the Lord, I had to remember the sign that he had given me previously. How did all of this tie into what we had just experienced?

Everything had happened so fast, I couldn't comprehend everything that was going on all at once.

By the time I felt relaxed and looked at the clock it was around 4:00 a.m. and our day was starting all over again.

The respiratory therapist had came in to give Joshua a breathing treatment, I had told him that Joshua had a nose bleed earlier and asked for him to be easy with him.

I let him know that Joshua's breathing treatments had been given differently and that Joshua liked the new way better, it was easier for him.

I had asked the therapist to accommodate Joshua with the new technique but he refused, and as Joshua was given this treatment he showed a great deal of distress and discomfort, his face started to turn blue.

Joshua wasn't breathing the way that he had been this was too much for him.

I asked the therapist if he had any children. And he said two boys. I asked him what he would do if one of his boys was admitted in the hospital, and he had to undergo breathing treatments. What if his boy was resisting the way Joshua was and he knew that there was another alternative and the therapist refused to do it? Again I asked him what he would do.

He quickly finished and didn't say anything.

I was doing everything that I could to hold my tears back I told him to remember what we were experiencing could happen to anyone.

Joshua had another nose bleed before he left and he simply said that it was due to the resistance that Joshua did during his treatment

SUFFERING

He gathered his things and left the room. I felt overwhelmed inside I couldn't tell Joshua everything was alright when I was physically crumbling to see this done. I felt like a failure, I continually apologized for what had been done. I cried and said to him if I knew what I could have done to prevent this from happening I would've, you know that don't you?

Joshua acted like he was choking and I immediately asked God to protect and watch over us to please give us a breakthrough, and to calm me for him.

I also asked that he would send us staff that would work with us and that they would have a heart and show compassion to us each day that we would remain at the hospital.

I needed him to get better, please Lord let him come through this no matter what and he did.

Tests were given each mourning; most of them were earlier than later it just depend on who was working.

The shifts would be changing soon; we would be working with other nurses in pediatrics.

Ex-rays would show if Joshua's food tube re-insertion had been placed far enough down his throat. This was his way of nourishment and was hope for all of us to see him have it. Remembering not to take one thing for granted.

I had the opportunity to take a small break; I went downstairs and received some fresh air. I was thankful for having Joshua but having these experiences made me feel weak. I had taken my vitamins and was sipping on tea, reading the Upper Room, wanting preparation for what laid ahead.

I needed help this was strenuous for me. The sun shined so bright and the birds sat close by. It was really comforting to feel such warmth so early in the mourning. I would watch the birds as they would come up next to me, I stayed amazed. The birds weren't startled at all, even when I moved my legs.

I felt that it was a sign from God, I believe that I had angels all around me, and Joshua was one of them. Even though I couldn't see these heavenly beings they were that close to me, I could feel there heavenly presence.

They were there to comfort, guide, and protect us at all times. To me angels move and function like a bird; like it says in Ecc. 10:20 (KJV) for a bird of the air shall carry the voice, and that which hath wings shall tell the matter. Angels transmit our request daily to Jesus for us.

It was time to head back, and I had seen a couple in the hallways that I had spoke with previously on the 8th Floor, again being asked how Joshua was doing? I responded with a smile and said great, remembering they had been there for months and hadn't received the break that we had. I seen this mother smile as she was encouraged by our testimony, I know that through our experience nothing could be taken for granted.

Although we had done so well previously, I wasn't ready to be tested the way that we had been.

I know that upon reading God's word that we will never go through what were not prepared for. As long as we trust in him and seek him we will receive his promise.

I had returned to Joshua's room to see him become restless, I called for his nurse and said he was due for his medicine and she said she would go get it.

This was our new nurse for the day but I didn't think anything of it.

Previously everyone had worked speedily and there hadn't been any hold ups.

Time had past and she hadn't come back, and Joshua was getting worse. I was doing everything that I could to comfort him but nothing seemed to be working.

I told Joshua that he was doing great, to be patient that I would be right back that I planned to get his nurse.

I went and looked for her and when I seen her and confronted her she said to me that they have a window, and as long as Joshua received his medicine within the two hours of his scheduled time, before or after he would be alright.

I wasn't too happy, I was mad I felt that it was done intentional to cause us to have a set back. I prayed below my voice and asked God to please help me with this, I don't want to sound mean I just want Joshua to have what he needs.

I responded to her with understanding and said Joshua had a difficult night and that maybe she could sympathize, I planned to rest but couldn't until he received what he needed I ended our conversation with please.

This was day 17; we had experienced many adjustments in such a short time.

As a sinner does when they find Christ, they adjust to becoming a Christian in such a short time there are so many things that you automatically want to do differently but it takes time.

Joshua was administered his medicine and after seeing him calm, I brushed my teeth and had planned to take a quick shower.

Everything evolved around Joshua and every decision made was based on what he needed.

Upon looking at the clock Joshua's bandages needed to be removed and his wounds to be cleaned again. I'll get around to showering after I attend to him.

I willing did everything except for his elbow and I would call his nurse and assist them with him. Joshua's elbow was very sensitive and I didn't have the confidence or the ability to do it by myself at the time.

Joshua flinched a great deal to the slightest touch of his left hand or arm.

To accurately do this area it took two to of us, you had to move extremely slow a half inch to an inch at a time to reach the desired height to clean and bandage it properly.

Joshua expressed pain by moaning or saying oww, I continually spoke softly to help calm, and comfort him.

I believe his arm hurt him, that it was that sore or else we wouldn't have seen or heard him do anything.

God was allowing all of us to witness his mercies and his grace there's no way anyone could deny what Jesus had done for us.

Countless times I had told the Lord that I gave Joshua to him, deep down I had no intentions of letting go of him. And selfishly I thought he would understand. I had felt that my need for Joshua was much greater than what he needed him for.

Remembering the times that I had prayed before and God met my expectations every time.

However this was the first time in my life that I had said Lord whatever it takes I will do; not realizing the sacrifice that I would make to keep my vow that I had made, as he had given and kept his.

God had moved and turned everything in my life around in such a short time. Everything that was important before meant nothing to me now.

God deserves the praise for what we had experienced it was by far greater than anything that I could've believed if I hadn't had this experience.

Many of Joshua's friends had called daily to check the status of Joshua's recovery, the receptionist took notes, and I had unplugged the phone in our room. I was afraid the constant ringing would upset him so I didn't take that chance.

A Legacy of Faith in 55 Days

I never returned calls there were to many of them. I believe in talking with our visitors, family and friends sharing my concern they would understand as different ones came to visit with us daily.

Joshua had become more restless and he seemed to be fighting to take breaths in and out comfortably. I was so upset I wanted so bad to climb in his bed and put my arms around him and hold him.

Please help him Lord; I don't want to see him hurt for me.

I had to take a shower, I told Joshua that I was just a wall away from him and that I would hurry. I liked seeing him move, but I didn't want to see him hurt himself to do it. Within minutes I was finished and after checking on Joshua he seemed to be more agitated. What was wrong with him was it his new medicine Joshua's face had swelled was he having a allergic reaction? I was filled with questions and no answers, but I continued to focus on God because it was by his grace that would get us through this.

I had some olive oil that had been brought up for various ones to anoint him when they came, I felt that by the same faith that I could do this and it would have the same affect as someone else in a leadership position.

And I believe it did. There was an uncertainty but God also gave me a wonderful calm.

I had started to read Psalm 23 and immediately remembered what we had already overcome. We were faced with a lot of adversity but there wasn't anything to be compared with the first day of our trial or affliction, to give us deliverance.

In our study guide for the day it read Deuteronomy 31:8 – And the Lord, he it is that doth go before thee; he will be with thee, he will not fail thee, neither forsake thee: fear not, neither be dismayed. I didn't have a preacher that I could confide in, I had to trust in Jesus to teach me and he did.

When Joshua would draw his leg up and then release, I much rather him knee me than to bruise himself with the bed rails.

Joshua had worked up a sweat and his sheets were wet, I prepared to give him another sponge bath and to replace his sheets. I wanted him to feel clean and comfortable; I would do everything that I could to see him have what he needed.

I was almost finished when I got to his feet; I liked pampering him and in times past I trimmed his toe-nails for him. I was doing it here without him asking me.

I had applied lotion to keep his skin from drying from his head to his toes, while placing it on his feet upon finishing I heard Joshua say

MEMORIAL

A Legacy of Faith in 55 Days

"I Love You Mum" I was overjoyed to hear his voice; I said I love you to Joshua.

My eyes started to feel with tears and I moved towards the head of him and asked if he would say it again this made me smile for quite sometime. I knew from that moment on that no matter what we would face everything was going to be o.k.

It was a great gift to receive after having faced what we had. My heart was still racing from hearing him say "I Love You Mum" we had said that to one another daily but there were times I felt that we had taken our love for each other for granted.

In an instant God gave me the courage and hope to continue.

Our day progressed and it was time, I had made arrangements with my sister Donna the day before, and was expecting her phone call at around 4:00p.m.

Like clock work she called and let the phone ring once so I would know that it was her.

Then she called back to complete the task that I had asked of her calling from my house.

I walked her through to complete the list that I had given her, if I hadn't she wouldn't have known where to find any of my belongings and wouldn't have brought what had need of up.

As soon as our conversation ended I unplugged the phone, so we wouldn't be interrupted. It had been about six hours since I had left his room, I was ready to take a break.

I enjoyed having breaks, it gave me time to refresh and prepare for all of our daily activities.

I had the opportunity to hear the beautiful melodies that the birds would sing and feel the warmth of the sun shine down on me.

It was a wonderful feeling all of it being God's creation and I hadn't noticed even noticed how beautiful everything was until now.

I was always asked how Joshua was doing when I had moments away from him, I always responded with he was doing great. I remembered what God had brought him from and I couldn't take one second for granted.

I soon headed back to Joshua's room, I knew that it was almost time for his respiratory treatments and I didn't want him to go through anything by himself and he didn't.

As I entered his room within minutes the therapist came in, Joshua started to stir in his bed and I spoke to him letting him know everything was going to be alright.

I remained with Joshua to keep him calm allowing the therapist to do there thing. I told Joshua that he was doing great and that I felt week seeing how strong he had been, holding on.

I believed in miracles and I believed in God and that was all that we needed forever being thankful.

Donna and Chris had arrived later than they usually did; it was almost 6:00p.m.

They had a lot of responsibility on them. Never once did they act like it was too much always doing what was asked of them. When your in this kind of situation that is exactly what you need.

Joshua hadn't had a very good day compared to what we had seen, but this was reality. No one can go through life without having to face trials and afflictions face to face. God was giving us strength to endure daily, we couldn't look at tomorrow because there was a lot to think about and do just for today.

Like it reads in Matthew 6:34 (KJV) Take therefore no thought for the morrow: for the morrow shall take thought for the things of itself. Sufficient unto the day is the evil thereof.

Chris had planned to stay with Joshua, and Donna and I went and grabbed a bite to eat. My eyes filled with tears and she asked what was wrong? I said, I was worried the transition had been too much on him, and it was causing a set back for him. I hadn't seen him become so agitated and staff had told me that was normal for the kind of injury that Joshua had had.

She grabbed me and held me and I just cried, I too needed someone to comfort me as I had with Joshua for a while. At that moment I too was coming short of the glory that would be given until she asked what she could do, and I just shook my head as if she couldn't do anything, but I did say I can't wait until you stay with me. I hadn't given up I was still holding on and looking forward. Upon returning to Joshua's room I had asked if we could stop in the Chapel to pray, I felt in my heart that we could join together and God would comfort both of us.

And God did, I received the confidence to return and continue as we walked back to Joshua's room.

As we entered and Chris greeted us with a smile and said Joshua had done great, he hadn't made a sound since we had been gone. I was relieved because I felt anytime that I took away would be to long.

I loved the idea that Joshua had his new bed, to keep him from hurting himself. However it was complicated to operate and it took more than a couple of seconds to get to him in a time of an emergency.

TESTIMONY

Joshua's bed reminded you of a large baby bed, and in a sense he was being treated very much like a newborn baby again. I believed in my heart God wasn't done showing us what he could and would do, this was just the beginning really because our experience would be remembered by many lifelong.

I was told that when we were released Joshua would be transferred back to a regular hospital bed that was fine with me. I felt that once we got home he wouldn't have need of it anyway, that's how I believed.

Donna and Chris didn't get to stay as long as they normally did, both of them worked days and they had a long commute away and it was getting late. As much as I hated to see them leave I was assured they would be up again the following day. We hugged and kissed saying our good-byes and believing in our hearts that everything was going to be ok. I thanked her again for making the arrangements to get everything that I had requested on my list.

Joshua was sleeping pretty sound this gave me a chance to remove the hindrance that I had had with my hands. The charms were coming out and I would never wear them again. I had to move quickly because I never knew when or what he would need. This was the first time that I didn't think it strange not to have anything but Joshua's ring on my hand. I had filed my nails down to the bed, so they wouldn't hurt when I changed Joshua's sheets.

I had the opportunity to read again in the study guide, I had also used my mom's Bible that she had left for reference; this allowed me to combine the stories- both biblical and in today's crisis that many face. I had received a better understanding that way.

All of this was new to me but God knew what he was doing, and was having his will and his way the entire time. God knew that deep down I wasn't ready to face the ultimate challenge that eventually would come.

However, contentiously I was willing to do whatever it took to prove my sincerity. God had my attention; I would do whatever was asked of me without question or hesitation it was a test of obedience and willingness.

I had a fear of God he had been very merciful to us and I didn't want to do anything that would change that he had showed us so much.

Everyday was a challenge, I found that I was stepping out and growing day by day in faith and belief and Joshua and I were being transformed daily.

I had to trust in God that everything would be alright, and as long as I looked to him to guide me I would see and understand with his eyes. At the same time I was holding onto Joshua's hand not ready for a sacrifice.

Earlier I had hoped Donna would stay with me this night. How would she know when I never asked?

God works the same way; ye have not because ye ask not. Scripture tells us that as his servants he wants us to ask and have enough confidence that he will come through with it. Remember I had told one of his doctor's before God doesn't limit us to what we can have, but we limit God in what he wants to give us.

Psalm 6:9 (KJV) the Lord hath heard my supplication; the Lord will receive my prayer.

Joshua started to stir; it was about time for our evening routine. I believe he was reminding me as God does that he was still there for me. I believe in my heart Joshua had to know in his heart that I was going to be alright before anything else would take place.

I loved caring for him as I always had. I let him know that I was there for him and that I knew that he was resting in God's hands. I shared with him the story from the study guide as I had daily, both mourning and evening to encourage him.

I never did more than one page at a time I couldn't understand all of it at once. One paragraph, one page was a lot for me being a beginner.

I also shared with Joshua that it really bothered me to see him be so agitated at everything as he had been previously. Joshua's nurse came in and administered his medicine within minutes came his respiratory therapist. I held his hand and I softly sang and talked to him. Continually saying relax, relax, relax, as it seemed to help and keep him calm.

As the therapist finished and exited, I sit back and looked at him feeling helpless. I had hoped that I was doing everything that I could to comfort him.

I pulled the sheet up wanting to cover him. I wanted him to feel warm and comfortable. The thermostat sat on 64 – 66 degrees all of the time.

Joshua wasn't hot blooded, every time we tried adjusting the thermostat he would start a fever. To keep his body temperature down we had to keep the thermostat sat the same all of the time.

As I looked at his bed could it make him feel isolated I questioned. All of the sides zipped up like a tent as he awoke did he feel confined?

I was always trying to do something that would help comfort him.

I talked to him continuously telling him everything that I was doing, or that they were doing to include him.

I didn't want Joshua to feel that just because we couldn't hear his voice, didn't mean that we couldn't communicate.

WISDOM

When you're working in a situation like this, you become very observant and notice different reactions without any words being heard.

Joshua had varying sounds some very clear words as oww, seeing the tears and his call out to me was enough for me. I didn't need anymore proof than what I had already seen, experienced, and heard.

Deep down I couldn't wait to have the opportunity to hold him in my arms and say I've got you Joshua everything is going to be alright.

They say no pain, no gain and I think they mean it; I was trying to smile and hold back the tears at the same time.

I noticed that when I had moved Joshua around he didn't seem as heavy, he had lost some weight. To me he was my baby and I never allowed the care of him to overcome me. Whatever it takes I will do. God keeps his promise now he was making sure that I was going to keep mine.

It was late and I knew that we would have a lot of company the following day, it was the weekend. My prayer was that God would use Joshua and I continually to instill hope with everyone that would come and visit with us.

God had preserved and strengthened us for every second, minute, and hour because it was no longer of us to feel that we had the ability to do it.

God blessed us supernaturally giving us the ability to do as those in the biblical days, something was given and happening to us everyday.

God had both of us in the palm of his hands; he was by us every second throughout each day.

Each day that came and went, I gave God praise for every minute even when we had to face the fiery darts of the wicked.

It felt good to lay down, I had taken a 15 to 30 minute nap before getting up and starting all over again. I felt at peace when I awoke and that I had received much needed rest that I hadn't had. God was having his way and I didn't realize the impact that it would have until later on.

Others inquired about my sleeping patterns and I would simply respond with when Joshua sleeps I do too and leave it at that.

I had the opportunity to take a quick shower before starting the day with Joshua, this wasn't the normal process but it was an exception for this day. I explained to Joshua what

I would be doing and why I was doing it and I hoped he would be patient, it was something that I really needed. Upon finishing I truly felt replenished, it was very much needed.

I felt if I didn't take care of myself, I wouldn't be of any good for him today.

Joshua was starting to have another extremely agitated mourning and I wasn't use to seeing this kind of behavior from him. It really bothered me I had mixed emotions I was feeling angry, sad and guilty all at the same time. Lord am I doing something wrong? Please Lord I liked seeing and being with him when he was calm, I don't understand why we have to go through this at all.

I had shared with Joshua where we were, how many days that we had been there, he was doing great and that everyone was really proud of him.

I was told that I may have to repeat myself numerously, Joshua may forget where he's at and when he awakes it would scare him not recognizing the surroundings or place it would be up to me to reinforce everything.

I apologized for me showering feeling he wouldn't have reacted this way had I placed him first. My heart raced and I began hymning a song it was all that I could do, there was such a lump in my throat I couldn't sing even if I had wanted to.

Soon the RT came in and said it was time for his treatment, I told him Joshua was having a difficult mourning, like he had the day before. The good news was that Joshua's treatments were decreasing because of his speedily recovery. Some would look at our situation and say you have to face the bad and then you get the good. And this was good news even though the circumstance at the time didn't look good. Joshua was having a dramatic recovery and the doctor's hadn't touched him.

The doctor's and the nurses couldn't take credit for what God was doing.

I had told Joshua that what he had gone through at the age of fourteen, that some would go there whole life and never face the challenges that we had faced together.

With all of my heart I believe and know that from the very beginning that God had used Joshua to leave a testimony for all of us to remember. And that I would be given this experience to share with all of whom would read it. At no time had God changed his mind, that what we had been given would last a lifetime.

I liked those who took the extra minute to pamper and encourage Joshua as he was in recovery. Joshua had begun to calm for a little while and this was an added blessing. I had began to arrange the necessary things to attend to the care chart given, getting warm water to sponge bathe him. He was making sound and I beeped for a nurse so she could witness this activity. I didn't want to be the only one to see this; it was proven too many what God was doing.

A Legacy of Faith in 55 Days

Some had been skeptical of all of the things that I had witnessed and said, this was for those who had never had anything to believe in, because of Joshua for some they now did.

As Joshua's nurse had came in and I had explained to her what Joshua was doing, he was following my voice with his head as I moved around in his room. As she had the opportunity to watch him and she smiled back at me she had said that she was to write all of the activity that Joshua was doing, and that it would be reviewed on Monday by his doctor's. Everything that had taken place was documented. His eyes were open and he looked at me every time I spoke to him. He didn't move quickly, but he did everything that I had asked of him.

Joshua's nurse tried to get him to do it for her and he wouldn't, and later the attempt was made several times by the physical therapists and again Joshua didn't do anything. I seen the glow and knew that God was with him and that what had been witnessed wasn't meant for everyone to see because some refused to believe.

There are those that have witnessed God's miracles and still deny his handiwork and existence. As the scripture says if ye can't believe in the earthly things how can ye believe in the heavenly things in which ye haven't seen. Please read John 3: 11&12 (KJV)

As everyone had wrapped things up and left for the day, I went to Joshua and said I know why you didn't show them what you could do,

I said if they had seen what we had seen you would be worked continually.

He smiled at me and then my understanding was much deeper, it was because he wasn't ready for all of the changes and neither was I.

God gave to us in increments and that would leave us a solid foundation and good understanding for the rest of our days.

It was late in the afternoon family and friends had came to visit with us, we had discussed the events that had taken place always leaving them with encouraging words. Minimizing the focus of negativity and having a genuine desire to bring Joshua home. Never looking at what he couldn't do, but at what he was doing. I believed that our entire circumstance and ordeal was in our favor.

Joshua's dad (Scott) had taken the news of the accident extremely hard after receiving and seeing his son fighting in recovery, thinking heavily about all of the lost time. Scott knew that God had spared Joshua's life for a reason.

Joshua's dad had made a life change and had accepted Jesus as his Savior; he had seen everything differently and had a new outlook on everything for the first time.

He had an immediate desire to change and he shared that joy he was feeling with me. I wanted to cry and said I'm so glad that this has happened, with God we were able to face anything.

I know that Joshua couldn't have been happier to know that his parents were saved and they were no longer hell bound but heaven bound and it was because of what I believe he had prayed.

And can you imagine how a child would feel seeing there parents who had argued for years come together and communicate agreeably not disagreeing. To be content in the same room with one another, and we would continue that fellowship even after our hospital visitation.

As everyone had taken there turns visiting, Joshua became more and more agitated and I had asked the nurse what more could I do. She had said that all of us should leave the room and give Joshua some time to himself. I know that it was good advice yet I found it very difficult to want to leave him for a little while. We responded to her suggestion and all of us gathered down the hallway to visit for a while. No one was really saying a whole lot; everyone was upset to see Joshua so agitated. I tried being confident deep down I felt like I was carrying an extra hundred pound weight on me and every time I took a breath I felt the weight press or crush just a little bit more out of me.

I had acted in times past like I didn't need anyone that I could do everything on my own, I was so wrong. If God would've left in the midst of our storm I wouldn't be here today to tell you of his great mercies. He sends different ones at the right time to help you through you're trying times. No matter where you're at and what your circumstance you're never alone. What God does can't be compared to anything seen or not seen it is truly amazing, the requirement is to be willing and obedient at all times. Family had witnessed the change and admitted that they could see God working with me too. Those statements made me stronger knowing that I was growing in the Lord in such a short time.

I knew in an instant the day the accident took place that life wasn't just about Joshua and I anymore, it was a wake up call and God had to be our #1 priority. I believe that for Joshua God was, and it would be through his prayers that God had mercy on me that day. Was that Joshua's final request I will never know, however I believe he had a big part in how all of this would work and end because he was willing and there are many thing that had and has happened to confirm and not have me think any differently.

That is why Joshua had the impact on others as he had had.

There was no one that could say that God hadn't done his part; everyone knew that what had happened with Joshua was definitely beyond our own way.

For the rest of my days I will continually giving God the praise.

LEGACY

I had been playing long enough; second place wasn't an option for Jesus. This was my last chance that I would be given to get to heaven, we choose our final destination.

Deep down inside I had the desire to find favor with God for all he had done, my love being greater for him today, than what it was, or what it had been ever.

I never realized the impact that at the age of 12 having been involved in a critical accident would have. Now that I've had the opportunity to really look back and realizing that God had spared my life then that I may offer our testimony as a sacrifice for many. He was with me when I walked the valleys of the shadow of death, as he was with us today feeling the intimate, closeness, and the reality of a genuine relationship with our Lord Jesus Christ for the first time.

We had a real connection that would last a lifetime. I can't imagine what life would be like without him. God had opened the door to real life and happiness without having to grudge or groan anymore.

The time was passing and I realized the importance of family as we waited in the waiting room with anticipation. We were tearing down those walls of perdition and replacing with love and comfort for one another without differences. During these difficult times family came together to encourage and uplift one another, all of us sharing our memories of Joshua as it were yesterdays and years.

Joshua had a way to make people smile without putting a lot of effort or thought into it; this was a talent that went un-recognized for a long time.

This was our opportunity to realize and hold these memories close to us, to allow them come alive in our spirits to be strengthened by it.

Many remembering and speaking the good of Joshua, there wasn't anyone that I had met or spoke with that had anything negative to say about him. Joshua was liked by everyone he definitely had a good name.

Time had passed and everyone had started to leave, we had made it a point to gather around Joshua's bed and pray again that God would send the angels down to mend and repair every inch of him. I was specific with my request having a list that was added to daily. All of us continually ending our prayer with God have your will and your way.

There was a difference in the surroundings a feeling of darkness that overshadowed us, not realizing what had caused it. There were many hugs and kisses as everyone was leaving, I was trying to understand the entirety of our experience the circumstance that we were facing.

Joshua had been so agitated it wasn't easy to see him this way, and to realize that there wasn't anything that I could do that would help him or comfort him. As Joshua's mom I had tried everything and nothing was working.

Donna had stayed with me and this would give me the chance to lean on her for the evening.

I had felt previously that everyone had been leaning heavily on me and that they had felt that it was up to me to change the circumstance if I were able or had the power to change it I would've.

Donna and I were working closely together throughout the evening; this was a necessity to comply with the requirements of bringing Joshua home.

I was teaching her everything that had been shown to me, I introduced her to staff and let them know it was important to have her assist me in everything that Joshua would need.

After finishing with our scheduled care plan, I was looking forward to an evening of much needed rest.

Our initial plan was for her to stay up with Joshua and allow me to sleep; I hadn't had the opportunity to sleep for more than an hour in two weeks. I would need rest to continue facing our many challenges.

I had asked Donna if she would lie beside me and put her arm around me until I fell asleep, we were sisters I was hurting and needed to be comforted and she agreed.

Moments had past and the shifts had changed, we were working with different staff. Our new nurse didn't know that Donna was my sister and as she entered into our room, it caught her by surprise, both of us lying in a cot. Donna quickly explained and the nurse began to relax, she took Joshua's temperature, administered his medicine, and checked his blood pressure and then exited.

Joshua always let us know that he knew when someone was in our room, Joshua had a difference in his breathing and he would start moving this was a definite indication that he was responding to voice and movement.

I had tuned into the difference of sound that Joshua had made when he was sleeping and was able to sleep when I knew that he wasn't in need of anything.

I had fell asleep and awoke to hear Joshua moving. I got up to see if Donna was in the room and she wasn't. I let Joshua know that everything was ok and I had started to unzip his bed to get to him and comfort him.

As I managed to get to him within minutes Donna had stepped back in, she had left to take a break and to move around to stay awake. She felt bad for leaving not realizing that in those minutes she would be needed.

I was upset, it wasn't anything that she had done but it made me realize that no one would care for Joshua the way I was. I spoke to him softly and prayed with him too, I said Lord you know what he needs I don't know what to do. I love you Joshua, and I need you please don't do this to me. Donna tried comforting both of us during this time.

I wanted to grab and hold him but I wouldn't, I was afraid that I might hurt him. As difficult the situation I reminded myself that Joshua was in God's hands and that he had been from the very beginning. I had to remember if I wanted to get through this with victory. Donna and I prayed in agreement to receive relief, even though what we were faced with didn't look to have any promise.

Joshua was breathing very irregular and was having a lot of difficulty. I tried repositioning him only to have him go back to the same spot that we initially started. Joshua had been restless and agitated all mourning and it was very difficult as his mother to sit back and watch him struggle.

I took minutes away and began to cry and pray. I asked our Lord what was happening to Joshua that I didn't understand. I had said Lord whatever you want me to do I will do but please Lord don't make him go through this to get to me I pleaded. Our situation had already affected and had a great impact on me; I didn't want to experience anything more. I felt that what we had experienced was enough little did I realize that we were still in the beginning stages.

I tried finding a quiet place to meditate somewhere I could feel the connection with my Lord, but there was so much commotion and there were so many people that I had seen that in order to help me I was and did pray for them and there circumstance willingly. God being my witness, and knowing that is what he had needed of me. I will never understand why he chose me other than believing he had enough confidence that I would do what he asked of me.

While I had found a place in the garden to meditate, deep down I heard a soft voice say that the accident had been to much for him and that Joshua was tired of fighting and didn't want to stay he already had his place, he was in God's hands. I was also told that I had to tell Joshua that he had received a messaged from the master.

I was confused and wasn't sure what to do, I rebuked it thinking that it was the devil trying to take what God had given. I immediately started to walk back, I was seriously thinking and I knew that Joshua wouldn't leave me unless I said it was ok. God was preparing me then and what was to come. As much as I said God have your will and have your way I was really saying Lord do your thing and give him back to me ok.

A Legacy of Faith in 55 Days

I hurriedly returned to Joshua's room I was afraid in what I had just heard. I wasn't giving up or giving back we had come too far for anything to happen. I didn't want Joshua to suffer for me. It wasn't fair to him; I had to be willing to do what was right when the time was right.

I was greeted by Donna and her husband Chris both of them having a certain look about them as I entered in, Joshua had flipped over and was lying on his stomach he was close to the rails, his head to the left and Joshua seemed to be sleeping quite peacefully. What was going on, I wondered?

Joshua had done it on his own I was told this was beyond my understanding, beyond my comprehension.

I was looking for signs of hope and God gave me something beyond normal. I had remembered this had been the same position that I had encountered with Joshua from the first day that the accident took place, I was startled seeing this, after hearing the voice that just spoke with me in the garden what was the real meaning?

We worked together to reposition him, thinking the position that he had been in probably wasn't good for him. Was he getting tired of lying on his back and that's why he chose to flip on his stomach? No. I believe this was needful to see to remind me about our beginning journey and that God had him in his hands instantly.

I had made a vow from the very beginning and I would have to keep it. Upon having days like this I wasn't sure if I was able to do what I had promised. I had the desire to please but to see Joshua go through so much for me to see was taking a lot from me.

It would only be by the grace of God that would get me through this and the days to come taking each day one by one. I had been a part of Joshua's entire recovery; this was a sign but was it a good one and was it the right time?

I switched places with Donna and she asked if I was alright? I nodded as they had planned to break away for a few minutes. It was day 19 but it seemed like we had been there longer than 3 weeks.

I knew that Donna and Chris had planned to leave she was tired after being up all night. They planned to share the news with others of what we had just seen. Some wouldn't make it up even though it was the weekend. I was holding onto every scripture that I could read and that I understood. We prayed, hugged, and kissed and said our good-byes for the day for her it felt like night.

At this time in my life the Upper Room had been so needful and helpful for me to get through these days; each one teaching scripture and letting me know that no matter what I felt like or what I was going through that I wasn't alone.

The scripture that I held to for this day was in Isaiah 43:2 (KJV) When thou passest through the waters, I will be with thee; and through the rivers, they shall not overflow thee: when thou walkest through the fire, thou shalt not be burned; neither shall the flame kindle upon thee. Having this scripture strengthened me and was very helpful during our days of trouble. I hadn't anyone to really confide with scripture the way it was given, God gave the interpretation daily that I would have the understanding. God cared for me and showed his love and grace towards me daily.

Most of Joshua's procedures seemed routine being cautious with every move, we had one more thing added daily but God gave me a wonderful memory to remember.

Although Joshua's test and ex-rays looked great I felt deep down it was of necessity to be careful with everything we did for him.

God gets the credit in everything. Healing and repairing every inch of him.

Man gets into trouble by rushing a healing, or turning a positive into a negative through conversation. If all would be patient and wait we would receive the good reports were longing for.

We were given good reports no matter what the circumstance had looked.

As the afternoon had progressed and many had come to visit, I had overheard some conversations taking place outside of our room of those whom thought I couldn't hear them and wasn't listening.

I was disappointed and hurt by some realizing that they had lost focus on what God had done for us. God knew my pain but I didn't have to express or make it known to them, I spoke to Jesus he was my immediate comforter.

I could only imagine what Jesus must have thought when he saw them doing this. Jesus had been done the very same way throughout his days and stay.

I stepped out making myself known although I didn't have to say anything, the amazing thing was the one's that were speaking negative didn't react or continue conversing on what they had when I was in front of them.

I was affected by others and there actions but I would simply pray for them that they would see the way God showed me and that they would say one day that they had blessed like me.

Everything was happening quite rapidly, I believe you can transform speedily when you don't have all of the worldly distractions right at you. God will talk to you directly and you will know his very presence. The conditions to his promise is this you have to be willing to commit, submit, and change into the likeness of him and he will take care of everything else that means all of the details.

Time past so fast visiting hours were over and we had planned to see everyone either through the week or the following weekend. We prayed, hugged, and kissed and said our good-byes everyone was readily waiting to see Joshua come home. The anticipation was great and our faith and hope was at one of its highest points in all of our lives.

Having been given this extra time it was needful in leaving a testimony for others and for me to understand how God had his way from the very beginning, we didn't have lack of anything.

After everything was done and we were getting settled for the night, I took the time to tell Joshua the message that I had received in the garden earlier that day. A part of me was very thankful for having that connection and then there was a part of me not willing or ready to accept anything other than what we had prayed for or had been praying for. I needed him and I didn't want to even think that I would have to do anything without him. I love you Joshua so much as I felt the tears coming down, please don't give up. I promise I will be here for you, I'm going to do a lot of things different when we get home, you'll see. You're my baby; you're what I've lived for. I had shared with him that upon returning home that we were going to take a vacation and that we could go anywhere, I had God in my life and that having him has changed everything. I said we would do whatever he asked but he had to keep fighting back.

Joshua smiled and then his heartbeat began to rise, throughout these past few days Joshua had seemed to be more agitated than any of our previous days.

I know that God took the time to share with me the difficulty of Joshua's injuries, in bits at a time because that is all that I could handle at the time.

We would have another difficult night and my smiles had faded as I seen Joshua struggle for his life. I had asked God why? I didn't receive an answer then it was much later in our stay when I realized that in scripture we have to be willing to carry the cross as Jesus did. I didn't understand the extent of it then the way I do now.

God had his hand on Joshua and Joshua was presented to us in perfect condition that was for all of us to always remember.

As we creped through the evening, every hour seemingly like an eternity when you've done all that you can and nothing is working. I had access to anything that money could buy, the one thing that I couldn't do was to have anyone or anything to change our circumstance to save Joshua's life was only by Jesus Christ. I felt overwhelmed inside at the time but later I would realize that as Jesus was there for me he would be all that I need for the rest of my life to carry out the testimony that he had given to us.

I broke away for a little while to pray and focus again on how good God had been to us. It was so important for me to stay in constant remembrance of the good things, and not allow the circumstance to take away our victory.

I was relieved to have the opportunity to sit outside and receive some fresh air; anyone that has had an extended visit in a hospital room knows just exactly where I'm coming from. I sat quietly watching and waiting with anticipation as the breeze past through my hair. The entrance doors constantly opening as many families gathered together outside talking and waiting to receive results for there loved one that was just brought in from a serious injury. It reminded me that I wasn't alone there are thousands of families who are faced with trauma and that are affected daily just like me.

I had Jesus on my side, I wondered did they. I wouldn't be able to share our story with anyone if he hadn't directed my feet the entire time.

I had to get back but I found that I wasn't as excited as I had been in the past. I wasn't sure what Joshua would be doing and I didn't like feeling that I couldn't do anything for him to help him. Why were we receiving mixed signals? I had stopped in the Chapel to pray again and I had continually carried the Study Guide in my hand I also had the little notebook in my hand.

I was being double-sided I was praying faithfully but had allowed the things that I had wrote in this little notebook to slowly take away what God had given our victory.

We had been given many good days as all of us had witnessed, it was when I started writing everything down things seemed to go wrong. I was confused on what I needed to do whether it was to continue writing or to put it up. I was seeking with everything in me it was important for me to do the right thing, what God needed of me. It was through him that he showed me.

I returned to Joshua's room seeing him be in a relaxed state upon entering he seemed to awaken and become agitated. I told him it was just me that everything was ok and for him to go back to sleep, we would have another busy day the following day. I told him what time it was and that I had went to him and prayed for us.

I opened his bed to lean in and kiss him on his head and I told him how much I loved him. He wasn't ready to go back to sleep so I sat and read to him, I told him that I knew that he was in God's hands and that God had gave him back to us.

Joshua lie with his eyes opened listening to me talk to him. I couldn't wait for us to get home; I was excited and had a fear at the same time. I said to him that his room made me feel confined, and I wondered if it made him. I had talked to Joshua as I always had not thinking any differently of our situation.

Joshua's breathing patterns were a lot different than I had ever seen. Joshua was considered to be a posturing or storming patient, I wasn't convinced of there interpretation by any means. Joshua had little episodes that would come and go lasting only momentarily. He would eventually calm and it made me think our circumstance was different that anyone else's at the hospital.

I had said that whatever we would go through was part of God's plan knowing that Joshua was in Gods hands.

As God gives to each of us it is up to us to seek him and receive good understanding. Joshua was a miracle and his story deserved to be shared with as many that would listen.

I know that Joshua had favor in God's eyes but I hadn't prior to the accident and in my wrongfulness I had to be willing to pay the price and sacrifice.

God shows love even when he's angry with us, I know that this was needful for me to experience and see to do what was requested of me, I had ran out all of my chances.

Mourning came and it seemed to go routine as staff came in visiting saying that he should really be on the 6th Floor, they weren't equipped and staffed to handle him on this floor. This was news shared that was unexpected and wasn't appreciated by me at all.

Joshua was really agitated and nothing seemed to comfort or calm him he was in a constant state of storming, or was he having an allergic reaction to the medicine that they had given him. I didn't know I wasn't qualified to make that determination; I would have to wait and watch until I had the opportunity to speak with his doctor.

By the grace of God he gave me the ability to be strong and calm, I had to do what was needful to help Joshua and others heal. There was no one else that God chose to do what he gave me to do.

Our ordeal was needful for me and helped me to heal before I was given the opportunity to help anyone else.

We were well into the afternoon when many had come to visit with us again; I know that it was difficult for others to see Joshua when he was having a bad day.

It was almost too much for me to see the many visitors because I felt that I had to carry the burden and the weight for them also.

I prayed for continual protection and strength before, during, and after anyone came to visit with us.

I had to know how to speak to them whether in a group or done individually.

I had to encourage them regardless of how they had seen him. We had to take each minute one by one as they came.

It reminds me of how a preacher does; A preacher will spend a lot of time with God to give a sermon the way God would want him to give it, before he ever preaches on it. He will also be willing to work with you daily and give you scripture to lead you in a path straight. But, in the end it's up to you to receive and act upon the way God had intended for you.

Everyone was quite upset with the doctor's and staff feeling like they could do more in helping with our situation. Whose report were we focusing on men or the Lords? This was a transition and a conditioning process that all of us would go through and I hope that for Joshua's name, will last a lifetime.

I had planned to ask Joshua to be released the following day I had seen enough and wanted him home and safe. I was trying not to point fingers but I knew in my heart no one could love or care for him the way I did.

Family was excited and nervous at the same time; this was a big responsibility that I had attempted to take on. No one disputed what I wanted to do, some inquire how soon I would know. We can't rush things or we will get ourselves in trouble.

I have found that until you're grounded with what the Lord says, and you admit that he's honest with everything in sight you can't understand his way of doing things.

I made a point not to partake in any negative conversation continually being reminded what Jesus had done for us from the very beginning. I had been saved for two weeks, and all of those things that I had tucked away and learned as a child were in my heart and very fresh. I had questions to ask but I never voiced them aloud, to anyone other than Jesus. I was truly taking one day at a time and not looking for tomorrow for we had enough to deal with today.

Visiting hours were over and everyone was leaving and showing a lot of emotion knowing that I had a big question to ask of Joshua's doctor the following day. All of us gathered around to pray for Joshua and our hearts were feeling heavy, we continually asked for his recovery and that every inch of him is made whole again.

Throughout our entire visit Joshua had been protected, were we allowing our remembrance to be altered by a negative situation?

We had immediate expectations with everyone who worked with Joshua and everything that they did. Not taking into consideration that there were others that had need of the same things that we did. We felt that after being transferred the protection that had been given now failed. None of us wanting to understand or sympathize we expected our needs to be met at anytime.

As the evening progressed and keeping everything on a timely schedule, it may have appeared easy but was very difficult.

Joshua's breathing treatments had been decreased and in the beginning when it was done gradually he seemed to do ok, but as time progressed he seemed to have difficulty, and struggled with each breath. I could tell with various staff who did there job and had compassion and I knew those who did not.

I was upset with certain doctor's and medical staff, the trust that I had placed in them in the beginning had now been broke. I had no confidence in what they did or said after our traumatic weekend experience. It would take some time to believe in someone else to help us.

I waited patiently for the mourning hours to come, I looked forward to seeing Joshua's doctor and was prepared to ask for our immediate discharge upon her arrival.

The anticipation can get to you if you're not prepared for what is needful to be an over comer.

Ms. C finally arrived and I quickly filled her in on our weekend, and I let her know that I had requested for her to be called but that was denied.

I didn't want either of us to stay any longer as I would exclaim.

I shared with her that in my heart I believed the only way Joshua was going to get better is if he came home with me. Without any hesitation she denied my request and I was heart struck and wondered why. She explained the many factors and risks that our situation involved, I told her that I didn't feel we were safe and that the hospital and staff had disappointed me greatly.

She didn't stay for very long seeing how upset I had become but said she would make immediate arrangements to have him transferred to the 6th Floor where they were equipped and staffed to help us in this situation.

God knew why we were denied, I wasn't told because it wasn't the right time. I struggled believing that she would be any different than the ones that I had already met, deep down I wanted her to help us, I would have to give her a chance. I had immediate decisions continually that I had to make in a difficult situation.

I'm glad that our requests are not always answered, if they were everyone that believes and prays would oft make a mess of things.

We had asked God to breathe life back into him in the beginning and he did.

That is a praise report for the Lord, it has been important for me to remember what we were faced with from the very beginning continually to get through this and through every second he was with us.

I understand that when God moves he's not obligated to do anymore than what he wants to do. Remember to continually be thankful for your blessing and not take anything for granted.

As his doctor left, Joshua had staff and therapists come in working with him and taking there turns with the visits. I didn't like how some of them worked with him and I was afraid to say anything not wanting to be separated from him. I was placed between a rock and a hard spot; it was the grace of God that kept me calm through all of it.

Joshua wasn't handled cautiously it was whatever it took for them to get the procedure done, that was one of the reasons why I was eager to learn everything. I wanted to bring Joshua home and I knew that I wouldn't do anything that would hurt or harm him.

Even when you're in Gods hands that don't mean that you won't endure pain. I believe that Joshua had already seen the ending and he was able to do what others couldn't do because God was in it.

The oddity about our stay was every time Joshua was worked with by staff or me he always tried to get out of his bed, I wondered what God was trying to tell me through watching him do this.

We had another doctor that came in to visit with us and I expressed my concerns about our situation and our stay. He had said that I worked quite efficiently whether someone was there to help accompany with the tasks. I smiled and didn't say anything; I recognized the spirit in me that was doing the moving it wasn't me.

I was told the arrangements had been made to move Joshua the following mourning that would be relief for me. I smiled as he finished in conversation and was leaving.

I've realized that sometimes when you're faced with someone that has a big title as he had it can be intimidating but when God is having his way he will take that fear away.

Our day was progressing and I didn't feel sleepy but I did feel semi-fatigued. I had always believed that once we got to the 6th Floor we would be out the door.

Joshua had started on a new medication called Baclofen and it seemed to relax him, he needed a good nights sleep considering all of the agitation that he had within these last few days of the initial transfer of him. It was a Blessing to see him resting. I liked when nothing seemed to bother him, it was then that I felt he was comfortable.

A Legacy of Faith in 55 Days

I did everything that I could for him and then I would take care of me, it was a relief to take a 5 minute shower and brush my teeth. I did everything with speed. I had a deep ache in my heart that no matter what was going on even in our good days that wouldn't go away. Joshua hadn't already left us had he, how could he after everything that we had witnessed and believed. What was God trying to tell me. I didn't share with anyone the deep ache that I had, I wasn't about to have anyone say that I had given up on him. When you're not saved you don't see and feel for others the same way and I wanted to encourage them, deep down I don't believe anyone could've handled the truth the way God had given it to me.

Anytime my spirit was telling or showing me something different than what I wanted to see or hear, I had a hard time with it.

With everything in me being thankful for Jesus taking such good care of us daily.

What we had been given wasn't for me to keep but was for me to share with as many that would believe in Jesus with me. And to witness of his great signs and wonders all being a part of his wonderful mystique.

As it reads in Luke 16:20 (KJV) And they went forth, and preached everywhere the Lord working with them, and confirming the word with signs following. Amen

I had an obligation to share with others the good that God does and he is merciful and gracious to each of us. The problem that many face is they won't ask feeling that they can figure life out without asking anything of him. It was good for me that at no time did I feel that I had been abandoned and that whatever I was seeking I would find through him.

In between times I found myself wondering through the halls to relieve myself of the daily responsibilities. I always kept an eye on the clock making sure that I wasn't away for more than fifteen minutes. And although I wasn't a preacher God had given me the opportunity to minister the word to others, to share our glory with many that walked through the doors.

I had the opportunity to go outside and I was always looking up; It seemed that the Sun, Moon, and Stars were following me those were three things that man couldn't touch. I was also reminded that even when it seems so dark Jesus shines his light throughout all of the darkness around that made everything feel bright.

Moses was given with tables of laws and commandments to the people and children of Israel, not everyone had the wisdom to understand what God had given to him to instruct them from the beginning. I felt the same way God had given me a testimony that at the time not everyone could understand. I wouldn't have understood the entirety of it had I been given it all at once, or had seen the ending from the very beginning.

The evening progressed and I had returned to reunite with Joshua again. I loved watching him and continually seeing a glow all around him. I sat in a chair resting and as time past we were given our 21st mourning. Joshua had started to stir in his bed and I made my way to greet him quickly with a smile to talk to him and calm him. Joshua was easily agitated and I believe that it was caused from the injury of his accident. We started out everyday with prayer and being continually thankful for having another day, I always asked that both of us have strength and to receive what was needed for each day with everyday that we take one should pray that way.

This was a big day for us because mid-afternoon we were scheduled to be transferred to the 6th Floor, and I just knew that after that we would be out the door.

I wanted everything to go my way, but deep down I couldn't help but say Lord your will and your way every step of the way.

I didn't want to second guess anything anymore; I knew that when it comes from God it's right no matter what.

We had experienced little consistency on this floor and it was a relief to know that we would soon be transferred to another floor.

I followed procedures with his care plan waiting, and watching the therapist work with him. As everyone exited I remained beside him encouraging him to continue as we waited for our transfer. Donna and Chris had come up to visit and to share this moment with us. Donna helped me pack all of our things we had twice as much than what we had when we had moved previously.

Minutes later a nurse came in administered medicine and said he was about to be transferred down. I was excited and nervous at the same time we had experienced so much in such a little time. As we moved Joshua he didn't seem to mind, he was handling the transfer just fine. Upon entering the 6th Floor I was amazed to see that we were placed in the first room on that floor.

I said we were first class all of the way not realizing the extent of what I had just said.

We were adjusting and within minutes staff came in and was greeting us that made me feel so much better. It was around 3:00p.m. And I know they were on a schedule but to take those minutes out of there day to let us know they were there for us at the time meant everything. Compared to others our stay was quickly wrapping up. I smiled greatly and responded with saying it works like that when you pray and believe in Jesus to change things around you. And I didn't think anything more of it. We were so blessed.

I was prepared by other family members not to get to excited that within a day or two after we were a little more settled that the physical therapists would really become aggressive. I can tell you this from my experience that is not something that I wanted to hear. I said they have been stretching him from the very beginning in Intensive Care Unit how much more will they do? One of the dads's said I won't tell you, you will see soon enough. This is something we had to do, if we planned on being released anytime soon.

That left me wondering and yet I agreed not knowing what the initial outcome would be. I would agree upon anything that would help him and not hurt him. Staff was checking in quite frequently and that was good it gave me a sense that they really cared about there patients and what they were doing. Joshua and I was left alone for most of the night having the routine awakening from the night shift staff. Both of us were to adjust in such a short time allowed before I knew it we had past through another day and again praying for the strength to get us through another day.

I gathered the things needful to properly tend to his wounds always being extremely careful.

Joshua didn't openly talk, he did moan and make sound and he said oww.

Remembering his last words to me was I love you mum. For me remembering where he had been and where he was now was truly enough for me to remember always and forever to stay with me.

I took a break and maneuvered quickly to be ready for anything that would take place throughout our day. Soon after I returned to Joshua's room his therapist made a visit and started working with him.

I watched very carefully as he was worked with and seeing that some of his expressions showed him hurting. Joshua wasn't able to speak and it was up to me to be a voice for him. I spoke without hesitation when I would see the tears come from his eyes. And no it wasn't because his eyes were dry. I would continue to tell Joshua everything was going to be alright, he was in God's hands and that we were going to see this all of the way through. I would sing the song God gave leaving me a continual melody in my heart.

As Joshua was responding to there work being done, it was up to me to do all that I could to keep him calm.

I was limited to what I could do I had to trust in God, and I had to believe the staff had his best interest at hand even though that was very difficult to do.

I felt the burden as Joshua expressed the pain.

It was day 23 and we had adjusted to the transferring of floors. Joshua had continued to go without the ventilator and was doing great. I was told that by the end of the week they had planned to have Joshua in a wheelchair, to have Joshua sitting up again this was great news and what we had been waiting and praying for. For me that was enough to praise the Lord all day for a good report and his mighty works.

All along I was thinking, saying, and believing it wouldn't be long before we were out those doors fulfilling Gods plan for us. In the beginning everyone seemed so friendly and good to us, it was a relief and very exciting.

I made mention of Joshua's food tube coming out twice on the previous floor and staff had told me that this was very common and it would happen many more times. Often when a patient is in recovery and they realize they have a tube down there nose the first thing they do is pull it out. I wasn't too excited knowing this thinking of how much blood was expressed when he done this, yet thinking of the good because he was in the recovery process and every little bit was a blessing to have the opportunity to witness.

I had kept everything on a schedule and liked having it that way. I shared with his doctor my concerns and requests and she was attentive and helpful that made me happy.

I felt that if there was to be any changes made that it was to be shared with me first because I too was keeping record. I had placed myself in a position to be a 24 hour caregiver.

At the time I didn't realize that when the doctors make changes there not always charted the way the doctor said. And if the doctor wasn't able to share those changes with the shift changing staff, the patients care can be neglected because there wasn't accurate communication or information given. Eventually we would have to experience these situations and if it falls on the weekend it can be quite scary.

To most of the staff I appeared very young and wasn't given the benefit of the doubt to help out. I proved myself worthy and able on all occasions. From the beginning to the end and to have that behavior allowed me to stay with Joshua at all times.

We had a lot to prepare for not realizing the extensive process of his recovery.

God was always placed first throughout our stay and that made our situation feel like we were doing great even when we had hard days.

I had set everything up to make it breeze as I did his dressing changes, everything was placed within arms reach. I would bathe and wash his hair; he didn't seem to mind because he wasn't moving around. I always used baby oil and conditioner for his hair and then I used a large pick to comb his hair out.

Our mornings always went by fast; there was so much to do and little time to do it. Many of the staff was in and out frequently leaving very little quiet time for us. Trying to stay focused that after going through this it wouldn't be long before we were home.

Ex-rays were continually being given and a part of me couldn't understand why there was so many. I know that in Joshua's recovery the ex-rays and records was evidence of his miraculous recovery. Joshua was breathing and moving efficiently, after ex-rays he would become agitated and move vigorously and yes that bothered me to a degree. He wasn't getting a lot of rest and there were many that were testing him heavily because they couldn't understand that God had a hold of him.

There were many that had shared there thoughts with me and when they had heard the news of Joshua being life-lined they had no thought of him every making it past the first day. That day has stuck into the minds of everyone, God moved that day there is no other explanation. God breathed life back into Joshua when man couldn't do anything for him. I would smile at the staff and say Gods ways are great, not being upset at what they had said or how it was directed because I had been a part of this miracle making process. There were many that knew a lot about me and my past even though I hadn't personally spoken with them. Jesus had made a change in me that was all that I needed.

Joshua had coughed, swallowed, and moved his eyes to follow, he'd move his feet and legs as if there was no tomorrow. He didn't do it with speed but that was ok with me he was doing it. All of it was needed to receive healing before, during, and after.

Reminding myself that when we had first arrived I could hardly see, and my heart was broke. God took the time to mend and repair every inch of me.

I had stayed with Joshua through everything every physical therapy session, except for one. I was there for every tests, ex-ray and surgical procedure with the exception of two that would later be given.

There were days that I had tried to schedule a shower for me but because of Joshua's needs, I wouldn't take one at all.

The staff was nice but I hadn't connected with them, after all we were still adjusting we had only been to the 6th floor for a few days.

As I watch Joshua lye in his bed, being quickly reminded of how big a part of him he was to me. The many times we were out for outings how he was just a few feet a way from me, or how he would make a way to stand beside me. I held onto our good times through all of it. Jesus showed compassion to Mary as Jesus was showing compassion to me. I believe, I believe, I believe we will see this to the end everyone else will see it too, I said continually.

I was given the opportunity to do a lot of things without asking for assistance, but when God is in it you're able to do things that normally you couldn't or wouldn't.

In times past I had been given many opportunities like Pharoah, but I had aloud my heart to become hardened and refused to be obedient and be humbled.

PROMISE

Our situation caused an immediate life changing experience that would humble me forever. To do the work that I was called to do I had to be broken to do it. I know that my judgment was not what God wanted for me but the lifestyle I chose left him no choice and I know that in his heart he grieved and mourned for me and when the spirit was moving inside of me and I was crying out aloud. I still had to face and take what I had caused to be sentenced out.

James 5: 20 (KJV) Let him know, that he which converteth the sinner from error of his way shall save a soul from death, and shall hide a multitude of sins.

I had made a commitment and would hold to it until I was given an ending.

I was living and speaking on the other side of the life I had once known as scripture reads in Romans 5:19 – For as by one man's disobedience many were made sinners, so by the obedience of one many be made righteous.

I was given the voice to speak, to leave a testimony for everyone to remember within our community.

There was so many staff it was the perfect opportunity to share the load, as a

Independent single mom I had a hard time believing that anyone would care for Joshua the way I could. I had to be there to protect and comfort him; I had the time to care for him without agitating him.

How would I know that I could trust them and that they would be responsible if I didn't give them a chance? I believe I was still holding on to our previous and negative experience.

Being youthful in Christ I seemed to be alright as long as my faith wasn't tried.

Joshua was enduring the suffering that he was faced with, and that isn't something I wanted to see him do for any of us. And then I thought really hard about what Jesus had done for us, he didn't know us yet he offered himself as a sacrifice out of love for us. He did it because he knew the importance of doing it. Our lives should be offered to him the same way no matter what were faced with.

At times throughout our entire stay I felt that I was being tested and was failing.

I didn't speak doubt aloud; in my heart I felt that there would be a day that I may have to say good-bye to him and until we meet again, yet we had our faith renewed and deep down that wasn't something that I was ready to face.

I told Joshua what the weather was like outside and how everyone continued asking about him. I would read the letters and cards others were sending. I knew that there were many that were praying within our community and nationwide, to have this kind of support was very uplifting.

Joshua hadn't disappointed any of us he was fighting until Jesus said when.

No matter what kind of day we were facing I knew that we weren't alone there were many that had faced and went through what we were going through without asking for help.

My promise to Joshua was to let everyone know that he was a miracle and God had blessed me to be his witness and when the time was right I would tell the world what God has done for us, Joshua knew that I had always kept what I had said.

As the day progressed the doctors had left, and the hallways seemed to be much quieter. Donna and Chris had come to visit and I shared with them my excitement the plan to place Joshua in a wheelchair the following day to know that we were still moving God was doing wonders for me.

We joined together in prayer and I believe that she was in agreement with me even though she hadn't committed to being a born again Christian.

She believed with me before asking Jesus Christ for anything different in our lives.

We had made arrangements to go down and eat at certain times daily, before realizing the length of our stay. When I ate I felt that I was eating for the two us wanting Joshua to receive all that God had given to each of us. I enjoyed making sure that I always had bread for the birds as the Lord had given to us I wanted to give to them. Our visits were soon over and it would be just the two of us again and whoever was working during the evening shift.

I loved there company it meant so much and was very encouraging, I looked forward to there visits daily.

I prepared for the evening as I always had, learning how to do the care needful for his stay. I asked for help when it came to cleaning his elbow.

I changed his sheets wanting to keep him comfortable, propping his pillows and working with his hands, I was asked by his physical therapist to do this for him and I did. It was just one more thing added to our list.

I was so proud of him and I hoped he knew just how much I loved him.

The doctor had written a request a sleep order that was to allow us to have 8 hours before any interruptions; I was looking forward to having a rested night.

As our evening progressed Mrs.C order was denied the nurse for the night refused what had been charted and didn't allow us the quiet time to sleep.

A Legacy of Faith in 55 Days

She came in continually every fifteen to thirty minutes, her name being RC letting me know that even though she had read those orders and that I was his mom she had a responsibility to care for him.

I told her he didn't need anything I was doing all that I could to take care of him. I didn't sleep a lot during our visit just minutes. When someone was working, testing, or ex-raying I was beside him to comfort him. I wasn't medically educated but deep down I knew when something didn't appear or sound right, that was a gift that God had given me during our stay.

The respiratory therapist came in to give a breathing treatment it was to strengthen him during breathing. Previously Joshua had had a bad experience with these kind of treatments and he appeared agitated when he knew what they was about to do. I sang to him and assured him that he was doing great, and that he was in Gods hands and if he called out to him he would take that fear away. I helped all that I could for every storm that he faced I faced it with him.

I always expressed my thoughts with Joshua and I shared with him what my plans were and I would tell him when I was leaving and how soon I would return to him. I made sure every one that visited spoke to him the way I did wanting to hold onto all that we had been given.

I felt that our love for one another was like David and Johnathon please read 1st Samuel 18, there wasn't anything that Joshua and I wouldn't do for one another this trial would test our faith because our love was great.

Nothing should mean more to anyone than having God 1st in your life and having family ties. Regardless of how you may feel in certain times not having that convenience or that break to set you for life. God's ways are more important than man could ever imagine.

As we were growing in the Lord I truly understood the love he showed us and felt it at all times.

Joshua showed signs of his days and nights mixed up, during the day he seemed quite sleepy but of the evening he was awake and listening. I didn't mind I was trying to understand our purpose and meaning. It was already 4:00 a.m. and that is when our daily schedule began, we had finished early with our mourning schedule. The night shift nurses wanted to do things early so they could leave as soon after they had there brief meetings.

I didn't mind as long as I had someone help us, when it came time to do his elbow; Joshua flinched greatly and I didn't want to be the one to clean or pack it at the time because it was so close to one of his main nerves and it bothered me greatly. God gave me extra strength during these times because as Joshua's mom when something seemed to hurt him I wanted to cry and was weeping on the inside, I made it a point not to express to anyone my deepest fear or pain until later on and that would be my last time.

Everything that Jesus did for us through Joshua was exciting for me. Joshua had been involved in a serious accident, yet he didn't have the numerous surgeries that other parents were facing. Joshua was regular in a lot of ways, there were so many not just one to say about them.

I had read new scripture daily but what did it all mean. Today's scripture was in Romans 8:25- But if we hope for that we see not, then do we with patience wait for it. Our experience was going rapidly, I knew that I was being prepared for something quite powerful yet I didn't understand it completely.

It was good to finish early it would give him a chance to break before the time of our big day to have Joshua in a wheelchair for the first time. Our prayers had been answered like our requests at the time.

I couldn't wait until they would say they were ready, I paced the floors with a lot of anticipation. I prayed and spoke with God one on one all of the time; I knew that he was up to something and he allowed me to have the opportunity to share it with everyone who would listen to me. I also knew that once Joshua was up and out of his bed that would give me the opportunity to hold him again, something I greatly missed. I asked over and over when, I didn't want them doing it unless I was right there with him. I wanted to share this spectacular event with them and encourage him.

For my studies it was much easier to understand this little guide because I hadn't picked up the Bible to read in such a long time.

For quite sometime I had said that I would take Joshua's place numerous times, if it had bee me Joshua was so young in the Lord would he have resented him and not done what I had done I was reminded that were not to think on things that didn't happen because that wasn't part of Gods plan. I quickly rephrased Joshua already knew Jesus as his personal savior and I didn't in the beginning, but I do now.

I may not have received the mercy and intervention as he did because I had been living a life as a sinner previously. My heart was broke I was crumbled and humbled, and I know that God grieved for the punishment that was placed on me, however I had made a choice as Moab and now I had to face the consequence of my actions without deliverance.

Some had even thought that this was a phase for me and as soon as we were released that I would go back to my old ways. When someone doesn't have God in there life they have no idea how he works, how he transforms and changes every inch of you, like a potter he remolds everything about you.

I know the real hold God shows and wouldn't change it for anything. I knew that it wasn't important to prove to anyone God already knew the place he had made in my heart and it would stay, as long as I live my days to him and am a faithful servant for him I would be ok.

IN HIS HANDS

I believe with everything in me Joshua was in the palm of Gods hand from the very beginning, and God used Joshua as he did many others in Biblical history to leave a testimony for all to remember as partners he used me to assist in the speaking.

This was the day the Lord had made; we will rejoice and be glad it is.

Donna and Chris had arrived waiting for the move with just as much excitement. It was now a little after 1:00p.m. we had decided to take a little break, no one said anything as we were leaving. Moments passed and we headed back sharing the anticipation of when they were going to have Joshua sitting up for us. As we entered his room Joshua's room was filled with nurses and attending staff all watching and helping with anticipation as he was placed in an upright position to sit up. I was a little overwhelmed and rushed to be beside him. Joshua was sitting up with his doctor Ms. C behind him holding and propping him up at the same time.

My eyes began to feel with tears, I wanted to be the one to hold him like she had. She had asked if Joshua had a curvature spine or any injury with his back, I responded with no and asked why. She had said that she felt vertebrae's out of place and weren't positioned right. I said he had perfect posture before the accident and there was a picture behind us to prove it.

Her phone rang and she asked if I wanted to switch her places, I eagerly accepted. To have the opportunity to hold him and share with him how much we loved him. I know that this was part of God's plan he knew the ending before the beginning and didn't change anything in between. The attending nurse had placed pillows behind me to help support us while we were placed in that position. Joshua's response to the adjustments was received as a victory to many. We were allowed 20 minutes and for him that would be a long time because he hadn't sat up like that in a little over 3 weeks. That was a great moment for me to hold my son in my arms for a little time. The doctor had ordered an ex-ray to see what was going on with Joshua's back. Through prayer God changed the appearance of those tests it was never meant for man to do anymore than what had been done.

This was just the beginning we would allow Joshua some time to adjust about two hours and then we had planned to place him in a wheelchair before the end of our day. Jesus deserves the praise throughout our entire stay. Donna and Chris stayed and waited with us, we had rearranged some of his things in his room to allow everyone space to move.

Finally the time had arrived and we had the opportunity to see Joshua in a wheelchair for the first time. There were many of us that helped place him in his chair we did on the count of three, we would do that again and do it together on count. This was so exciting we placed pillows under him and all around him to protect and cushion him at the same time. I was so eager to get behind his chair and wheel him out; we were allowed to go anywhere as long as we remained on the Rehabilitation floor. To see him out of his bed and sitting up was such a blessing. I took him to the activities room this room had an array of sunlight and there were many children running and playing. I had hoped to see Joshua do this again soon.

A Legacy of Faith in 55 Days

This room had inspired me from the very beginning of our arrival, in watching the children when they were faced with obstacles they still managed to find a way out.

Deep down I felt that way with Joshua and I God was making a way for Joshua and I to detour our obstacles and one day we would share that victory together with a smile.

I pushed Joshua towards the window and sat for a few minutes. He hadn't seen or been in any direct sun in a long time. I had hoped that he could tell in my voice how proud of him I was and I was so glad that he was there with me that together we were being strengthened and receiving a healing. Donna and Chris had been downstairs but they were just as happy when they arrived and seen us walking through the hallways.

As I watched him sleep he soon began to open his eyes this was more encouraging than I had already been. I told him that it wouldn't be long that as soon as we were finished on the 6th Floor we would be out the door.

I didn't want him to become too stirred so we began to walk some more, and as we were walking down the hallway I stopped at the Chapel that was on our floor and I stood for a moment and looked at Joshua in amazement his foot was touching the floor.

At first I thought that maybe it was because the pillow needed to be tucked in a little bit better, but that wasn't it at all. I placed Joshua's foot back on the props and as we started to move he did it again allowing his foot to slide across the floor. I smiled and laughed seeing Joshua do this made me happy, there wasn't anything that I would've rather done than to be with him and see all of these positive changes.

Joshua seemed to quickly become agitated and as we headed back to his room he began to arch back and it didn't look good, my smile was quickly removed as we hurried back to his room asking for assistance to get him back in his bed. I was speaking softly to try and calm him, at the time it didn't seem to be working. We had been out for over an hour and for it being his first time many said that it had been too long for him, we quickly placed Joshua back in his bed and he was quite restless as he laid there.

God had allowed Joshua to sit up and this was progress to take another step. Joshua was given the opportunity to rest for the rest of the day and that was a relief after seeing him become so agitated.

I couldn't say when we would be home, but God knew the plan for us even when I thought we would be going home soon. The change that takes place when we come to him is great, even when he corrects us its out of love and when were hurting he still comforts us.

Donna and Chris had left for the evening and I knew that when they shared with everyone the news that they would come up and want to see Joshua in a wheelchair too.

Joshua wasn't relaxed for the rest of the evening he was really having it rough. I felt crushed, had I expected to much and I was doing all that I could surely there was something more that I wasn't doing. Lord if I just knew what it was that you wanted me to do I will do it, please Lord Come to him. I went to take a small break and I told Joshua that I would return soon I had to get a way for a few minutes, I too felt like I couldn't breathe and was struggling on the inside.

I can only imagine what it was like when Jesus was crucified; he had done all that he could for the people and this is what they chose to do to him.

Was I willing to experience the same pain to gain his promise, yes from the very beginning and not looking back?

I couldn't explain or converse on what Jesus had given to me he gave me complete understanding each day throughout our entire journey, I headed back ready to face our circumstance. I entered Joshua's room and he hadn't calmed at all, I just prayed as I had tears well up in my eyes.

As we progressed throughout the evening I stepped out to go down and get me some ice for my mountain dew, I knew that I was going to be up for another night at the time I thought that I needed it or else I wouldn't have been able to stay with it. God had me in the palm of his hands taking care of me or else I wouldn't have done what I had done daily without him. As I stepped back in Joshua was face down and his food-tube was out of his nose again and there was a lot of bleeding, how could he do this I had only been away for two minutes. I screamed for the nurse as she quickly came to help us, I was so upset there was a lot of blood where was it coming from, I said.

We quickly got him repositioned and Joshua seemed to have a gurgle and she did an immediate suction to remove any excess fluid that could choke or affect him. During our tribulation I felt very weak I hadn't thought much about the voice that I had heard in the garden, yet I felt that God had prepared me yet I wasn't ready to let go of him. I closed every prayer with "not mine will, but thine be done."

Finally we had him relaxed and comfortable again, I sat in a chair next to him and on occasion I would fall asleep, only to wake up to Joshua with the slightest sound or move and immediately I would tend to him. I would say it's alright I'm right here, your doing great the angels are truly coming down and mending every inch of you, and he would soon fall back asleep.

It was a little after 2:00 a.m. and I decided to take a small break again, one would be surprised at the many people walking the halls at this time of hour, but when your in a hospital there is activity every second, minute, and hour.

There will be many that will speak to you seeking a friend someone that they can confide in.

I had certain spots that I liked to sit, one for the day and one for the night. I kept my conversations minimized because I too had a lot going on. I sat sometimes in a daze and had always looked for a sign.

I seeked Jesus daily and all that he had for me. It was very needful during our stay and would be continually in later days.

As I sat on this bench and I looked over there was a door that opened and closed, but no one was there. I watched for other types of activity like lights, movement anything would've been nice. I sat dumbfounded, startled and scared then I headed back and asked what did it mean? God reminded me that he had opened the door that no man could open, and he would close the door that no man could close. That was very needful for me to see at that time, keeping in mind everything is God breathed.

I soon returned to share with Joshua the experience that I had just had not holding anything back. After entering his room I made it a point to hop in his bed to be next to him, he started to move and I said it was just me I wanted to be beside him for the rest of the evening, I was a little scared and needed to be close to him.

I told him that there wasn't anything that I would ever be able to do without him, and he was going to have to stick it out. I loved him so much and I needed him. I hadn't expected to have a temporary solution but was looking for a permanent resolution. I didn't understand the full meaning of what God had given me, I asked Joshua to give Jesus a message for me and have him extend his patience with me until I was in line of what he had asked of me.

I shared everything with Joshua knowing that he was in God's hands; laughter, joy, sorrow, pain, excitement with each new day and what it brings.

Joshua didn't seem to mind me sharing his bed, I fell asleep holding his hand. I awoke to the sound of the zipper moving and it was his nurse administering medicine to him. Joshua had awoke too and started breathing heavily knowing someone else was in his room, I spoke to him softly knowing that often times in doing this it seemed to immediately calm him. I let him know that it was just his nurse, and she would be done soon. Being with him made it easier for me to know when someone had come in and it gave me the opportunity to help calm and comfort him immediately.

I always told Joshua how great he was doing, and I was there for him I wouldn't leave until he did and I meant it.

I hadn't planned on sharing his bed with him for the rest of our days; I felt he was safe knowing that I was beside him to help protect him.

I would speak for him when I felt that someone was doing what they shouldn't be doing.

I loved having the opportunity to be beside him and it kept me from feeling becoming so overwhelmed inside.

We were taking one day at a time, nothing more I couldn't even if I had wanted too.

It was early mourning when the nurses had come into to start there routine with us. They had been required to draw blood daily and from watching Joshua I knew that he didn't like this. He had been stuck with needles everyday that he had been there and it showed that it bothered him as well as it had me. Joshua had tears in his eyes as his nurse began to stick him, one tear rolled down as I wiped it away and said it's alright Joshua you're doing great. Everything that has affected you affects me. I love you!

I shared with Joshua it was day 25 and that he had came along way from our first day. We started out our day with prayer and I asked the Lord for Joshua to receive rest from all of this.

I too was being strengthened daily to have this opportunity to witness Joshua's miraculous recovery.

As the nurse had finished and left our room, I had told Joshua that I was going to take a small break before our day actually began. At the time I had started out each day with a certain amount of caffeine and several cigarettes, I can tell you that it's been 2 years and I have been delivered from those harmful habits.

Upon leaving Joshua's room this gave me the opportunity to extend my ear to others that had been hurting on the inside. I would share with them what God had done for us he would do for them. And almost always I would have the chance to pray with them and I would gladly accept with everyone.

I had been gone for 25 minutes and this for me had been a long time, I hurried back feeling a little overwhelmed maybe I was gone too long; please Lord let him be alright. In returning to Joshua's room, I opened his door and he was alright I was relieved to see he hadn't needed anything or done anything since I had been gone. I wanted so bad for Joshua to come home with me, every time I was away from him I felt that he was going to leave me. I wasn't ready nor did I think that I would ever be.

I told him how much Jesus loved him as I was taking care of his wounds and bathing him, and I had thought that Jesus love couldn't be as great as mine that I had for my son but we were sharing him. We needed one another we had always shared everything.

Jesus knew my pain and had extended Joshua's life that he may gain other lives through the testimony that he had given us and he did.

A Legacy of Faith in 55 Days

I had finished with Joshua's care earlier to be prepared for the visitor's that would be coming to see and spend time with us.

I had music playing not allowing the volume to be turned above 2. It was just enough to hear the music and be in tune with the promises that God leaves with us.

I was looking forward to the many that would be told of Joshua sitting up in a wheelchair for the first time since he had been there.

There were many challenges and obstacles that we would face, but there were many battles that had been fought and we had already won.

To remain in victory is to keep in focus of God's way of doing things and not man.

I did worry as his mom, but I believed in God and what he had done and that eliminated the fear and the anxiety as I continually prayed.

Joshua was really agitated today was it because he had been overworked in his wheelchair the day before that I will never know? Or was it because he needed a back-brace and wasn't given that?

Ex-rays were given daily to monitor the fluid on his lungs but they weren't given to check the correctness of his spinal column along his back with any vertebrae's or discs that may have been out of place, I'm not a doctor so I can't be certain of why some of the procedures were handled the way they were.

I kept the victory in my heart but sometimes it was hard because of the trials that we were facing.

Joshua's doctor had shared with me the charting of his medicines was changing and that she had planned to introduce a new medicine to help him. Joshua's daily doses were changed; the plan was to give more medicine to keep him stable and comfortable until they could regulate what worked for him. I had readily made available to her my requests of certain situations that I wanted addressed

My scripture that I had been given for the day was in II Chronicles 4:18- (KJV) While we look not at the things which are seen, but at the things which are not seen: for the things which are seen are temporal; but the things which are not seen are eternal. I had to remind myself that although I wanted to bring Joshua home, I also wanted to see him have a place made in heaven. To build our faith we would have to trust and obey what God was saying because he had both of our best interest in his hands.

I believed that everything that we were experiencing was part of God's plan; it was needful to go through to share the gospel – which is God's news.

One of the issues that I had addressed with Joshua's doctor is that he had continued having difficulty with the food-tube that was going down his nose; it had caused him to have numerous nose bleeds and the respiratory therapists hadn't been sensitive to our needs or the suctioning process that was done through his nose. It caused more irritation and lots of blood to flow this grieved me deeply and as his mom there wasn't anything that I could do.

Joshua's doctor and I had discussed having a jagosteomy tube in place up to three months until Joshua could eat and swallow food on his own that was great news for me. God was moving we were given extras everyday to continue, I was relieved to know that she had showed compassion in caring for both of our state of well-being.

We had been in agreement and made the arrangements for Joshua to have this surgery done the beginning of the week, we couldn't any sooner because the request had been made coming upon a weekend.

Staff handled the procedures differently daily, there were some that I liked and there were others that I didn't like. There were ones that I wouldn't turn my back too when they were working with Joshua and there are many reasons why. I remained humble throughout our entire ordeal, I knew with everything in me that this was out of my hands. And every day we would be tested.

I had been blessed to have the opportunity to stay with Joshua throughout our 55 days. From the very beginning I had always felt that if I had left during our stay then Joshua would have too.

As the hours seems to pass and it was around 3:00 p.m. our visitors started to arrive with the anticipation in there eyes.

It was difficult for everyone to see him have a trying day, for all of us prayed to have Joshua come home and be safe. No one would believe or want to hear that God's way would be done differently in all of this.

It was a test of faith to hold onto Gods word believing with all of our hearts that Joshua was alright with having seen him struggling with every breath that he breathed at certain times. It was through this humbling experience that I realized the extent of Gods love for us.

I continually requested everyone to keep praying that we weren't finished with what God had begun. I felt the presence of the Holy Spirit within me at all times, it was giving me the strength to carry on.

I hadn't had a lot of rest since day one; I had little sleep and little to eat but God was with me. There was always something to do and yet with the listed being added to daily it didn't seem to bother me, it was needful for me to do.

A Legacy of Faith in 55 Days

As many of us continued to visit Joshua seemed to become frigid, I checked closely to see what I could do to help calm him. I was aware that his sheets needed to be changed, he was aware of what he had done.

I asked everyone to leave us for a few minutes to give me time to change him. As I had attempted to help Joshua he acted as if he didn't want me touching him, this really bothered me, as I held back the tears that filled my eyes.

I told him if he continued I was going to have the nurse come in and do it for him and he continued being restless. So I called for his nurse and asked them to do this for me, I wasn't sure why he was being like that but I didn't want to be the one to upset him. I felt like crying the only thing that I wanted to do was help him, I said.

Staff had said often times in the recovery process as Joshua's they will react differently to the one who is with them the most. I was seeing all of the varied reactions due to the accident both physically and mentally. It was caused by the injury it juggled many emotions and Joshua expressed them allowed to me. This was one of the hardest challenges that I faced, remembering that when Joshua was brought into this world and for fourteen years was a perfect boy, we were starting over and I had to care for him as a mother would that had a child with extra special needs.

I reassured Joshua that I would be there for him continually remembering the promise that I had made, and the promise that God had gave.

We were finally finished and I asked family and friends to come back in and visit with us. All of us continued to encourage Joshua to keep on going, but it wasn't us that were struggling like he was. I had let them know that I wouldn't have Joshua in a wheelchair today; we would try for the following day when he wasn't so agitated. He had been through a lot and I wanted everything to be easy for him as our time progressed and permitted as God allowed. We hadn't had any problems until our first encounter of Joshua sitting up, and everything seemed to snow ball beyond our comprehension after that experience.

As time had past Joshua's dad had asked if he could be included with the care plan process. I had agreed believing this would be a great opportunity for Joshua and his dad to build a greater relationship.

Having this would also allow me extra minutes to relax and breathe as I would have someone else helping me. We had planned to begin working together for the following week. I was excited and at the same time I had started worrying about Joshua's well-being, I shared my concern with other family members as I did Scott and allowed them to see that I was deeply hurt by seeing Joshua struggle so much. I wasn't giving up but as Joshua's mother, I didn't want him hurting continually for any one of us.

We had many children that had come to visit with us that evening, many greeting our immediate family.

Joshua was extremely agitated by now and that allowed only a few minutes with him. I asked each of them to talk to Joshua one at a time, instead of all at once. I tried keeping a smile to enlighten everyone but deep down I was crumbling, and no one knew but one.

Visiting hours were over and everyone hugged and said there goodbyes, some had planned to come and visit with us the following weekend as we said our good nights. Joshua and I were given some quiet time. I sat in a chair to watch him for a while; I grabbed a Bible that had been in his bed. As I opened it up to Psalm 91:1&2 I had originally been feeling weak after reading this scripture it would give me a new strength.

(KJV) He that dwelleth in the secret place of the most High shall abide under the shadow of the Almighty. (2) I will say of the Lord, He is my refuge and my fortress: my God; in him will I trust.

This was a test question was I really believing in what I had been saying from the very beginning? Did I really believe that Joshua was in Gods hands as I had said he was answering with an absolute yes?

Joshua was in a spiritual realm of things why on earth would I want him to step out of God's protection to be with me.

God continually reminded me of what I had asked of him from the very beginning and when he does it there's no confusion with the way he does things.

Man couldn't take credit for what had taken place; God makes it possible when no one else can.

I would keep in continual remembrance knowing that without the mercy and the grace of God I wouldn't be able to tell you what God had done for us during these days.

Joshua started to make sound and I immediately stood up and stepped towards him. I let him know that everything was alright and I held his hand. Joshua began to smile as he did it made me tingle inside and return with a smile to him.

I believe that everything I had seen had been given for a reason. We took every day by seconds, and asking for nothing less than what God had given.

I began to work with him until I finished with our evening routine of doing things; I even repositioned him and put everything away until I would need it again. I had noticed that Joshua didn't appear as restless when the light was dimmed, that too had been adjusted to accommodate him. I realized that when it was fully lit it really seemed to agitate him.

There had been a lot of time that had past, I finally had the opportunity to take a break again. I avoided many of those who were on our floor that was heavily focusing on the medical terminology, conditions and the doctors' words for everything. I knew that they weren't believers when they would say I know God is good, but he can't do this for us only the doctors' can. When I was approached by others that had made statements like that, I would simply ask who gave them the wisdom and the understanding to make the difference to help the patients. Most wouldn't answer and often walk away.

I soon returned to Joshua's room, wondering when we would be able to come home.

As I entered Joshua's room him being sound asleep, I moved towards my bed that I had made in the corner. I knelt to pray and asked the Lord repeatedly when we would be able to go home, with tears flowing down my face. Can you hear me Lord; I know I've asked for the same thing numerous times my request hasn't changed. I need to know how much longer our stay is.

I was reminded that through my transgressions Jesus had paid the ultimate price; it was through his life that we would have life. Joshua was innocent he didn't deserve to have this happen to him, I did as I pleaded. I felt empty and when I quit seeking pity that was when God really gave me the understanding that I had been seeking.

I was walking on thin ice, but during this time God was giving me so much more he was repairing and restoring my life and giving me the opportunity to stand up and take a stand for him and what is right for our lives, I finally seen the purpose and plan that he had for me and it took our experience to get it through to me the many reasons why things happen the way they do, it is for our benefit if we would look through it as did the eyes of Jesus Christ.

As I made way to get some sleep it seemed that within minutes Joshua's Respiratory Therapist had came in, Joshua stirred in his bed making sound letting me know that someone was in there with us. I immediately let Joshua know that everything was alright that it was just the RT doing the evening routine, I waited patiently as he finished and when he would leave so I could go back to sleep. I had to always tell Joshua that I knew when someone was in the room with us to calm him, to keep him from breathing so heavily. I believe he did it this way it was his way of communicating with me, it let me know that he was listening.

I felt that confirming my presence continually would take away any fear that Joshua may have had being in such a big place and knowing that he wasn't facing anything alone. At the same time I was reminded of the scripture I will never leave you comfortless, I will come to you. (KJV)

I will be with you Joshua until the end; I won't leave without you I assured him.

I lied back down only to be awakened 40 minutes later by staff doing routine visits again, we would be tried daily because what God had given and done for us made many curious and they wanted to see if they could speed up or enhance any part of Joshua's recovery process.

Time had past by so quickly it was now 4:00a.m. and Joshua was wide awake ready to take on the day. I was glad to be greeted by him every mourning sometimes with a smile and other times just having the opportunity to look into his beautiful green eyes made it worth the while.

I let him know that I was doing things a little bit different I would take a shower first because it took longer to care for him and I would be done with everything in just a few minutes. This would've been a good time for him to argue with me and I wouldn't have minded. I scurried quickly making the most of such little time.

I was finished and routinely did everything that was needful to care for him, not hurrying to ever hurt him but always taking time to do it right. I had learned to do a lot and became quite fast than I had when I originally started.

I sat back feeling satisfied waiting for the time to strike 9:00 a.m. Joshua had a visit with a physical therapist and a speech therapist at the same time. I watched carefully as the physical therapist had braced him while sitting up and his speech therapist placed a swab in his mouth that caused Joshua to suck on it getting all of the water from it, he really liked it. She had asked him to swallow and he did this was great progress that he had showed. All of us were smiling and were very pleased in the way he was doing things. God was working every inch of him for us to see and remember all that he had given. Joshua had been in therapy for approximately 20 minutes when he arched back, they continued to work him while he lay down instead of sitting up. I wasn't too happy after seeing him become so agitated; he was resisting anyone's touch to him at this point including mine the one who was always trying to comfort him.

There time was up and they wrapped it up with the plan to come again in a few hours, I didn't say anything as I nodded my head and watched them as they were leaving.

My heart was racing I prayed with Joshua and then I told him that I had to go to the Chapel to pray at this point my heart was really hurting and I didn't want him to see me that way. I had to trust in the Lord, or I wouldn't make it. I had to learn his way and my way had not been the right way.

Upon leaving him I had met with a couple through the hallways who had just arrived Michelle and Roc were there with three year old daughter Olivia.

We were introduced and I was told they were placed in a room next door to us, I didn't know them or there circumstance but they had heard about mine and let me know they were praying for us and Joshua's recovery. I thanked them and proceeded to leave as I went to the Chapel to pray my heart feeling very heavy.

God was first I know that from speaking with them it was genuine they were committed there wasn't any second guessing.

As I was learning and growing God was so merciful to energize and strengthen me continually. And as I began to understand his love it made me become more vibrant as the sun in which followed me. I know that it does with everyone but in times past I had taken it for granted, and didn't realize how beautiful it was and how it's needful for all of us until now.

Jesus Christ deserves all of the praise for it is through his eyes that allowed us to be over comers. I felt embraced within minutes and immediately returned to Joshua's room with that strength. As I entered in Joshua seemed agitated I started overlooking him closely to see what could be bothering him and noticed his ivie area was red, bleeding and looked irritated. I called for his nurse and she came in and said it would be ok she would keep an eye on it and recommend having it changed later. I felt in needed to be changed then but there was nothing that I could do except continue asking and reminding them of this area every time they came in to check on him.

We had continued with our plan of placing Joshua in a wheelchair for those who hadn't seen Joshua sitting up when they came to visit. My mom and Joshua's cousin Cody were one of them that had come to see us. I wanted it to be a surprise for everyone so I had them wait in the waiting area while we placed Joshua in his chair. It was exciting to have this opportunity once again and after securing Joshua in I wheeled him down to let them see him. As I entered it was truly an emotional moment upon seeing everyone's eyes gleaming for what had been a long time to see Joshua sitting up for us.

This was just one more thing that God had given us to witness and it instilled the beliefs of many, his greatest breathing life back into him. To have Joshua up and out of his room made all of us feel that it wouldn't be long before we would have the opportunity to bring him home.

It doesn't take long to cover every inch of a hospital when you're grounded to one floor only. Everyone was excited to walk with us through the hallways this was one of the happiest days that we had shared.

We had kept Joshua out for about an hour changing his elevation slightly every 10 to 15 minutes as the nurse had said. Joshua started to breathe heavily and became agitated suddenly it was immediate for me to take him back to his room right then. I stopped at the nurse's station and let some of them know that we had to get him back in his bed immediately and everyone gathered around to transfer him quickly.

Moments passed and Joshua had started to relax, we patiently waited and had decided to go to the cafeteria and grab a quick bite to eat. Before leaving all of us had gathered around Joshua's bed again, joining hands and had asked the angels to mend and repair every inch of him that we wanted to see him recover and bring him home with us. Amen

We left and I let the staff know that I was going to get a bite to eat and I would be back soon, I always asked if they had planned to do anything different before ever leaving and they had said there wasn't any changes made for that day in particular. They assured me that they would check in on Joshua for me even if he was sleeping, that made me feel a little at ease. So we left I felt like my mom and nephew were in slow motion upon arriving at the cafeteria, we sat and prayed and within a few minutes I was done and excused myself to return to Joshua again. I apologized for being in such a hurry but deep down I felt I couldn't stay away for very long. They had just started to eat and I was already done.

I rushed back not wasting any time, as I returned to the 6th Floor and entered in Joshua's room seeing him sleeping sound, I didn't want to wake him but it was time to change his bandages again. I was continually thankful for every minute that I had with him.

I knew that it would be a little while before my mom or Cody returned I had completed what was needed in the time frame aloud.

I waited quietly in his room watching in amazement the wounds were healing they really looked good.

I never once looked at what I was doing as anything more than what I felt needed to be done.

Time had past and my Mom and Cody returned to let me know they planned to leave, I nodded my head and knew that there were others that would be up and I gave a hug and kiss as we said good-bye. Before they left Donna and Chris had made it in and there was a few more minutes of sharing the great news of what Joshua was doing. God had blessed us so greatly not one is to be taken lightly. I was so delighted to see Donna and Chris; I had complete trust in them from the very beginning.

I never had to worry what I said when I was with Chris or Donna they never misinterpreted anything. It was difficult for me to have a conversation with others because by the time they left the truth had been completely twisted than what it had originally been given. I wouldn't be told until much later, what others had said but deep down I had an uneasy feeling with many I had guidance from the Holy Spirit and I could feel if it was right or wrong deep down even with the visitation.

Joshua's dad (Scott) and girlfriend (Deanna) had come to visit with us too; Scott was really struggling with the situation that we were facing. I found myself speaking calmly and positive during our visitation, I wanted him to be encouraged and see him strengthened through our experience.

I let him know they had planned to perform surgery on Joshua in the beginning of the week; a replacement for the food tube that had been inserted through the nose would be placed directly in the stomach. That would lesson his irritation and would eventually allow them to increase his food intake with the tube, the overall would be much better for him. I wasn't sure exactly when, but as soon as I would know I would tell him.

Joshua had close to 14 nosebleeds during our stay, my decision for this surgery was to eliminate the irritation that had been made to the lining and tissue of his nose. I know they had said it was common for the numerous nosebleeds but for me and being there with him I felt it was too much on him.

The time had come and visiting hours were over, before we had said our good-byes we joined together and prayed with Joshua again.

I knew that I would see Donna and Chris again the following day; for every day that we would have to stay they would come and visit with us.

I prepared for our evening care, as if it were the beginning of our day and never requiring a lot of sleep to stay with Joshua.

I had to stay consistent with all of the changes. I had kept extra moisturizer on Joshua's lips, hands and feet to keep them from drying out. I had kept extra drops in his eyes too. For other patients it was common for them to have bad skin and irritant eyes but for me and Joshua it wasn't. I told Joshua that I knew that he was a miracle child and I would share his story with everyone that would listen.

We had been so blessed but Joshua already knew, and was in the palm of God's hands being used to touch many not just mine.

I knew everything would be different for us upon being released, no more doubts my faith was growing more and more everyday and I was truly learning to trust in God completely.

Joshua had continued to be breathing on his own without the assistance of a machine; however he was given breathing treatments that was to strengthen his existing patterns. The respiratory therapist had come in and said eventually I would be taught to do them. I hesitated for a moment and realized that it would be much later in our stay and I didn't need to give it much thought until then. I stood by Joshua waiting for them to finish and shared the excitement with them as we talked about Joshua's recovery. He was amazing. Some of the staff shared with me there difficult times that they had with a loved one, as some finished with the comment "went through" I believed we were going through too. It helped to know that there were caregivers who could relate to our traumatic experience and it was heartfelt.

I would find myself taking a break between 1:00a.m. and 2:00a.m. it was during this time that I would stay away the longest trying to get as close to God as I could and to remember everything that we had been given.

I would walk downstairs and find myself during those quiet times really pouring my heart out to God. I was thankful and hurting in the same breath.

I couldn't understand how God could love me as much as he had Joshua and I sure couldn't see me making a difference in other peoples lives the way he had used Joshua.

Joshua was in his youth and he still had his innocence. He had a life to live I didn't I exclaimed. Lord let me know that I'm going to take him home and everything is going to be alright. That's what I wanted answered and that is what I had prayed.

No matter what you achieve in life, it means nothing if you can't share it with the one that you love most.

I loved Joshua he was my son and he was my life for the longest time. And then I realized at that moment that without God his mercies and love my life would've been gone and I wouldn't be able to live without God allowing me to see the way he did. I had to seek his purpose and plan for both of us; it wasn't just for the one of us.

I finished my prayer and had my break ready to return to see how Joshua was doing. Upon entering his room Joshua began to breathe quite heavily and made sound, I reassured him it was just me (mom) and we had a couple more hours before he really needed to start moving around.

I would unzip his bed pull up a chair and sit next to him, holding his hand. I was holding to him and letting him know that I wasn't giving up on him.

Mourning had came it was around 6:00a.m. it was time to start with our planned schedule again, Joshua seemed more agitated than usual this mourning and I couldn't understand why.

We started out our mourning with prayer and I asked for guidance to do what God needed me to do and it was evident that he was using Joshua to get me to do this.

Every day we shared was a blessing and a gift given to us!

After caring for him as I had, I asked the nurse to come in and help with his elbow again. I felt I wasn't able to do it myself, and I wasn't sure how far it needed to be packed. I had to hold his arm up while they clean, packed, and wrapped it and it was difficult to do because this caused pain to him greatly. I could tell by the way he reacted every time we had to tend to this arm.

I had asked our Lord to heal his arm, and I believed Joshua had received a touch and was being healed inside out but at the time that isn't how I prayed in this case until much later on and that too was granted with or request that had been made, it was amazing.

The technicians were coming down to take ex-rays again, it was part of our daily activities for the longest time until the incident took place and then they were no longer requested daily again for part of our care plan.

I reassured Joshua they were there to take another picture of him, and that I was right there going through it with him. I didn't want him to be or feel scared ever.

I was asked to step out; I felt it necessary to stay and was granted my request. I was given a protective vest to wear during Joshua's ex-ray. I put it on feeling like I was placing a piece of armory on, I too had lost weight and this piece felt extremely heavy. I will never forget what Joshua had endured for everything he had went through I was there.

I wanted so desperately to have the opportunity to make up for all of those lost years; I had been to busy doing stuff and had limits with a lot of our time. It was during our stay that I had realized that he was almost a grown up as our time together shared had flown by over the years.

I was telling Joshua what my plans were, what I was anticipating upon our release and he lye comfortably and listened. Even in discomfort he smiled for me.

I planned to take a break as I watched Joshua start to move around and he was making sound. I gave him a kiss and zipped his bed and told him I would be back very soon. I moved quite quickly feeling the minutes that we had been given daily. I still had that ache that no matter how great our day that pain wouldn't go away.

As I went downstairs and looked out the window, it saddened me to see that it was dark and gloomy. Throughout our stay it was like a preparation given daily of what kind of day that we would face based on the weather conditions. As a newborn babe in Jesus Christ it was easier for me to understand the difference in weather conditions and compare these parables with our Christian experiences in living. Although we would be faced with another difficult day and it would be quite challenging, God gave us the strength and ability to endure.

Even after knowing I loved the care for us Jesus was showing!

For all of the extra time given with Joshua was truly a blessing.

As I had taken my break and headed back, I stopped in the Chapel to kneel and pray again, looking at the stain glass was an instant reminder of the love this mother had shown. She held her child in her arms but she knew that she couldn't help him the way he could and she was giving him back as Jesus reached out to help them and that's exactly the way I had felt. I couldn't do what he needed me to do without him.

I finished praying and eagerly headed back to reunite with Joshua again. I was always happy to see him upon entering his room. I went and spoke softly too him, I unzipped his bed and placed my head on his chest. I could hear his heart beat loud and clear and that assured me of the life within him.

Again I told him how much he meant to me and how much I loved him and he had to know, I believe this was a time that I realized that everything that we had been through he loved me just as much. I zipped his bed up and I had gathered the laundry that needed to be washed, it was done daily to keep everything up.

I left and hurried back always pacing in the time it took.

I prepared to take a shower, I told him that I was just around the corner and just steps away that within minutes I would be finished and then it would be his turn.

I was always listening upon bathing to see if there was anything different than his normal breathing. Joshua had a way of letting me know someone else had entered our room, this was his way of communicating with me.

I moved quickly to keep everything on a consistency to prove that I would care for him and do what they were doing, I remained attentive to his every need.

I knew the necessity of staying focused of Gods will and way each day. I prayed with Joshua and shared with him the scripture that I had been given with my reading for this day. We had to trust in the Lord, for it is he that had never failed us. It was through Gods grace that allowed Joshua to be with us.

Time moves by so quickly when you have so much to do in keeping with the daily schedule and activities. Everyone had been given a certain amount of time with him. Family and friends had started to arrive having the opportunity to see Joshua in a wheelchair again was exciting.

Some had made the comment that I didn't really have a lot to do because they had seen how quickly I moved to accompany Joshua. What they've forgotten was the continual repetitions that it took for me to become that way. I smiled to each one not holding any grudges against the conversation being made. I wanted to give to them and show them what God had given to us deep within. I loved each one in a different way some making it easier than others to be around. In society people are taught that you have to prove yourself worthy for recognition, but in God's eyes it's not needful at all.

Everyone had exited for a few minutes giving us the opportunity to place him in his wheelchair again. On the count of three staff and I worked to properly place him in his chair and we did. I again had the opportunity to wheel Joshua out having placed pillows round about him to keep him cushioned and comfortable.

In the eyes of everyone that had witnessed; you could see the gleam in each ones eyes as they watched him. They too were reminded of Joshua's accident and where he had came from compared to day one. Jesus Christ continually getting all of the praise and glory for it wasn't any of us that were doing anything different than what had already been done. This was an expression of God's love when you place it in his hands and not mans.

A Legacy of Faith in 55 Days

As we wheeled him through the hallways Joshua made it a point to show off for us today. Joshua kept placing his foot on the floor as we were moving across the narrow pathway. He was doing this repeatedly with his eyes closed, and I said to him as we stopped Joshua open your eyes for everyone to see what you've been showing me, at the time he wasn't doing anything. And then I told him Joshua if you don't let them see your pretty green eyes as you've shown me then I'm going to cut your hair and you know what, he did what I had asked of him with a moan.

Joshua had been growing out his hair from the childhood chili bowl cut and he could hear us and knew what I was asking and responded that was very pleasing, even with a moan. I had assured him that I wasn't going to cut his hair but I wanted them to see what he had been doing for me as I gave him a quick kiss on his cheek.

We continually walked the floor and stopped as Joshua had placed special attention to a balloon that was on a desk in our path. All of us gathered around and prayed and gave a moment of Thanks.

We had only been out of his room a few times, but he seemed to adjust so well as long as he wasn't rushed. This was the first time in our stay that I had spoke with his dad without getting mad. We had our differences and there had been many contentions between us before the accident, God was removing the old and making the both of us new.

Joshua loved the both of us; he didn't want to choose which one he loved or liked more we were equal as most parents are to a child if you don't spoil there minds.

It definitely was time to put the past to rest once and for all and that is what we had done.

We had been out for about an hours Joshua had immediate signs of agitation as we quickly moved to get him to his room. As I came around the corner I let the staff know he needed to be immediately placed in his bed as they followed right behind to accompany me.

I had watched Joshua so closely on a daily basis I could tell when he was going to move before anyone else did.

As I positioned myself across his bed to help with the lift in placing him in his bed, his nurse for the day being at the head of the chair and the other one being at the feet and I was in the middle. I had asked the nurse to keep an eye on his head so he didn't hurt himself with the metal rail before lifting him on count. I wasn't in a position where I could immediately help him the way the attending nurse was that I was addressing.

He didn't respond thinking he had plenty of time and about that time Joshua arched back and really hurt himself against the rail of his chair, which made me mad because his nurse didn't believe that Joshua needed assistance when I had told him he did. I reached for Joshua and wanted to pick him up myself and place him back in his bed but on a quick three all of us did.

I hadn't realized the impact of this incident; God was giving me the ability to see things happen before they did. All of us could be better prepared in acting upon those warning signs before the storm ever takes place if we would acknowledge what they are when they are given to us.

The staff had left and family came back in to visit with us, it was mid-afternoon and some of us were ready to grab a bite to eat. I had lost weight and many were concerned that I wasn't eating like I needed to. The continual consistency of Joshua's care was taking everything that I had eaten from me. There were many times that I would eat when I wasn't hungry; I had realized that my body needed the nutrients to keep me going. I believed that as long as I stayed strong that Joshua would to and that meant everything.

Joshua's dad was concerned about the upcoming surgery; I assured him that I would contact him as soon as Joshua was in recovery. He wouldn't have to go all day without knowing, I had planned to call his mom and she would contact him and give him the information that I had gave to her. We had said our good-byes and anticipated on the surgery for the following day.

Joshua and I was to ourselves again, he was really agitated and I felt overwhelmed to see him express so much discomfort and there wasn't anything else that I could do that I hadn't already done. I believe that it was because he had been sitting up and it was too much for him in just a few days. I would tell him that I believed that it was God's plan and that I believed that he was being used to get all of us to believe again and we did.

He was healing nicely as I had prepared to change the bandages on his wounds again. I hummed a song to him and said to him that he looked as handsome then as he had the day that he had came in.

His hair was growing out fast, getting rid of all of that black and his natural was coming back.

His evening nurse came in to let me know that she would be working with us as I finished up. She was extremely efficient with her procedures and very knowledgeable which some appeared to be lacking. She had a very loud voice and I had asked her to tone it down a little bit, it may have been because she was an evening nurse and she was awake that she assumed all of her patients would be to regardless of what time it was.

We had a great day it made me appreciate everything that we had been given, the things that we had always taken for granted even sitting up had now become a challenge. There were many families who faced daily the same challenges that we were facing.

A Legacy of Faith in 55 Days

Through it all we would be over comers if we didn't loose sight on what God had given to us.

Time had past and I had a few minutes to rest my head my cot was positioned directly across from Joshua. I prayed and had asked to experience the same thing Joshua was going through so I would never forget the tremendous sacrifice he was making for us.

I had fell asleep and awakened to have the most excruciating pain that was in my left arm. The pain was so bad that it felt like every bone that I had had been crushed, like I'd been hit with a baseball bat. This experience lasted for about five minutes, my eyes filled with tears and then the pain left.

Joshua had started arching in his bed, I went to him and said I know how your feeling and told him that I would go ask his nurse to give him an extra dose of medicine to help him. I found his nurse and asked her to give him something extra and she said no, if she gave him his medicine early than he would have to wait longer for his next dose. I walked away hurting knowing that there wasn't anything that I could do for him, as I entered his room tears filling my eyes and the only thing that I could say is I'm sorry there isn't anything that I can do. I had never had to tell him that until now. God would give him what he needed, and what I needed to.

I picked up the Bible that was laying next to him in the bed and opened it up to read Psalm 46:1 – (KJV) God is our refuge and strength, a very present help in trouble. This was confirming the scripture that I had read the previous mourning in the Upper Room; this was teaching and renewing in me the hope to keep believing.

After reading this scripture to Joshua it didn't seem to calm him, but it reminded me of how merciful and strong God is and how he extends his love to each of us, knowing that it will help us.

If I hadn't had this extra time with Joshua, I would've questioned if he made it to heaven or not. What God gave to us there is no doubt in my mind I know that he made it and that one day I will reunite with him.

Joshua knew that his life would end soon; he had shared that with his dad previously. Weeks later his dad had shared that with me only to tell Joshua that he had his whole life ahead of him and there wasn't anything that was going to happen to him. I had been given the warning and ignored it thinking, maybe to someone else but not to us. The truth of the matter is you never know when your life will end there is but a step between life and death. All of us should make it a necessity to be ready.

I thought Joshua had said it to be mean, being a teenager and saying this to persuade me to let him have his way but it didn't change the rules that I had for him.

Just three weeks before the accident there were some boys that had came to our door, they appeared to be much older than 14 or 15 year olds. Joshua had asked me to tell them that he wasn't allowed and couldn't come out. I did as he had asked and after these young men had left I had asked who they were and what they wanted; I had never seen them before.

Joshua had been avoiding them and now they were coming to our door. He told me not to worry he had met them through a friend, and he had made the decision not to hang around them. I didn't know what was going on but deep down I knew that Joshua was making a wise decision and he had put thought into it before ever saying anything. This was one of those times he needed me to help him and I did because it was too big for him to handle without me.

Later that evening Joshua had asked me to share a Bible story with him and I had asked why? He said it was the way I would tell it helped to comfort him. I shared with him what Jesus had done for us to receive forgiveness and I ended it because I was starting to feel guilty sharing with him this story and the life I had been living.

Joshua was restless and arching back like he was about to do a complete back bend. I was told by many of the staff this was very common with brain injury patients. Throughout our mourning Joshua became more and more agitated wheezing while he was breathing and to me that wasn't a good sign.

I tried praying and was having a really difficult time concentrating seeing him this way. I told him everyone was praying for us and he had to come through this we would share with everyone what God had done for us. I had also said that we had come too far for him to even think about giving up.

It was easy for me to say because I wasn't the one physically experiencing what he did. Deep down it was effecting more and more to see him go through so much knowing that it was taking a lot from him daily and I believe Joshua was starting to get tired of fighting.

I wanted Joshua to be like he was before the accident, he looked like he always had and as far as the mobility of everything that would take a little bit more practice.

I was trying to build a relationship with his doctor, nurses, and therapist knowing how important it was to have trust and good communication. If I couldn't trust in them and there training how would I ever trust in God completely?

I really began to feel overwhelmed and decided to break away for a few minutes, as I moved through the hallways being greeted by many recognized as Joshua's mom and being asked how he was doing, normally I said great but not today. I was being honest in saying that he was having a very difficult mourning and we needed extra prayer today to get through the minutes.

A Legacy of Faith in 55 Days

As I walked outside proceeding to get to my chosen spot, I came across a man named Brian whom I'd never met this was my first time visiting with him. Brian was from West Virginia and had survived a terrible drowning accident many years ago as a teenager.

I had said whatever it takes I will do but having this encounter with Brian was not something that I had thought or was even prepared for.

He had asked if I was a patient, and I said no my son was and through compassion he had asked what had happened. I had shared with him briefly that Joshua had been struck by a mini-van and was pinned underneath and that was what I had seen upon arriving at the scene. I had also said that by the grace of God he had intervened and he was caring for him I had placed Joshua in the palm of his hands saying it with confidence for a minute.

I stated that I was a strong believer in miracles and he said he was too. He had asked how long we had been there and I said that this was day 28 for us.

I briefly answered his questions and finished with a smile and then Brian looked me in the eyes and began to tell me about his traumatic accident and dramatic recovery.

Brian had gone out for the afternoon with a few of his friends to go swimming, what was planned for fun ended in disaster.

Brian had swum out farther from the banks than the rest and planned to turn around and go back when he realized he couldn't catch his breath and began to panic and started to go under the water. Those who were watching him from the bank thought he was playing and watched him pop up and down as he drowned and went a float. Moments had past when they had realized that he was in trouble and needed help.

None of them knew the proper procedure to get him out of the water without being at risk for them to drown.

Some stayed while others went to get an adult to help them, it took approximately 20 minutes before they had someone to dive in and rescue him.

Brian was given CPR with no response; they used a defibulator to get a heartbeat. Brian's mom arrived at the hospital and immediately started praying for him. Brian had been a believer all of his life and through prayer was given life again.

Brian was in the hospital for 1 year and every test that they could think to give him was done, him remembering the pain that was endured but because he had lost his voice he couldn't tell them. They had said that he was in a comatose state and had given up on him and wanted to send him away but his mom hadn't. His mom was told to take him off of the machines but she refused to do it this was hitting the very core of my heart because I too had been experiencing the same thing as Joshua's mom. This made me to realize that there are many who are able to share the same pain that I was feeling.

INSPIRATION

The demand was too great for his mom to care for him and Brian was eventually transferred to a nursing home; He had been there 6 months and was one day awakened. Brian had received extensive operations from the loss of oxygen; he has scars from his head to his toes but was thankful for the air that he was breathing.

Brian had a difficult time talking, walking, and having the ability to use his hands but he was doing it. Here he was standing in front of me what a tremendous testimony!

I had tears filling my eyes as he had finished sharing with me what I felt was very personal; he asked if I was alright? I said, no. I apologized and excused myself I wasn't but steps away and the tears were really flowing. I hurried to the Chapel and no more than I entered in I fell to my knees, I begged and pleaded Lord please don't put Joshua through that for me. Lord I know that you're scripture says that you will never put any more on us than we can handle, well I think this is it I exclaimed. I had said I was willing to except all of the changes, was I really? Joshua had come into this world perfectly formed and was a healthy boy, I didn't want the memories that all of us had shared with him to be changed or altered in any way. I knew that deep down that this wasn't something that I would be able to handle, although in the beginning I had said I would accept anything. I finished my prayer and was eager to return and be reunited with Joshua.

Upon entering his room I moved close to him letting him know where I had been and who I had met as he vigorously moved in his bed. I said Joshua I know that this is very challenging for you, please don't give up, I need you and I love you so much. You know that don't you? I was really missing him talk to me like he used to.

He wasn't at all relaxed and expressed a lot of difficulty but his therapist continued to do his physical therapy as it had been scheduled and knowing that he would be proceeding with surgery later in the afternoon. I was then told about an hour later that it was re-scheduled for the following afternoon. I was relieved and I also watched as I felt helpless as everyone else expected and took so much of him and made him so agitated.

After the room was cleared I shared with him my visit with Brian, and I felt that he had been God sent to send a message to me in the form that I could relate. Joshua had started to calm for a few minutes before he would become agitated again.

Joshua's doctor had came in and said that they would start the weaning process of one of his medicines today. He had a lot going on for one day.

I was briefed in as she consistently made her rounds to each of her patients.

I proceeded to tend to the care and needs of Joshua's daily activities that were necessary and also charted. I always let staff know what I was doing and when I was doing it so they could mark it.

There was so much to do to keep everything going smoothly.

When I had the opportunity to look at the clock again it was almost 5:00p.m.

Joshua had therapy three times today and the sessions are for 45 minutes that a lot when you've been out of practice. I always looked forward to the clock striking five-o-clock I knew then that no one would be in to bother him.

I believed greatly when Joshua was having a good day, like today when he wasn't I would doubt. I continued to pray and seek strength to have the faith that I had claimed from our very first day.

Donna and Chris had made it up again to visit with us I shared with them our ups and downs all day long our experiences. I enjoyed visiting with them daily as I know Joshua did too. We had been in Joshua's room for quite some time and we had agreed to walk down and grab a bite to eat, as we left telling Joshua not to do anything until we returned.

As we entered the cafeteria I shared with her my fear while standing in line and having tears roll down, she grabbed and hugged me and said everything is going to be alright.

She was the only one that I could really express how I was feeling and instead of making it more difficult she just wrapped her arms around me and loved me.

We managed to find us a seat and between the three of us there was minimal talking. We were focused on Joshua and it was difficult to say anything when we had seen him have such a difficult day.

Donna and Chris had been given a tremendous gift as I had they had been given the opportunity to witness everything as I had and even extras. There were a lot of things Joshua wouldn't do with others in the room, it was with specific ones. A great testimony had been given to us and God trusted us with his anointing.

We had finished eating and left the cafeteria to take a little break outside. It was great to have some fresh air and to feed the birds because I had done this every evening before returning to Joshua's room.

Time had always gone by so fast when I was given this opportunity to visit with them, we had headed back and I had asked Donna if she would help me in caring for him.

I had been asked by his care coordinator Deb to have someone in the family be able to do the same thing that I had been doing.

I felt comfortable with Donna and Chris and I trusted in them. She had agreed as we had returned to his room.

After entering in and seeing Joshua as restless as ever we had read some of the cards given to him, and then I had asked her to read the Bible to him so I could take another shower. I knew this was going to be a long night and I needed to rejuvenate while someone else watched him for me.

I took longer than the normal five or ten minutes, afterwards I felt really good, I was ready to face another evening without any expectations of what it would bring.

It was getting really late and they had to leave, we prayed and she had said when the time comes and you need me I will be here to help you, and I knew from speaking to the coordinator she would have to come up soon, we had planned on him being released very soon.

I felt overwhelmed as if I wouldn't be able to continue to do everything on my own without her being there to help me, failing to keep in mind that God had his hand on us the entire time.

My brother-in-law had told me before leaving to keep an extra eye on the way Joshua was being handled and what staff had given him. It had been made known to him that patients that have insurance the way we did often have continual set backs for the hospital to receive the maximum benefit and it's at cost of someone else life. The maximum hold on any floor was two weeks at a time, there had to be something significant happen with each patient to keep them in the hospital. In our case we were a prime candidate for release because the care that Joshua needed was minimal compared to others who were sharing the 6th Floor.

I had been writing a lot of incidents in that little blue notebook for quite some time, this was one more thing that I had been reminded of. What I had started out with good intentions in doing having the opportunity to share with Joshua later in regards to his recovery was ending negatively.

We hugged and said our goodbyes as Joshua had continued his arching and posturing. I remained with Joshua and had tried everything and a last resort I moved his legs to the edge of the bed, and he relaxed them with a bend.

I then moved him in a position to have his legs resting in the bends of my elbows continually supporting him. I stood and began to rock or sway back and forth and he had immediately began to calm. He became so comfortable with that position that he had fell asleep. I had stood in this position for almost 2 hours with just a few minutes lacking. I was getting really tired, yet I knew that he had such a difficult day and really needed some sleep.

I looked at him with admiration and how peacefully sleeping he really was. I asked God to continue working through me to give back to Joshua and others as he had given me.

Joshua awoke and pulled his left leg back and when he did, I placed him comfortably back in his bed surrounding him with pillows and making sure certain areas were elevated for him.

Joshua had lost some weight because there was a three inch gap from his back to the mattress. And I felt without having extra cushion that probably caused discomfort. It really seemed to be helping him and I needed to see that I could contribute something that would help satisfy him being his mom.

It was really difficult to keep everything in perspective and on schedule when he was so relaxed and comfortable. I had to do his dressing changes and was learning to administer his medicines to him. I moved with a little hesitation really not wanting to disturb or awake him. He was so beautiful and he was resting. I finished much later than usual wanting him to get the maximum benefit of sleep that he had needed.

After finishing I had pulled up a chair and sat next to his bed, again carefully holding or caressing his hand. I had looked down to read the verse that I had been given when our day began which was Psalm 91:1 (KJV) and was still trying to grasp the full meaning of this verse. I believe that he was dwelling with the most high my God, and he had him protected under the shadow of his wings. If you're and heir to the kingdom having his shadow upon you is all that you need when you're faced with a situation like this.

Joshua had started to become agitated, his breathing patterns had changed rapidly. Did he wake up afraid, I'm not sure but I immediately started to do what I always had to calm him?

Then I got in his bed and lay beside him, telling him everything was going to be alright and had hymned the melody that I had been given. I prayed with him and said I give you to God and we will see this through.

I wondered who the angels there to help us were. And I wondered if one of them had been my brother.

I thought for a moment of how beautiful heaven must be as I asked him what did he think heaven would be like? He began to calm and I know that he knew that I was there with him through everything.

I had big plans for us when we got home; we hadn't been able to call it ours for very long. Together we had made our house feel like a home and it was wonderful to have had those talks, and quiet time something that money couldn't buy.

The reality of this was I couldn't buy or give anything that was going to change our situation for us. But, God would give us the strength and peace to continue.

It was around 3:30a.m. And I was feeling really tired from all of his moving, I got out of his bed and was really cold although he was very warm. I had to wear winter clothing the entire time, because the temperature was set so low in his room.

I had told him that I needed a nap and that I would be back.

I went around the corner where the play area was and laid my head down on a rubber mat. There was a fish tank that was in front of me and that seemed to make me feel real sleepy. I closed my eyes and awoke fifteen minutes later by the sound of an automatic door opening.

I sat up and grabbed my things and hurried back to see where the technicians were going, to see what time it was and to reunite with Joshua, deep down hoping that I hadn't stayed away too long.

I went in to see Joshua all rolled up and breathing heavily. I said a loud it's alright Joshua I'm right here calm down ok. I had always felt that he would only stay if I was around, if I had left the hospital within our stay Joshua would have left too that was emanate I felt. God knew how much I loved him and he loved him too, God gave us this time that he could use the two of us to leave a gift from heaven a written testimony.

Joshua had been calmed for a little while only to be disturbed by the nurse to draw blood again. This was part of the daily routine, Joshua had track marks up and down his arms from all of the procedures that he had been given. He was awake for me to see his eyes fill with tears as they did there thing, during there procedure I let Joshua know how proud of him I was and how courageous he had been for all of us.

This was a time that I would have loved to step in and go through all of the testing for him, that wasn't a choice that I was given to make. Through it all he managed to give me a smile and after being beside him and watching I too had experienced and shared his pain.

We were to start our daily regimen again and I wasn't too excited to have the therapists working with him again, he had another difficult night and I really didn't want anyone working with him. I wanted him to get some rest; I had been actively supportive in everything that involved him Joshua had moved around so much as if he really didn't want anyone touching him. And this was a day planned for him to have surgery for the gagestomy tube.

At the time no one really knew what was going on other than God and Joshua.

I struggled with allowing certain actions and comments pass that had been directed towards me as a slam. I didn't have a degree and the past I had lived had been held against me by some. To get through this the way God would have it I had to look past the remarks that others had stated. I knew that I was walking in newness and it wasn't important to prove myself to them, but to the one that sees all of us.

It was mid-afternoon and we had visitors to accompany us as we had prepared for his upcoming surgery. I had felt some contentions in the air but didn't want to say anything that would upset Joshua so I waited. We had transferred Joshua down to the West Wing that was where they had planned to do his surgery. Nothing about this day was going smoothly and for Joshua he seemed to be fighting for his life, there wasn't anything that I could do that would calm him. We had stayed side by side Joshua until they actually planned to take him back to surgery. It was finally time as the nurse had came back to inform us we said a prayer, remembering to ask God's mighty hand to be with him and it was done in agreement. I insisted on walking back with him and wanting to be with him through the procedure, he had to know that I wasn't leaving him that I was there for him.

I was told that it was against hospital policy for me to accompany him during surgery. I had said that throughout all of the other procedures I had been aloud, I was denied and asked to step out of the surgery room and wait outside. I was told that it was a fairly quick procedure and that in minutes the doctor would be finished.

I wasn't sure if they had planned on putting him under anesthesia but I insisted that they did before I exited he was so restless. I watched them administer it before leaving.

I was so upset to see Joshua uncomfortable and restless as he was. I let staff know that I would be waiting in the waiting room, to please come get me when they had finished with the surgery.

I paced the floor waiting and every minute feeling like an hour as my sister and mom stayed with me. We had left to take a 5 minute break and hurried back waiting with anticipation.

I never stayed away too long always feeling anxious if I was gone for more than 15 minutes.

My mom and sister were talking and I was thinking about Joshua as long as I could stand next to him, hold his hand, or watch his heart beat and help take care of him I was alright. Oh how I was holding on!

I never thought of anyone else as I did him.

Finally the time had arrived Joshua's doctor had informed us that his surgery had been a success, and Joshua has just been transferred to the recovery room. She had handed me a picture of Joshua's stomach and said it appeared that Joshua had the start of an ulcer and had prescribed Zantac for him to be used as a preventive 24 hours after his surgery. She had asked me if Joshua had been under any stress at home, I said no but our visit there had been very stressful. She didn't comment but smiled and said that as soon as possible they would send for me to be with him and then she left.

EXPERIENCE

We waited again with anticipation it had been almost an hour, and then the door opened and the nurse called Ms. Hobbs. I stood and said, "that's me" and she said "I can take you back now to be with your son".

My mom and sister wanted to go but they could only allow one person during recovery, this was a critical time for patients and they needed no distractions. Without question this was a call for me, I told my family that I would be back as soon as I could.

I followed the nurse and as I walked I felt that I couldn't get to him fast enough.

We had an extensive walk and arrived in a secluded part of the hospital, for recovery patients like Joshua. We went through a set of automatic double-doors and it was extremely quiet you could've heard a pin drop. I was quickly reminded of our first day as we walked down a pathway and reached the end and behind some closed curtains it was there that I would find him.

There he was sleeping so peacefully, I went to him and gave him a little kiss and said you've done great I'm right here baby.

I was given a chair to sit beside him until he became awake; I wasn't aloud to touch him because it can cause problems as there coming out of anesthesia. I knew that from my own experiences.

His nurse had stated that he came to find Joshua really stirring and moving aggressively coming out of his recovery, and he immediately administered morphine to help calm him.

Joshua had been there about 10 minutes before anyone had told his nurse that he was back there. This upset me greatly, but the good thing was God had his hand on him and didn't allow any harm to come to him.

I was supposed to walk back and tell my sister and mom how Joshua was doing. After speaking with Joshua's nurse, I didn't feel comfortable with leaving him until we were able to return to Joshua's room.

Almost daily with the later part of our recovery we were faced with a great deal of turmoil and despair. My confidence and trust that I had once had with the hospital and staff was severed and during this time I felt beyond repair.

Joshua had started to move around again and the nurse administered more morphine to help stabilize him. His nurse had asked if Joshua had a binder in his room to help keep everything in place, I stated no and he said that he was going to go get one for him. The way Joshua did things and in watching him, I knew that his nurse would have to move quickly in order to assist us with this. Within one minute he was back and we moved quickly to place the binder on Joshua, as soon as we had finished Joshua arched back and jolted with his leg

A Legacy of Faith in 55 Days

and then began to calm again. In a matter of seconds Joshua began to arch again. If he hadn't had that binder on he may've pulled the food tube out. We were blessed to have had one.

His nurse had asked what was Joshua doing and how often did he do this?

I had answered with the information that had been given to me, and also said that it was part of the plan. He looked at me strangely and I said Joshua is a miracle and we have to go through this to see the end, its part of our healing.

The required time was up to stay in recovery, so we headed back to Joshua's room. His nurse didn't say anything looking curiously as I briefly explained our ordeal, upon arriving to Joshua's room he just smiled and said I hope you have a happy ending. I said Thank You as he had walked away. I believe that we were, everyday was an extra blessing to have him with us.

My mom and my sister quickly rushed in and had asked what happened they hadn't any news for hours and then I had explained to them in detail what had transpired through our recovery. I apologized for not telling them any sooner to keep them waiting, but I couldn't leave him again for anything. They had said they understood.

Joshua was completely out of it when they got to see him, sleeping like a baby quite sound. We gathered around him and joined together in prayer thanking our God for what he had given and done for us today, and for the days to come.

There had been so much time that had past that they would have to be leaving soon. There were many phone calls that they had to make many wanted to know how Joshua was doing. My family handled all of the questions; I spoke with discretion being careful not to have anything mis-handled.

There will always be skeptics no matter where you go, unless you've shared the same or similar experience you too would doubt how God moved. Those are ones that I ask God to open there eyes and ask him to give to them as he has me. And to allow me to give to them to help them heal no matter what the circumstance may be.

Hugs and kisses were given as they were leaving and they had planned to come and visit with us again the following day.

I waited for a while not rushing into cleaning his wounds or changing him, the surgery had been difficult for him and he was hurting and I knew it.

I sat in a chair re-reading the Upper Room that I had since the beginning of our journey. Joshua began to make sound; he curled up into a ball, and was groaning, I went and asked the nurse what would be administered to him to relieve him of his discomfort? She said," give her a minute she would read his chart and come tell me." Joshua was extremely agitated and needed something, she came in to let me know that the doctor hadn't prescribed anything, and it wasn't up to her to give him anything extra.

I had said as his parent I'm asking you to do something, give him what he needs to help calm him and she refused and walked out of our room. I followed her out and asked," why are they doing this I asked?" How many patients do you know that has surgery and aren't given medicine afterwards to help them in there discomfort and pain?

Why would you want him to struggle and go through this all night, I exclaimed. He's just a boy; he's been through enough already. She stated if I got any louder, that she would call security. She was going by the doctor's orders, I said I'm his voice what about his rights? And then I made myself walk away and return to accompany Joshua. I approached him again with tears rolling down my eyes, as I had felt like I had failed him there wasn't anything that I could do. I heard a voice that said, "He rest with the Most High. That reassured me Joshua was alright.

Satan knew the testimony that had been given to us and he was mad that I made a decision that would change the direction of my path, and that in the newness of our walk; he would use Joshua as my weakness trying to change the avenue of my testimony. God had already used Joshua to reach the heart of thousands of people and it was given to me to tell the world the specifics of what he had done for us.

I had to be patient and wait continuing to believe Joshua was going to be alright at the time. It was a very, very, long night. I had done his dressing changes but everything took twice as long wanting him to relax in- between.

By the Grace of God we were getting through this evening, and I was given the needed strength to do what I had been doing for him. "It's when you're hit with life's toughest challenges that you must not quit! And we didn't.

It was around 3:00a.m. I went and found his nurse (Sherri) and asked her to call his doctor, the one that had done his surgery. She said she had to attend a few more patients but she would, she had also said the doctor was probably still sleeping and I said well I'm not, and he's not so she needs to do something. I walked away returning to Joshua and letting him know that help was on the way. I was going to take a break there was very little that I could do until she received the news from his doctor, both of us waiting for that call.

I went downstairs it was around 3:45a.m. I would be back to here the conversation as she would make it sometime soon. I knew that around 4:00a.m. or a few minutes after that's when she had planned to call the physician I would be back before she had the chance to do anything.

As I walked and found a place to sit, I looked up and there was the most beautiful star that I had ever seen shining so beautifully down on me. As I sat and watched feeling that it was moving towards me, knowing that God loved me and was there too to help me feel better and get well.

I had a broken heart and having been given this extra time, with all of the signs and wonder was the only thing that would allow me to have victory over our tragedy in the end.

God works with each of us in different ways and for all of us individually the way he moves, you know that it's him without having any doubts.

The Lord strengthened me to keep myself together continually.

I found within minutes I was heading back to Joshua's room with anticipation.

I had to remember to be thankful for each day given, not to ever take any of our time for granted.

I needed help in releasing all of the negativity that I was building against those who had been working with us.

I was quite aggravated with the doctor's, nurses, therapist, and any additional attending staff. I had continued to write every incident that happened with each individual in a little notebook that I had been given.

I had planned to use all of the information that I had gathered at a later date, after having Joshua released from the hospital. I was quite emotional at the way they had been treating us. And I was going to use it to speak against them, but that's not the way God does thing I later learned.

Satan was trying to take our victory away and in the days of my weakness, I was letting him.

I knew from the beginning of our journey, I had made a commitment and had a life changing experience. Having made the decision that for the rest of my days I will serve the Lord with gladness and that I will lift him up for all of the joy he had given and instilled in us throughout our days. I had to pray, pray, and pray again to have the joy restored in me daily. I was seeking with everything in me to have and do the right thing at all times.

Upon entering in Joshua's room I knelt beside his bed and asked God to give him peace that watching him made me feel so overwhelmed and helpless. I loved him so much and I didn't want to see him have any struggle or difficulty. Without our experience I wouldn't have had the ability to share it with others the way God had moved with us.

I had ended my prayer and found myself repositioning him in his bed. I had experienced a great tear and had a sharp piercing pain all the way down my back. I kept moving not allowing this to affect or slow me down; I had to take care of him not allowing anything to interfere with God's Plan for us.

I had some music played on a very low volume and one of the songs touched me so greatly which was one touch can mend a broken heart, and words can heal the pain. Oh how wonderful God was to us.

Joshua's surgeon was finally called and I had heard the nurse as she was speaking to her, I went outside of Joshua's room and asked if I could have a moment to speak with his surgeon.

The nurse handed me the phone and I had quickly informed her that Joshua had been extremely agitated all night and that he needed something for his pain. She stated, "That she understood my concern, but she wasn't his attending physician and couldn't give him anything." My heart sank, I had asked all night for her to be called and then after having her called she said she couldn't give him anything. Why they did this to us, I said. I handed back the phone, and said I have no more to say as I walked away. I hadn't planned on having our conversation end that way. Tears were streaming down my face as I entered Joshua's room feeling so helpless. I was concerned about Joshua's well-being and safety, I didn't feel they had his best interest at hand.

I went to the bathroom grabbing tissue, and sat and sobbed. I had to pull myself together, within minutes I found myself washing my face and brushing my teeth. This was something that had helped distract me.

As time had past it would soon be time for the day shift nurses to come in. I paced the floor waiting knowing that God was sending help through one of them; I just wasn't sure which one.

I had to remember that I had placed Joshua in Gods hands, and although we were faced with extreme difficulty situations periodically. Both of us remained in Gods hands. He never said the road was easy, but he did leave us a promise to hold on and look for the fire (light) again.

Joshua had experienced several troubled nights throughout all of the adjusting with his medications, aggressive therapy, and now surgery. Joshua had been deprived of sleep with all of the excessive movement. I had always been one to believe that when your sick and feeling weak than having sleep was the best medicine to restore you back to good health.

It was well into the mourning and it was time for me to prepare for the care of him again. I gathered everything that I had need of eagerly addressing each area of him that needed attended. Joshua had made a great deal of progress, it was in steps and it was a slow process.

To look at him you couldn't see the severity that the accident had had, it didn't strip everything that we had in remembrance of Joshua. We had been blessed daily to have been a good report, the reports were always changing. Everything that Joshua had done was significant to each of us.

Joshua didn't have to do a lot to get me to smile or be encouraged, it was having all of these little things given that was so big and left a lasting impression.

There was never a time that any of us could say that what God had done and given us wasn't enough! God had proved that what was impossible for us wasn't for him.

Help had arrived, Joshua's nurse for the day had came in to administer morphine to him, I was relieved and at the same time had asked what took her so long? She didn't understand and I had explained, she apologized for the other and that made me feel a little bit better. Finally Joshua was starting to calm and seeing that was giving light for us all day.

I watched as he soon fell asleep and then I made my way to take a break. I knew that I wouldn't be long; I needed to break away for a few minutes again. Before you could look at the time and notice that I was gone, I was back in his room watching him, and helping take care of him.

We had so much adjustments take place throughout the week, I wasn't sure if I wanted to laugh or if I wanted to cry.

It was day 30 and I knew that we would have visitors again very soon. I had to be careful with everything that I had said not to discourage anyone from coming. I didn't always succeed because of incidents that had happened, I was hurting and my short-comings with others were often tolerated during our stay.

It's not an excuse to get your way by any means but often people will over look many instances when they can feel what you must be feeling (showing compassion). With people it seems to be temporary but for the Lord it's everlasting.

I found that I was doing a lot more listening than talking and that had been a big adjustment than the way that I had once lived. I was undergoing a lot of changing, I had acknowledged these changes and it felt really good. I had pressure from every side but the Lord had sustained me throughout it all!

It was only by God's grace that my faith was growing day by day.

The time had arrived and our family and friends had come to see how we were doing, they were eager to see Joshua sleeping. They couldn't comprehend the difficult evenings that we had faced because they hadn't seen him the way I had seen him. I know now there was a reason and it was needful or intended for everyone to witness this. We didn't need anyone that would be hindered from being a faithful witness that the Lord wants us to be.

I had always believed that God wouldn't hurt Joshua, but man would. I had to put all of my worries and doubts in Gods hands. There were only three staff members that I had really trusted, and when there are so many to work with that seems like a very limited number.

Family had stayed and visited with us; before I knew it we were again hugging, kissing and saying our goodbyes.

It was Joshua and me again getting ready to go through another evening. I shared with him that I knew that it was up to me to leave a testimony that God had intended and for a moment he smiled again.

In working with varying staff its sometimes difficult to express to ones that doesn't believe that miracles do happen. A non-believer will be skeptical and also will question everything not looking at anything as a blessing, but part of a medical procedure.

God gives us blessings but man will take it away from us if we allow it. Not just strangers but it can happen with your immediate family as well.

Time had past and I continually cared for Joshua as I always had. I repositioned Joshua to give him a different view of his room. And he seemed to really enjoy the new look of his room.

He lied there with his eyes open responding when I placed my finger on his nose.

He knew what was going on God gave him to be a messenger for us.

I asked Joshua if he was comfortable and to blink twice if he was, and he did. Oh how great it was to have all of the extras!

With every opportunity taking the time to re-read the study daily and read the following scripture that tied the meanings together. Knowing the importance of keeping God's word fresh, to remember his works.

I was so blessed to have the opportunity to stay with Joshua throughout our 55 days. The doctors and nurses were over worked and under staffed and I knew that Joshua had his own nurse attending to him and that was me. I watched every move so attentively. I knew what he was going to do before he did 98% of the time. I wanted to be the best that I could be for him in everything that he would need, even when there were times I had to speak for him.

We were facing the weekend with many visitors; I needed extra strength and had to have wisdom to know how to speak with each one individually. Our lights had to shine too many of them that was living in darkness and it did. With everyone that we had come in contact with we expressed our glow.

As the time progressed before I knew we had many visitors accompany us.

Everyone who came shared our joy and had commented on how beautiful he was and how well he had been doing. He looked so well that any minute he could've hopped out of his bed and stood with us.

Joshua lied in his bed looking at us as we were standing around and talking to him; his dad had came to visit and hadn't said anything to Joshua as he was in the room with him.

His dad had a visitor enter our room and left to speak with him instead of Joshua, as he had left Joshua started moving and appeared to be upset.

I told Joshua everything would be alright and that I was going to get his dad and I did just that.

I immediately left and found Scott and said that he needed to be in the room with Joshua, he had upset him for not saying anything to him when he was in the room with us. Everyone else had talked to Joshua and Joshua knew that he hadn't. Scott followed me back to Joshua's room and upon entering and talking to Joshua it was immediate that Joshua started to calm down. I was relieved and agitated with Scott for doing this at the same time.

Scott wasn't sure what to say he was hurting in his heart and I knew deep down he wanted to have more time to make things right. I wanted to give him something to hold onto and I had asked if we could get Joshua in a wheelchair while everyone was with us visiting. I had no idea this would be our last time seeing him up and about with us. My request had been granted and this was a cherished moment that would last a lifetime.

We didn't get to keep Joshua out for very long just a few minutes, he had became so agitated I felt that it would be best to have him back in his bed so he couldn't hurt himself. The labor of love I had expressed to Joshua would keep me going for the rest of our days until we both could get home.

We rushed back to his room placing him back in his bed, everyone gathered around to pray and visit for a little while longer. Visiting hours were over I knew that with most of them I would see them again during our weekend visits. All of us were still holding onto the request of bringing Joshua home, nothing else to consider after we had been given so much.

Our evenings seemed quite subtle compared to all of the hustle throughout the early mourning and day shift, however that was about to change.

I had cared for Joshua as I always had keeping everything on a timely schedule, cleaning his wounds daily as they had been requested. I was being extra careful with the new incision not wanting to cause anymore discomfort than he had already had.

I was so careful knowing that he needed sleep and I didn't want to be the one that had caused him to awaken or become agitated. I was blessed because during most of his wound care cleanings Joshua slept peacefully, and that was a relief to me.

When other nurses had came in to care for him as I had been, he would start to stir as if to let them know that it wasn't needful for them. I hymned songs all night long to him and myself it seemed to be comforting for both of us.

I had a constant reminder right in front of me that Joshua had received a touch from the heavens above. How wonderful it was for God to be using me as he was him to touch so many. I finished up and put everything away sitting next to him watching him as he lay awake knowing that it was all given by God's Amazing Grace. God was talking and preparing me for a new way during this time.

As the days and nights were passing by us we were given God's promise throughout Joshua's entire recovery process.

Our evening passing and a new day was to come I would soon learn that a faith walk isn't always about getting your way, in every circumstance or situation. But, whatever the circumstance may be God will give you what you need to get you through it.

I wouldn't be where I'm at today, if God hadn't have taken me under the shadow of his wing.

Joshua's medicines seemed to always be changing, and he had complications with the jagesotomony in the beginning but he seemed to handle the many adjustments just fine. But, later I seen and realized that the many changes that he had went through with his medicines, various therapies and tests was really starting to effect him and cause more agitation than he had previously in our stay. This was effecting me greatly, I knew the importance of the testimony that we had been given, could I continue was the question.

For a short time I believed that in sharing our victory with others was causing trouble. There were some it seemed didn't want Joshua to get better within the facility and certain staff.

This was a difficult time for me to say you're in God's hands and it's part of his plan because Joshua was suffering to leave a good name. I hadn't read 1st Peter 4: 1 & 16 yet. I had always been one that believed Christians weren't suppose to suffer for Jesus Christ name that was how I was raised, later I realized it was those that did that left a good name for all to remember.

God's word of truth was the only real comfort to me! Everyday that we had been given was something given in greatness from him.

It was early in the mourning and Joshua's granny had come to visit with us.

Joshua wasn't having a very good day he was quite restless and breathing heavily. He hadn't been on a respirator in almost a weak, we had new challenges to face everyday and we were living by faith.

Granny was having a difficult time seeing Joshua struggle with every breath that he breathed, you could see tears fill her eyes even though at the time she didn't cry. I wasn't too comforting to her my focus remaining on Joshua entirely. She stayed for a very short time and had decided to leave, I understood and said I would visit with her later as she left our room.

One of the most peculiar things with Joshua was he appeared alright until someone entered our room, and then he would become agitated and appear restless until they would leave he did this on numerous occasions. I was trying to figure it out, wondering what it meant. I feel that part of this was because of what we had experienced and what I had seen wasn't meant for everyone to witness or see.

Our day had past like the previous days we had, we were making progress but it wasn't rapidly. I had spoke with Joshua's neurosurgeon and asked how the ex-rays looked, I hadn't dwelt on any tests Joshua had been given, until I had spoke to this man; he responded that Joshua was in the gray (which meant that he could go either way) it was too early to say.

This was a busy day with lots of information I had also spoke with his doctor whom I had placed my trust and confidence in, and felt that she was caring for Joshua as I had.

She pulled me to the side to let me know she had planned on taking a mini-vacation for five days, my eyes started to fill with tears and I began to feel overwhelmed inside. Everything was going so good she couldn't leave now. She had reassured me everything would remain the same with no changes in his daily routine or medicines until she got back, she was the only one that I felt that I could trust with Joshua's life. I believed that she would see to it everything remained the same with no changes.

Our conversation ended and we had separated, I was being prepared and didn't realize it at the time. I immediately remembered how good God had been to us nothing was going to happen; we were under Gods protection and I didn't think anything more of it.

It was then that I should have gone and prayed fervently in the Chapel on that feeling or ache that wouldn't go away; it was given as a warning and I didn't know I still had a lot of growing.

Until now Joshua hadn't had a difficult time adjusting from the transfers and changes that go with each floor.

I was standing by his side encouraging him to take it in stride; even on a difficult mourning to me we were still having a good day. There was a glow about Joshua that I had seen continually and no one else had mentioned seeing it from the very first day.

Some of our family and Joshua's friends came to visit with us; not knowing everything would soon come to an end. We had gathered around Joshua believing and praying together for his recovery and some had even said that we were soon to be released.

I believed that the same care that Joshua had received there he could get at home with me privately.

I wouldn't get too excited until I had time to confirm it with his doctor, but it was great news during visiting hours.

I was also told that a few of the staff had privately talked with my sister and brother-in-law wanting them to influence me in leaving the hospital for a day and take a break. I refused to leave, saying that I wouldn't leave until Joshua did and they understood and didn't pursue that discussion with me. I know that our ordeal had greatly effected me, I'm human it would effect anyone that has faced a situation as ours. Before I knew it visiting hours were over and we would see one another again the following night. It would then be just Joshua and I again.

There was a lot to do in one day having Joshua as my one and only focus, I did it at ease to keeping everything flowing because Gods hand was upon me. Having everything organized made it easy access when needed at anytime.

I had ordered extra supplies to keep from running out or having need of anything. Any information that was needed for his care I could repeat it at any moment, I also had the ability to successfully operate any and all equipment placed in his room (like the food-tube, oscinameter-for breathing treatments and suctions. How many and how much of it, whatever and whomever it concerned I knew it, because I cared and loved him so much. I could tell you any changes before the shifts changed; I worked at mastering what was needed of me, to help him.

Joshua was settled in for the night this gave me the opportunity to take a break for the evening, they were far between I always had a fear of leaving. I would whisper to Joshua that I would be back soon, to get some rest and not to do anything until I returned.

During this time I had been given the opportunity to witness to others what God had done for us.

With every chance given I entered the Chapel to pray and I could feel the Holy Spirit with me, as I cried aloud to the Lord and continually asked for Joshua's recovery. Every bone and every test to receive a victory report from me I pleaded. This was considered a church for me I didn't look at it as a room, I went to receive a healing for him and at the same time I was being healed. For me I had realized that there had been lots of prayer, laughter, joining of hands, and songs of praise in this small place as a temple. What a wonderful place to have, a place of healing it was a necessity to have continue believing in faith that I had received.

I always returned feeling renewed in my spirit, even during our most difficult and trying times.

You take your burden to the Lord and leave it there; no matter how small or how big you think your problem is, he loves you so much that he will work it out, you just have to trust him he does have your best interest at hand.

To know that you are loved by God and his warmth and comfort wraps around you, to feel him all around you is so awesome, it's not to be compared to anything that I've ever experienced.

Upon returning and entering Joshua's room he began to stir, I would re-assure him everything was alright it was just me and he would soon go back to sleep.

Our continual gift was precious time and miracles received that had been given to me by God and I will always remember it.

Before I knew we were facing another day with much anticipation with every procedure seemingly routine with his daily regimen or schedule.

There was never one day that I didn't tell him how proud of him I was and how much I loved him.

Joshua seemed to be more agitated with me helping him today than he had expressed in our earlier days, I understood and expressed it to him I knew that before the accident he had been very independent and that had been taken from him. I reassured him that what I was doing was temporary and one day I knew that he would be doing it for himself again. Staff had reassured me this is very common with all brain injury patients and with that information I could except it.

The time had gone by so fast it was almost 2:00p.m. in the afternoon. This was an easy place to loose time with having so much to do. Everyday Joshua was doing more and more with everything even his physical therapy than he had done before. We had quickly found that Joshua didn't mind sitting up, but he didn't want to be placed in a wheelchair from that day forward. The comment was made that with each patient the circumstances are different, and with each individual staff tries to accommodate each ones specific needs. They had planned on having Joshua a wheelchair custom made; this wasn't something that we needed today and would be addressed much later in our stay.

Everyday I took as much responsibility as I could, and having the opportunity to prepare him for our upcoming visitors was a lot of work, it ended always with a great reward. I was thankful that I had been given the opportunity to do it.

I had even said while taking care of him that if he got to heaven before I did, he had to come back and get me with a smile. It would have to be beautiful and calming if he had decided to leave. I knew how much he loved me and felt that all that we had been given he was staying.

I had even shared with him what I had thought heaven must be like, and to be an angel, to have the ability to race in the skies my, my!

To face Jesus my Savior and my Creator with delight. All of us had stayed steadfast in our faith believing in what we had been praying.

Everything was God given from the very beginning and a preparation to leave a testimony. God was showing me how much he loved me. Our visitors came always bringing something a card, balloon, flowers, or a simple memento just to keep us smiling. Nothing had ever been given that had went un-noticed or unappreciated even with others who had made a special trip to show there sympathy that didn't really know us.

Joshua had been quite agitated during visiting hours and I hadn't wanted anyone to see him having a bad day, but then for them to understand the challenges we had been facing they would have to see it first hand. God had given all of us the strength to withstand.

None of us had to experience what Joshua did, it was harder on him than anyone. As his mom I was making excuses of what must be happening to him, thinking that he had been over-worked during therapy and that had caused his agitation. I wasn't sure but it was easier for me to blame someone than it was to think the severity of his accident had done this to him. Through it all I had to keep in focus all of the good that had become of our experience; we wouldn't be helping anyone else if we didn't. And it was good medicine for our hearts and mind renewing the right spirit in us.

Hours had past and visiting hours were over hugs and kisses given during our good-byes. With (2) I knew that I would see them again the following day and that was big for me, I depended on them to help carry my burden and to uplift me and they did everyday. There was a lot of love flowing, not just with them; I happened to express my joy with almost everyone that I had met. This was an incredible transformation than I had once been.

I began to prepare once again for our evening hours regimen, keeping everything on a consistent schedule. I realized for the first time the importance of all of our body parts, not just one even our tongue. Whatever comes out of our mouth is in our heart and it was important to make sure the first fruit was pleasing to God. God spoke with me with much intimacy that I understood what he had given me.

It was late and everything had been given and finished for our evening hours. Joshua was settled quite nicely for the evening I had said a prayer and done some reading to him and then I had planned to separate from Joshua taking a small break once again.

The hallways of a hospital are full of heaviness with the people that you meet. Many had to face trauma with someone close in there family. And to find that they didn't have anyone to come and comfort them during there admission that weighed on my heart heavily. I was so blessed not to have had that experience.

This was a perfect opportunity for me to get rest and instead, I continually paced the hallways. I hadn't placed all of my trust in God; I was still trying to have everything go my way. I was afraid to sleep, I cherished every minute that I had been given with him.

I didn't express to anyone the hurt that I was really feeling, I felt the weight of the world in my hands and I was doing all that I could just to face each day, realizing the pressures of what we would face. God gave me strength in my weakest hours.

I returned to Joshua's room to find him very restless, and the deepest pain was when there was nothing that I could do for him to help him.

It was almost 4:00 a.m. and after trying everything it had made me very tired, my adrenalin was running low and I realized that I needed to get a few minutes sleep before having to face another challenging day that we had just experienced.

I told Joshua that I would be away longer than a few minutes; I needed to get some sleep and not to do anything until I returned. I grabbed a pillow and a blanket and took a few steps outside of his room, I pulled my knees up and rested my head for approximately 15 minutes and then I awoke. I heard Joshua struggling with every breath and re-entered his room only this time openly rebuking Satan for trying to destroy what God had given us.

No matter what we would face that he would not prevail over us. God was with us, he was our stay.

After being chosen to write, I truly understand the sacrifice it takes to leave a testimony and to have a good name for all to remember, as those did that went before us.

Joshua had been fighting for quite some time miraculously he did begin to calm, but also looked so drained from all of the restlessness and moving around.

Within minutes he began to start sleeping sound, this was an answered prayer; we had experienced so much throughout the entire evening. As Gods word says "come unto me all ye that labor and I will give you rest."

And God moved for us again. Oh how beautiful he was and to be given this extra time with him.

Our life is so limited while being here on this earth; to think about life there are thousands that loose there lives daily. We should always be thankful for each day that we have been given.

We can make a difference in other people's lives; just by one is truly amazing.

Our night slowly pressed through and soon his Respiratory Therapist had come in the room, we shared together how wonderful Joshua was doing. Joshua had been the talk across the halls, cafeteria, and break room areas everyone knew him and his story. God had used Joshua to make many believers from hearing and seeing first hand his miraculous recovery. This was a tremendous testimony to have the opportunity to leave with many. Knowing that by one many hearts were touched.

I was looking forward to seeing Joshua's doctor (MS.C) to share with her Joshua's progress during our weekend. She was a very busy person but she always took those extra minutes to listen. This meant a great deal to me. Finally she had come to visit with us, and she had taken a look at an incision on Joshua's right knee. She had insisted on a wound care team to come and give a second opinion, I agreed

If there was ever anything new to try we would to keep him as comfortable as we could.

Hours had past and the wound care specialist had came up they took one look and asked what I had been doing? In detail I explained to them the lengthy procedure to try and expedite the healing of his knee. The two of them smiled and said that I was doing a great job and in there opinion other than a special bandage to continue in what I had been doing.

I took it upon myself to say an extra prayer and within days his knee was healed. I was very thankful that I was being used in the many ways that was needful, I give God the praise!

There were many families in our beginning days that were starting to be released during this time of our stay, I held on with the anticipation of us soon leaving, what a relief that would be. Keeping in mind they had been there for a long time and they were ready to go home.

Time had past as it had, being thankful for every second that we had. Donna and Chris had come to visit with us and had planned to take me to the cafeteria to grab a bite to eat. We had a great day!

During visitation I was unaware that staff had planned to take Joshua down for ex-rays, no one had said anything to me before leaving his room.

Joshua was resting and for us this was the perfect time to make a run to the cafeteria. The three of us did and I didn't think anything of it taking a few extra minutes away. I was extremely joyful today, and Joshua was doing great. We had talked and carried on and before I knew we were on our way returning to Joshua's room. Our faith and hope was growing every moment!

I remembered our returning to Joshua's room, this had been one of my happiest days in Joshua's recovery and I was sharing it with two people that had a tremendous impact on my life.

I hadn't anticipated on any changes as we walked in Joshua's room. I walked into find that he was gone, his bed and all. Instantly I panicked walking out and asking the receptionist Where is he? Where did they take him? Why? I asked.

She had responded that the doctor had requested ex-rays earlier in the day but they had never said anything to me, I said.

I had been with him through every procedure and test; he couldn't go through this without me I exclaimed. She said he was down in ex-ray and I immediately took off running, I instantly remembered how to get to that floor but nothing more. I was in a panic state and felt like I was going to throw up any second.

There are a lot of tunnels when it's a new path to take; I bypassed all of the restricted areas not wasting any time just to get to him. We had reached the designated area and there was a technician or nurse that had came out of no where and helped us, I told her what happened as I began to cry.

She had made a call and within minutes she was directing me to get to him. I was relieved but also felt that I couldn't run fast enough to reunite him. I had reacted merely in fear, my mind not being at ease until I could be with him.

Within seconds and turning a corner a door opened and an ex-ray technician motioned me to come in. I walked in and there lied Joshua resting so peacefully and his nurse behind him, standing at the head of his bed. I was overwhelmed inside; I rushed towards him and then I burst out crying, and I apologized for not being there for him.

I confronted his nurse, asking why he took him without saying anything to me. He knew that I had been with Joshua through everything. His response was I'm his nurse, you're just his mom.

You shouldn't have been allowed to be with him through everything! I was hurt and lost for words.

I immediately knew deep down this was an attack from the enemy to do his best to get me down. I didn't respond the way he may've thought I would, because I knew that in this type of conflict then the hospital and staff could keep me separated from him. So I let the fusion end, keeping in mind that everything was in God's hands. The procedure was finished and we wheeled him back to his room, which was a big relief. Donna and Chris had patiently waited and they had made sure that we were ok before they had to leave, it was really late. We said prayer and hugged and kissed as we said our good-byes.

I know that God sees and hears everything, there is nothing hidden. There will be a day that those that who have purposely hurt one of God's children and that hasn't repented will be dealt with directly. What we do affects him daily whether it is good or bad, and knowing that all of us will face judgment I wouldn't want to be one that will stand in front of him having hurt one of his. If you don't have forgiveness then you don't have victory.

We were experiencing trial and tribulation as those that were wrote about in the Biblical days.

Our evening passing as we would be blessed to face another day.

It was day 35 Joshua was doing great, his medicines had been adjusted and he was tremendously progressing with and responding during his therapy. His doctor had mentioned us being discharged upon her return from her mini-vacation and I was confident in our discussion that nothing was going to go wrong. I believed that Joshua would have a speedier recovery after coming home.

We had tried to increase the amount of his food intake within the last couple of days, Joshua didn't tolerate the adjusting and we had decided to wait and try it again at a later date.

I was reassured that the attending physician wasn't to change anything, everything was to remain the same until Joshua's doctor returned. She would be gone for five days; and had planned to leave that evening at least it wasn't for ten days I thought. I really didn't want her to leave until we did but there wasn't any way that I could convince her to stay, after all all of us need to take a break.

Our day was passing but I couldn't wait for visiting hours to share the news. We had always believed that Joshua would do much better in his own surroundings. I had repeatedly done enough procedures to have them done in a timely manner.

Sometimes with the anticipation and waiting it seems like the time will never arrive to share great news with those that you love so dear.

Donna and Chris had made it up to visit, and they shared with me the joy of Joshua's upcoming release.

Our time had past and we had agreed on having a bite to eat. But after our previous experience I had decided that I wanted to eat in Joshua's room not leaving him unattended. Chris agreed and had made arrangements to get something for all of us while we stayed with Joshua waiting in his return.

A Legacy of Faith in 55 Days

We had prayer and I had said to Joshua that it wouldn't be long that he would be able to have what we had, he was doing great. Everyone was amazed.

Donna and I had finished our dinner and then we had planned to take a few minutes away while Chris stayed with Joshua waiting for our return.

I loved every chance to step outside and have fresh air, hospital rooms have a tendency to smell like medicine. This also gave Donna and me a few minutes of quiet time, oh how I cherished all that she had done for me.

We headed back making it a point to stop in the Chapel to pray, being thankful for everything that had been given daily.

Visiting hours were over but I knew that Donna and Chris had planned on coming up the following day, and Donna was to stay with us and learn what was needful to bring Joshua home, I couldn't wait for the following day. We said our good-byes and looked forward to the morrow.

I handled the time as it past knowing that with every opportunity they had they would be there to share it with us. We had been doing great and the day had ended once again with great news.

I had prepared for the evening as I had in the past; taking care of Joshua and sharing with him the joy that he had given me in all of our days shared together.

We were interrupted by a knock on our door a nurse came in, her name was Judy and she let me know that Joshua was her patient for the night. We had already crossed paths once before, I had an uneasiness about her that wouldn't go away. It would be fair to say she was one that I didn't like, because of the carelessness and callousness she had expressed to us before. I reminded her that Joshua was soon due for his medicine and she quickly responded it would be administered to him in her time and not mine! I immediately knew that we were facing trouble, I just wasn't sure how much or when. I knew the difficulty Joshua would have as a result in the delay of his medications given, and I didn't want him to have to go through that.

I had started to feel anxious inside and at this time I had a difficult time trying to pray. I quoted Psalm 23 over and over again that was the only scripture that was coming to me. I wasn't sure what I could do other than stay close beside him.

Joshua had been wearing a monitor due to the new medication that he had been given, I sat in a chair next to him and there was a beautiful glow all about him.

It was as if someone had opened the roof and the sun was pouring in on him. I sat speechless and dismayed wondering why I had been chosen to see this when no one else was in the room to share it with. I didn't say anything I took deep breaths and just felt God was giving me this to let me know that Joshua rested in the palm of his hands and not in man.

Having been given this special moment will stay with me for the rest of my life. I was smiling ear to ear and then suddenly the alarm on the monitor started to sound; as I read the numbers and they had fallen below, I quickly moved towards Joshua and said wake up sleepy head, you are sleeping to sound. I went and told his nurse and she came in and looked at the monitor and said that he was sleeping deeply and had turned the volume down. She had said it was set to sound if his heartbeat went below 67bpm, and it had at 64bpm. After watching him she then adjusted it to 56bpm, and said that it should keep the alarm from sounding. She had also adjusted the breaths to 13 per minute before leaving our room.

I had been so eager to see him rest and now that he was I was scared. I took the remote that controlled his bed and started moving him up and down to get him to wake up and start moving around. As I continued to watch his monitor I started to doubt. The numbers on the screen continued to decrease, I started to cry and wasn't sure why.

His nurse came in and said don't worry it's good for him to catch up on much needed rest, I told her I wasn't sure what I could do for him. Maybe I had wrongfully judged her because she was being very nice to us for the first time. I didn't realize that there was a trap waiting just minutes away.

She had left the room and I had apologized to Joshua for trying to awake him. I had been praying to see him receive much needed sleep and now that he was, I had changed my mind. Joshua's numbers had started to rise and that assured me that he was starting to awake, his heartbeat read 70bpm and that was good news for me. I stayed around watching to see if there were going to be any changes in his numbers but they had remained steady and that was good news for me. It was a little test but we were ok.

It was getting later in the evening and after receiving calm of our situation I had planned to take a small break. I had informed his nurse and said I would be back in a few minutes, she said he was sleeping and wouldn't need anything until I returned. I hurried and was a way just for a few minutes. I still had a habit that eventually I would receive deliverance. I returned to the 6th Floor and as I came around the corner seeing Joshua's nurse on the phone talking to the doctor that was on call, the one that was assigned to oversee Joshua's care until Joshua's doctor had returned. I knew who the nurse was speaking with because I overheard her sharing the events that we had experienced in the last couple of hours.

I past by her to get to Joshua's room and upon entering he was awake and his monitor had read 78bpm with 17 breaths per minute. He was ok but what was she planning I wondered. I left Joshua for a few minutes to ask who she had been talking to. I already knew. She had told me that she had just finished speaking with the doctor on call and had shared with her Joshua's experience that we had earlier. They had felt that Joshua had received too much medicine and refused to give him anymore for the remainder of the evening for fear of him bottoming out. I said you said he was sleeping and everything was going to be ok, go look

A Legacy of Faith in 55 Days

at him now his numbers look great and he was awake. Please, please Judy don't do this to him! I pleaded.

She said there wasn't anymore that she could do, that it was the doctor's orders. I immediately requested her to call Ms. C and she refused, she said that as long as she was away it was up to the attending physician to make adjustments and have the final call and then she walked away.

I returned to Joshua's room to find him starting to move around and leaning on his right side. I told Joshua he was going to have a difficult night and I explained why. My heart ached so bad, I prayed and asked God to take care of him the situation was out of my hands. I continued to stay beside him as our evening was slowly passing, and seeing first hand the progression of his agitation from the withdrawals of all of his medication all at once.

Joshua was having difficulty breathing and was staring right at me. I felt so helpless I was trying everything to calm him. I went out pleading to his nurse over and over to give him something even the one that didn't have him as his patient; there were only two of them for the evening. I repeatedly asked to see his chart knowing that I had that right and was refused and told if I didn't settle down they were going to have security come down. I had began to cry and I apologized to them willing to say and do anything to get help to him. I love him so much and need him please, please don't give up on him! They walked away from me refusing to say or do anything to help him.

As the hours past I helplessly watched Joshua's physical abilities and accomplishments that we had, deteriorate in front of me. His response after this evening would never be like it use to be.

I wanted to go get help but was afraid to leave, I had thought about the 8th Floor I.C.U. it was two floors away. I wondered what they would do to him when I walked away, so I stayed.

His nurse came in and gave him one shot of something he hadn't had. I asked her what it was and she didn't answer me. I had asked about his oxygen with his numbers reading low, she shook her head and walked away not saying anything.

Joshua was sweating, and shaking greatly after all that he had been through I still didn't want him to leave me. I told him that I was going to call Donna we needed help; I would make the necessary call and quickly return.

My legs felt like jello as I crossed the halls to get to a phone. I called her at 3:00 a.m. and she quickly answered. I told her what happened and she said she would be there within the hour. I had asked her to purchase a mini-tape recorder I needed proof of our conversations; I wanted to hold them accountable for denying us our rights.

She agreed to get it and would have it when they came to see us. I was crying a river; the tears were flowing as I made my way back to reunite with Joshua. Words cannot describe the hurt that I was feeling on the inside.

I told Joshua to hang in there he had been doing great help was on the way.

I had been praying throughout our entire evening and couldn't understand why at the time we would have to go through something so horrific after all that we had already experienced. I know now that it has to be whatever it takes to leave a legacy of faith and to have a good name. God needed us to help him fill his mighty plan. When you're given a testimony it's meant to be shared with everyone, or at least those who will listen. It's not up to us to decide what we should do with it.

Donna had finally arrived it was just a little after 4:00 a.m. as she entered into our room, she took one look at me and then she seen him. I was so broke down she just moved as closely as she could and just held me for a while. When I had the opportunity to look her into the eyes hers filled with tears but she didn't cry. She would express herself to her husband Chris later; she knew at the time what I needed.

I made it known to the nurses that I was no longer alone, and that she was there as a witness of our experience.

I had hoped that in having her with me they would administer medicine to Joshua as we know that it was needed. I hid the recorder and made my request, with having it once again denied. However after going all night they had decided to send a respiratory therapist down to give him a breathing treatment. I was recording everything for the next several hours.

Beverly was the therapist sent down to help us, she had placed him on 6 liters of oxygen and it still wasn't increasing the numbers on the screen. I could see the compassion she had; she was as upset as we. She had insisted on us doing again what we had already done, I did only to be refused once again. She said if I needed a witness, I could call upon her and she would do it.

I told her that I wanted him out of that hospital as quickly as I could and she said she completely understood. I had tears rolling down my eyes I was breaking inside; she finished his treatment and then left the room.

This was a point in our stay that I had felt God had abandoned us; I was so wrong he was there with us and would give us victory in the end. I didn't understand the importance of what we had just experienced until the days that followed ahead. It would've been void if I was given it any sooner, I wouldn't have had the heart to understand then why we had to go through this.

It had been a very long night I was heart broke and very confused. Donna and I took a walk as we did I continued to cry, she grabbed me and held me tight. I told her I didn't want Joshua to go through this; she said he is going to be alright.

After this night it would be difficult to think the hospital would be able to convince me of anything good.

I had pleaded with many tears wanting to know what more that I could do? We came around the hallway and entered Joshua's room. There he was struggling desperately for his life right before my eyes. I asked repeatedly for him to hold on help was coming as I would have to wait for the mourning dawn. I tried praying but I was very weak and few words were coming to me, I didn't have that joy that I had experienced from before.

I had set up a camcorder and continued taping the conversations with a mini-recorder. I was so upset and I knew that with the entire evidence put together that I had planned on our release of suing due to medical negligence.

We were definitely under attack, Satan was mad. And he was going to do all that he could to try and influence me to turn my back on God. I was holding on by God's word, his promise and his mercies that he had expressed to us from the very beginning. God had showed his love and I wasn't about to let go of the good God had given us even by this experience.

I hadn't comprehended the greatness of resting in God's hands, however I continually said it and believed in it and knew that what we had experienced would soon come to an end, the shifts would soon be changing. It was the break of dawn there was light to see even after all of the darkness. It was time to focus God would send someone in that would be there to help us, her name was Jennifer. She would care for him all day and she remained so calm throughout all of it.

Our circumstance was really bad, Joshua was moving profusely every limb of his that had been receptive to therapy was now to tight to do anything with. He continually expressed difficulty in breathing with having an extremely high heartbeat consistently.

Jennifer administered medicine to him immediately and I looked at her and asked "Why did they do this to him, as tears flowed down my eyes. He's my boy they've tried taking him away from me last night.

She never even tried to make an excuse she said that what we had went through wasn't justified, wasn't right and the only thing that she could do is help today as much as she could.

She was doing everything to calm him and stabilize him; she was in every 5 to 10 minutes like they do in the I.C.U. If I had of thought then to have had someone from I.C.U. to come down and look at him I would've. I feel that if it had been the way God had intended than I would've done it then, but I didn't. I requested her to phone doctor C; I had planned to ask for our discharge immediately. The call was made and to my dismay the doctor had acted as if I would put him at risk by discharging him then, putting a side our horrific experience, to this day I wonder what she had to have been thinking.

I hung up the phone and walked away in dismay. Donna was right there and had asked what she said, I cried again as I repeated our conversation and how it had ended with being denied. How could they make us stay after what we had just experienced, it wasn't fair.

At this time I had questioned God, Why would he allow this to happen to us? Keeping in mind not everyone would lift up God's name after having had this experience. I had to trust that God knew at all times what he was doing, even when we hadn't a clue. Great men and women of God had gone through horrific experiences to leave a testimony and a good name for all to remember. And that is what God had chosen and given us to do and prepared us to carry it through.

Please Lord suffer me but not with him. This is what it took to get me to do what had been asked. For me this was the ultimate sacrifice that I had to make, in order for me to get to heaven. I would unite with Jesus and share the joys with all of my loved ones that had gone on before.

There would be a point after coming home that I would read (KJV) Psalm 119:71 and completely understand it. "It is good for me that I have been afflicted; that I might learn thy statues.

Many hours had past and after realizing that we had continual care without any minutes wavering, I was relieved and broke away to take a break. I was crushed inside; I felt the weight of the world or heaviness as I walked the hallways. I had planned on having Joshua come home with me, not looking at it any different until now.

I found myself outside and for the second time I had asked God to go ahead and take Joshua's life. I couldn't understand why Joshua had to be the one to go through these horrific experiences; I was the one that had lived a life of sin and not him. Although I had repented and had asked Jesus in my life, was this payback for the life that I had lived?

Regardless of the emotional roller coaster I was facing it wasn't my choice to make, of whether Joshua stayed or that he went.

God had already prepared his place and called him to heaven's home, I didn't know.

The day had been long and God had begun to restore the joy, I began to sing and hymn a song as I once did in the beginning.

I felt God's presence all around me, he shared everything with me! I could not see him, but I knew that he was there. (KJV) Psalm 34:15 – The eyes of the Lord are unto the righteous, and his ears are open unto their cry.

A Legacy of Faith in 55 Days

I had originally held my head down during this time, but I was moved to look up and when I did there was five birds within arms reach to me.

I had always been given signs in threes, and had an amazing story of how birds do things. This was the first time to see them in five, my, my, what did it mean? I had been immediately answered, my thought of God's mysterious ways and this was a sign given to me that he had sent extra angels to be with us and help us.

I knew that I had to get back to Joshua, in given these signs I had felt renewed and relieved. As I walked through the halls this was the first time I made sure that I didn't look into anyone's eyes, I was afraid they would see the hurt in mine and I would begin to cry again.

Upon returning to Joshua and entering in his room, he seemed to be at ease really calm again and I was so relieved. I smiled to see this as Donna did to, to share this with me, oh what a victory! I give God the praise.

I was also relieved knowing that the rest of my family had not seen Joshua the way we did, it would've been too hard on them and God knew it.

I had also made sure that I hadn't discussed what had happened to other parents that were on our floor, not wanting to discourage any of them. I knew that some had not had the opportunity to stay with there child as I did.

In all things knowing what it's like to lift up and not tear down.

It was getting late and Donna and Chris had to leave, we gathered around praying again for his recovery. Donna had offered to stay another night but I really felt that we would be alright

We were told before the shifts changed the two nurses that had been responsible for the events that had taken place the previous night were given a few days off. We were relieved; I don't think I would've been able to go through another night during that time and have to work with them.

The information that had been given was a temporary solution to our situation, to us was a victory. This would give me time to be renewed and strengthened in my spirit as needed. For today there was no more that I could handle.

PREPARATION

A Legacy of Faith in 55 Days

I began to prepare for Joshua's evening care and taking extra time to let him know that I was so thankful that he was there for me. I was so proud of him for continuing to endure so much for us. I couldn't wait to get him home to have the opportunity to cook for him and talk with him like we use to do. I really missed all of those special times that we had. I had made a mess of things so many times; God had both of us in the palm of his hand and under the shadow of his wing now.

After finishing I hopped in bed to sleep next to him. My head was towards his feet and I leaned over and kissed his feet. I was so thankful to have all of him with me. We needed rest to visit with everyone during the upcoming weekend. For several hours both of us slept so peacefully.

I was blessed everyday to have had the experience that we had shared together during our stay.

As we awoke during the mourning hours I was immediately reminded of one of the afternoon visions that I had during a walk out into the hospital garden.

I didn't want to let go of Joshua but I also knew that it wasn't up to me to keep him with me.

I think this was a time that I had challenged God, I knew that he had created me and Joshua and it was up to God to determine our ending. He already knew from the very beginning, what he was going to do. I had a pull deep down and it was then that I knew God wanted Joshua and yet I insisted on keeping him, "I'll be good I continually said"

It was during these last days that I had a genuine desire to want what God wanted or else I would never see the promise that he intended.

I continued working with Joshua as I had and hoped that extra effort would allow us to find favor in God's eyes and with attending staff.

I was very particular about every procedure, and when we had a rough day or evening it caused me to feel frustrated and overwhelmed inside. God calmed the storm and restored the peace that I had lost inside.

I can say that although we were facing numerous challenges, my continual focus stayed upon Jesus and he is the won that give us victory.

I had been a perfectionist the biggest part of my life what if I didn't do something right; this had been one of my greatest challenges.

One of the most satisfying rewards is to know that God chose me and had faith in me to take a stand for him. There are no words to describe what that feels like inside.

Our day passing as it had and we shared the evening with many visitors that had come to see us. I expressed to everyone what had happened within the last 48 hours to us, I was angry for what had been done to us. This news stunned everyone and I was amused at the way they had behaved. No one really saying anything almost in dismay or belief because they hadn't seen what Donna, Chris, and I had seen.

I had to let these feelings come to pass and hold onto the good days that we had. We allowed our evening to pass with discussing other things that would cause us to smile and not frown. What a joy that was, I referred to God's word as my continual source during our recovery.

All of God's chosen ones that had a high calling on there life faced much affliction, and endured long-suffering. As Abraham, Issaic, and Jacob had followed God's plan. These are great examples to remember what it takes to leave a good name for all to remember, holding onto Jesus promise to the end. Times past, is in text with times present.

A willingness to suffer and glorify his name is to inherit the kingdom of heaven, with haven chosen him to be your life and your guide.

Many of our experiences were never discussed directly with us (Joshua and I) they were done away from us like in Biblical days to Job, Jesus, Peter and John.

In Job's experience some of his family had felt that he must be doing something wrong, to have been tried and tested as he was. Job knew that he hadn't and held onto God's word and his promise. And in doing that his days would be fulfilled.

In all of our days and experience I had to trust and believe in God's judgment, his way was the right way.

During visitation it was important for them to talk to Joshua as they always had, I insisted. Our visiting was soon over as time passed quickly during our weekend stays everyone started leaving, but we gathered around to pray once again with him in agreement. It was important to do this it added to their believing as it was strengthening me.

I loved and cared for Joshua with all of my heart, I couldn't imagine God's love being much more than mine, but it was. And not just to him but to both of us.

I hadn't realized the significance of daily preparation and devotion, just knowing that I had the desire to do it. God was preparing me for a new way of living and a new way of thinking as it read in (KJV) 1Peter 5:10- But the God of all grace, who hath called us unto his eternal glory by Christ Jesus, after that ye have suffered a while, make you perfect, stablish, strengthen, settle you.

I had the desire to give back to God for all that he had done for me, knowing that no matter what I could possibly do I could never repay the debt that I owe.

A Legacy of Faith in 55 Days

As our evening was progressing Joshua was expressing agitation. I felt overwhelmed tears filling my eyes not ever forgetting what he had already gone through.

I had stayed with Joshua throughout every hour and became tired; I needed to be renewed in my mind. I told him that I was taking a small break and that I would return in just a few minutes. I unzipped his bed and gave him a kiss on his forehead, I loved him so much but it was so hard to watch him have to struggle so much.

It was around 2:00a.m. Most people would be sleeping, I found myself walking the hallways. I tried avoiding others when I was having a difficult day or evening, knowing God doesn't work that way. It seemed like it was then that I had many others intervene and ask me to pray with them or there loved ones this was such a moving time in my life. When we forget about our situation and offer to help someone else during there crisis, it is then that God answers our prayers and sends help for healing or divine intervention.

God was using me the way he had wanted to and this was the first time that I had submitted to doing what was needed and asked.

I had found a place to sit quietly outside as I wondered, how often do we ask God what does he need of us? I was quickly moved by a lady who had seen me and asked if she could sit with me. I said absolutely, I moved to allow her to sit comfortably beside me so we could talk. In looking in her eyes I knew that she had a broken spirit, I asked what I could do to help. She immediately opened her heart to tell me that her husband of 20 plus years was in the Intensive Care Unit battling with cancer it was a struggle for his life.

He had spent the last five years in and out of the hospital due to the rapid growth of cancer that had taken over his body and there lives together. He had given up his interest for life and she was deeply hurt feeling that he would soon be gone, as she began to cry. I asked if I could pray with her and she agreed. Minutes passing and soon it was time for me to go back,.

She had asked why I was there and I had briefly shared with her Joshua and my experience. I told her Joshua was doing great but we needed continual prayer so remember us as she prays. As we departed this was another individual that God had allowed me to pray for, I was so thankful.

I was ready to get back to Joshua being thankful for all of the time that God has allowed us. I entered Joshua's room to see him continually struggling but I had also remembered reading the scripture where it said that Joshua was the chosen won, he had won the hearts of the people and he was called to minister. He was willing do to whatever it took to make the difference and see souls saved and lives changed.

I continued to have that deep hurt in my heart that wouldn't go away. I had felt that with everything that had happened, it had been too much for him and Joshua was called to be in heaven's home and not ours. What I was seeing wasn't what I was seeing, everything was God given.

This was a tremendous testimony and ministry for the two of us.

It's important to keep God first and then you will always have a praise report.

Our time seemed to be passing by so quickly, much more than it had ever been before. It was already Sunday we had just a few more days before his doctor would be back, I was so glad. I had held onto ill feelings that had been caused by attending staff, but until I truly gave it to Jesus I wouldn't

Receive the ending that I had anticipated. As family had came to visit I was agitated with some in there reactions acting as if I was to blame instead of the hospital or staff, when Joshua was having a bad day. Forgetting all about what had taken place with him just a few days prior.

I was with him everyday there wasn't anything that I wouldn't do for him, I exclaimed. I wasn't a doctor or a nurse and that makes a huge difference in authority positions and what I could do for him. I could make requests but it was up to them to have the final say. As Jesus says he will never leave you or forsake you, he was present with us the entire time. He is the only one that has sustained and kept me through everything.

Some didn't seem too excited in seeing me want to bring Joshua home, he had been through so much would it be safe to transport him, we lived so far away. This was a very difficult time for all of us, each one forming there own opinions about the entire situation. God knew how to calm each one of us in his own special way of doing things and in doing that and the way he did would allow us to have victory.

This was one of those times that I had felt in all that we had experienced, I would receive the answers that I had been praying for. I had a very difficult time in trusting God; there wasn't anyone that I had really trusted in my entire life. But by his grace he had faith in me and chose me to help leave a legacy.

It's terrible to think that often times we put God on the side when everything seems to be going our way, but, when the storms rage and we are faced with the trouble of life it is then that we are attentive and drawn so close to him. God's has to be #1 if he's not, you won't receive the promise or see the light that only he can give.

In caring for Joshua I had also planned to make the necessary arrangements to bring Joshua home. I would do everything that I could to expedite the process.

I had been asked when I planned to have him released and at the time I didn't have an answer, I believed I would have the opportunity I just didn't know when and had planned to have it done by the following weekend.

DECISION

We gathered around and prayed again with Joshua as everyone had started to leave, I was relieved. Any pressure that I had felt I always expressed after everyone had left. Everyone was hurting deep down and barely holding on; it took God's love to each of us to give us reason to hold on. As with any injury it takes time to heal, and when it hits you eternally it will take extra time, even then you wear the scar or scars for life. No one knows the extent of your wounds but God.

I prepared for our evening hours as I always had knowing that the three of us was keeping the circle of faith going.

And it had been left to us to give a tremendous testimony.

I knew the following day would be extremely hectic in keeping with Joshua's schedule and making the necessary calls to individuals that could help expedite our discharge process. I had feelings of both excitement and feelings of being overwhelmed, and found myself not doing anymore than seconds or minutes would allow. Keeping in mind I had always said that whatever it takes I will do.

Joshua struggled throughout the evening having difficult time breathing. I had asked for an ex-ray of his chest and was told that it wasn't necessary.

What was going on with him I didn't know but the way he was struggling over each breath, like he was choking for long lengths of time I knew that it wasn't a good sign. His nurse also made it a point not to give him his medicine on time.

I repeatedly told Joshua to hold on that we would soon be home, and then it would be all good. I asked God to deliver him from his pain and suffering not really wanting to except the fact God had prepared a place for him and called Joshua home with him.

We had been placed in the care of Nurse Judy the one who had caused so much pain for him and caused a setback in his recovery. I couldn't understand why this was allowed and had asked for someone else and was denied even by the administrator that had come by that night. I remained side by side Joshua throughout the entire evening, for added protection and for me to have peace of mind.

I pressed through the evening feeling overwhelmed and tired, it gets to you after a while. I felt pressured to keep everything going and yet it was until I felt that I couldn't do anymore is when God stepped in. I had been very selfish to compare my experience with what Joshua had experienced, or anyone as a patient that is on the receiving end.

There was no way that I could say God hadn't done anything for us, we were believers from the very beginning and he had given me the ability to see miracle after miracle take place with Joshua right in front of me. He deserves all of the praise not me. What God has given me will be a constant reminder of his great love for each of us and will be with me for the rest of my days.

As the evening progressed I had became more upset over the actions and carelessness of his attending nurse. It had come to a head as I confronted her and demanded his well-being at hand. She had called security and planned to have me removed from his room, but God moved. She had acted as if I was the one that had placed him in harms way and not them. I pleaded with the numerous officers and openly told them what she had done to him previously and that I couldn't leave him. They expressed compassion and told me that if there were any more incidents that I would be removed. I thanked them greatly for allowing me to stay. I desperately needed God to be my guide and to speak and do for me; I was so weak and felt like I was falling apart and that I was going to loose him, it wasn't the right time.

I had remembered in my studies as a young girl how Jesus and all of his followers were not always accepted and were falsely accused and persecuted for living there life in truth. Our situation wasn't any different compared to those that had lived before us.

Our weekend had past it was early mourning and day 40. I had made a list of people to call and an itemized list of all of the necessary things that would be needed to bring Joshua home with me. I had kept everything on schedule and had separated from him for a while, letting him know that it was necessary to make these arrangements and to place the calls. We had prayer and I gave him a kiss on the forehead as I left him for a while to make the calls. "Just a little while longer Joshua we'll be home" as I exited his room.

I shared our story with everyone that listened, pleading desperately for the help of many. I couldn't do it alone I needed the help of everyone that had titles or positions. There wasn't a physical tie that bound us there was no reason for anyone to risk there positions for us and they didn't. I cried helplessly for hours after hearing the rejection the numerous phone calls that I had made. It would be at least Thursday before anyone would get back with me, to me that was an eternity it was three days to man's calendar and our experiences was overwhelming. This was one of those times that I had to have faith and hold onto the hope of the things that I hadn't seen. (KJV) Hebrew 11:1

I knew that I couldn't return to Joshua in the shape that I was in. I took a few minutes away walking downstairs to take a break. I was crushed; I avoided talking with anyone today.

I walked with my head down as I proceeded to get to my favorite spot. What did I do for everything to be so wrong, I thought? Hurt me, not him I pleaded.

I sat in dismay without any words to say, it seemed like a long time even though it had only been approximately 10 minutes. I hesitated to hurry back as I began to shorten my path and walk through the hospital garden. It was then the Sun opened wide it had the biggest beams of light shining down, it was beautiful and as it glistened surrounding the hospital garden.

I set down my things directed myself in the center of this circle of light; I lifted up my hands and started praising God, for all that he had done was right.

HOME

The sun had come out of nowhere this was a definite sign for me the day had been so gloomy prior to this happening.

I felt the weight of the world immediately being lifted off of my shoulders and was given strength to continue. The peace that I had been given at this very moment and the tingling sensation that I had experienced all over was not to be compared to anything that I have ever experienced.

What a wonderful way as God did with Paul in Acts 26 to let him know that he had trusted in him to see this through.

There was a light cool breeze that had passed before me as I had been praising him and knew that I had to head back. I was faced with challenges, but God would see to it that it wouldn't become too great for me to handle.

I needed this today something to reassure me that God was with me through everything.

The biggest part of my days was spent in Joshua's room and I needed strength, I needed to be renewed. Today was different I felt this light and warmth all around me. It was overshadowing me every step that I had to take, what a great feeling.

I then realized that Joshua must have known what this had felt like because I had seen and felt a continual glow that had surrounded him. I couldn't wait to share it with him. I was experiencing in part what he had been given.

I returned to Joshua's room to see him struggling for his life, I leaned over to turn Christian music on. I loved him so much but there was nothing that I could do to help him, my hands were tied. I began to cry as I sat beside him; a nurse came in and asked if I was alright? I said, I will be when I can take him home with me. She smiled and sighed.

I told Joshua that I wasn't supposed to go through this without him, that I needed him. This isn't how it's supposed to be, you can't give up on me! Tears flowing down like a stream by the river. He had gone through so much this was the first time that I had realized it, and I didn't want to be selfish about it anymore. I asked God to help me see his way and not mine continually. With everything in me I didn't want to let go. Time had past and the day seemed so long. I declined his physical therapy for the day wanting to give Joshua a break.

I had turned his phone on in the room, not wanting to leave him because of the severity of his condition. Minutes had past and the phone rang it was part of another administration trying to help meet the requirements needed for Joshua's release. I had openly voiced everything that the hospital and staff had done wrong and at that point I didn't have any confidence that they could do anything right. I felt that Joshua's life was in danger and I was about to collapse with all of the added pressures that had been placed on us.

I was discouraged to hear that there was a process to go through even though we had a horrific experience and wouldn't be able to leave without having made the necessary arrangements and go through all of the necessary paperwork. I demanded an Emergency Discharge but was denied. Our conversation ended and I began to cry once again, I questioned why God would allow us to have to go through this. I believed that God would give me an understanding to all of it someday and a month later I realized that whatever we have to face, or whatever we will go through, it's our reasonable service is to be willing.

I stepped outside of Joshua's room for a few seconds after receiving the news of the other administration and heard the nurses conversing about my phone conversation. They had said they felt that it would be good if they could separate us; I stepped back into Joshua's room and was really discouraged. God was mad at me or this wouldn't be happening I thought.

I sat down in a chair beside Joshua's bed and I began to read some Biblical stories, for me it was good to speak aloud it was feeding my thought process. I asked the Lord to help me think more clearly, I had a desire to always remember the good that he had given us. Jesus sent his life-line for us on the very first day, there's no way that I could even consider forgetting what had been done for us.

I read aloud to Joshua as I sat beside him, reminding me of the numerous scriptures God had already given us. The drive inside that God gave was so strong I couldn't give up until he said my work was done.

I wouldn't have stayed focused on God's will if we had been separated, but the way God worked it was best for both of us.

My greatest desire is to always be grateful for what had been given to us. I silently prayed not knowing what to say, I had said made so many requests previously that the only thing that I could really do is open my heart and allow him to come in and heal all of my wounds.

Donna and Chris had came to visit and I shared with them all conversations and activities that had taken place. We had dinner in Joshua's room because I feared to leave him unattended. It hadn't seemed long while they had came to visit but before I knew visiting hours were over and they would leave and come again the following day. We hugged and kissed saying our good-byes not really knowing daily what to expect. Having them visit daily was encouraging and uplifting for us. I never felt any tension when I discussed Joshua's medical situation with them. I looked forward to there daily visits!

I prepared for Joshua's evening care as I always had, he was quite restless so I didn't take the extra time like I usually had. I wanted him to rest and not be so agitated. After finishing I gave him a kiss and told him that I was going to walk around on the floor a little bit. As I slowly past each room, and glancing at other moms eye to eye I could see the same pain that they had in there eyes. I continued to walk having this deep hurt, something that can't be expressed or described with words. My heart was aching I just wanted to take Joshua home.

God let me know that not everyone will glorify his name when they are faced with tragedy.

I returned to Joshua's room hoping that he was settled but he continued to be struggling. I had asked for him to have more medicine but my request was denied, he had already been given the maximum dose allowed and there wasn't anything more they could do at the time.

As I watched his heart racing mine was melting. I was crumbling inside to watch him suffer as he did. I was begging and pleading Lord, please there's got to be something more that I could do. We need help I can't do this without you or him. One day God planned to give us both a beautiful rainbow to see again, but when would I see it is what I was asking?

I told Joshua that I had walked the halls and seen some of the other kids fighting alone, and that there was some that had been more traumatized than he had. I expressed how sad it had made me to see some of the children had to be courageous without having anyone there to help support them. Some were visually mutilated with scars and others were choking on there own saliva and had a trachea to help comfort them because they were no longer able to swallow. I was so thankful to have been given the opportunity to stay beside Joshua entirely. And that we hadn't had to experience those countless surgeries as others had. Our experience had grieved me deeply to see his continual struggle for recovery.

Joshua had only two surgeries; just two (elbow surgery and then the insertion of the food-tube) we were so blessed. God had a plan and I had continually said that whatever it takes I will do, and God would see to it that I would keep my word as he had kept his. We slowly pressed through those aching evening hours. God allowed all of us to see his handy work a miracle in the making and it was continually by giving us Joshua as we had him before the accident.

By mourning Joshua's medicines had increased at a significant level but nothing seemed to be comforting him. He was administered morphine again along with other sedatives a reminder that our time was evolving back to day one with one to many similarities starting.

Our situation wasn't looking good and I had to consider and prepare myself for the possibility of loosing him. Even though I had continually said that we would walk out of those hospital doors and say never underestimate what God can do. And to this day we can still say that.

God better than anyone knew the pain that I was feeling as he had shared that same pain knowing that one day his son would bare the cross for all of us to have a Savior. The story of Joshua in the Biblical days he as a young high priest was also considered to be a Savior. I knowing first hand that the life of Joshua had touched and changed many, Joshua too was the perfect example for all of us to use.

Jesus was being prepared for the ultimate sacrifice of love God had for us he too was afraid; just like us was how he was made. Jesus wept. as the scripture says in John 11:35 (KJV). The examples we had been given for strength, guidance, and in the end victory. The number one key is to trust and obey. You have to if you believe in the promise of life everlasting on the other side.

It was through our ordeal that I realized how short life was and the importance of making sure everything is alright in God's eyes. It was only until now at my weakest point that God could show me and allow me to be a part of his wonderful plan; he really comforted me during this difficult time.

I had been doing everything but couldn't keep going. I had said over and over that Joshua rested in Gods hands and that what I was seeing wasn't what I was seeing. I believe Joshua already had a glimpse of heaven and there wasn't anything more that I could do to convince him to stay with me.

I said to him if he had seen heaven that was ok that one day I too would be given the opportunity to share it with him.

Joshua's dad and I were both saved oh how the heavens must have rejoiced when we surrendered and gave our lives to him. And I can imagine the beautiful crown Joshua has been given for all that he did in giving his life to see us have life.

I was given this testament for all ages to understand. I was crumbled and brought low, but what God had done for us was worth it all and in every word.

We were starting a new day as the early mourning came Joshua didn't seemed to be too relaxed. I had become frustrated and felt that I had made God mad and that is why he wasn't answering any more of my prayers the way I had asked.

I left Joshua's room overwhelmed with feelings of doubt. I managed to walk down to the Chapel ready to let everything that I had held in out. As I walked in to my dismay there was a congregation full of black people about to pray.

I moved in feeling weak hoping they would allow me to join in, I was greeted with smiles everyone moving a space to allow me to join hands as they were praying and uplifting many of the requests that had been made.

I hadn't said anything but there had been a request made for me that let me know that God seen and heard my plea. They didn't know that I was Joshua's mom but that is one of the requests to uplift and strengthen both of us during this time.

God's ways are so great it was important for me to share such a treasured moment; he hears all of us no matter what color of our skin. They were so nice to me as our prayer had ended everyone shook hands and even some extended a hug. I was ready to head back feeling that after our meeting I could face anything.

I had a song in my heart knowing that it was from heaven above no turning back, no turning back. I'm not sure who sings it but I knew in my heart there was nothing to look back to other than how blessed we had been to have so many extra days with him.

More than ever I felt today the love of God towards me as I returned to Joshua's room. After entering and seeing Joshua struggle I told him that I too received a touch from heaven and I thanked him for showing so much love for me to wait until I could start seeing it God's way.

He sounded pretty raspy and I had to suction him, it wasn't by choice but it was one of those things that I had to do. This was part of the agreement if I partook in this procedure to know how to do it, it would greater the chance of him being coming home. After all I did say that whatever it takes I will do.

I prepared Joshua before doing anything as I got things ready I would talk to him softly and tell him what I needed him to do, he would smile and do it for me and say mum, mum before finishing. He refused to comply when anyone else tried.

I would always reassure him that I was right there for him this was so encouraging for me. Having this time and hearing and seeing Joshua do this filed my heart with joy and hope of tomorrow.

I couldn't wait for others to come and visit, I loved sharing this kind of news. Our time had past and it was late in the afternoon Donna and Chris had came to visit as well as family and friends. Joshua's dad was one of them and he seemed more stressed today than usual. I tried encouraging him and saying that Joshua was going to be alright but he was so hurt you couldn't help from see the sadness in his eyes. I believe God gave this time and it allowed some to make mends.

This was day 42 and all of us had tried to be patient wanting to know when we were going to bring Joshua home. I had told them that I spoke with everyone that I could, but it wasn't up to me make that final decision. All of us believed Joshua would do better once we were able to bring him home. Visiting hours seemed to fly right by and before we knew it everyone once again was saying there good-byes.

As I was given the opportunity to stay beside Joshua daily I could see it visually having an effect on him entirely. No matter what I did, and I really tried nothing seemed to be helping him he was so agitated and restless. I lay my head on his rail and began to cry as I sobbed, I heard Joshua's voice above me and he said it's going to be alright. God allowed him to speak to me and I was so upset I let this great miracle slip before me. I looked up there he was struggling for his life. How could everything be alright without you, I asked as I continued to cry?

One of my greatest memories of Joshua is he always thought of comforting others even when he was the one who really needed to be comforted.

I had been given so much during a short time, yet it wouldn't be enough to last me a lifetime. Our circumstance with procedures and medicines seemed to be evolving back to our first day. But through it all I had gained faith and had a new outlook and prospective about everything.

Joshua was whole and he had a beautiful glow about him. I have compared my son's life to Joshua in the Biblical days and as long as I live I know that people will always remember him and his testament and memorial that he has left and given to all of us.

His story had a great impact on our entire community. It is truly a blessing to be given this gift to share our story.

I wasn't ready to give him back to our Creator even though that is what God had planned, that is something that I hadn't asked. I had a difficult time handling the rough days. The emotion was in a 24 hour cycle.

I had been waiting all mourning for the most important call of the day and that was to find out if the decision had been made that we would be able to take Joshua home.

I had waited patiently throughout the entire night, ready to pack our things and say good-bye.

I received the call and it wasn't my delight my request had been denied, it was against medical advice. I had a lump in my throat and tightness in my chest, and I again asked why? I hung up the phone and began to cry, nothing can describe the feelings I had inside. We had both been put through so much, why would they make us continue like this?

It was staffs negligence and we had to stay for punishment.

I was angry with most of the attending staff for the carelessness and selfish acts that they had expressed to us. I didn't want to get close to anyone; I had even stepped back from God being broken hearted.

We were in a bad situation and they had caused the setbacks that we had, how could I ever forgive them for all that they had done?

I had a little notebook filled with improper procedures and the many patient rights that we had been denied. They wouldn't get by with this I exclaimed!

I had video of our confrontations and recorded our conversations; I was setting myself up for nothing. Because what God gave us was not something man could take away.

God intervened and cleansed me of those harsh feelings and I would have to leave the matter in his hands and I did learn to do just that.

Our day had progressed with the physical therapists coming in I know they had to see the sadness written upon my face. I told Joshua that we were going to stay another weekend as they worked with him. His session was over and the therapists left the room, Joshua was so agitated and I was extremely upset. I went to him leaning over and kissing his head and holding his hand, it was then I felt strongly that the Lord was going to take him I didn't know when.

It was so important to regain focus on what God had done. I had said over and over as the Holy Spirit was my guide that God doesn't change his mind during a crisis, he knows the outcome before we ever receive it. He will do what is best for each of us he knows what lies ahead. God created each of us and knows when our time is up.

Although I had been extremely emotional, I began to sing and feel the joy that God had given me once again.

When our lights seem to dim, that's when God steps in and gives us the burning again.

Time had went by so fast that before I knew it mourning and afternoon had past and it was closer to the evening visiting hours.

Our visitors started to arrive and I had to prepare them that Joshua was having a bad day, all that came had clearly seen how it was affecting him.

I didn't want to face them with the disappointing news, but they depended on me to share with them if we were coming home soon. We had planned on leaving that weekend but without choice once again had to stay. There were many times that I felt that we were just a number, a reminder of the benefits of the insurance company and not on how we were doing.

Visiting hours soon ended, everyone had left but Donna and Chris. She had always been there for the both of us and stayed around a few more minutes.

I had reminded everyone that there were minutes throughout our day that Joshua breathed steadily and rested peacefully and to keep praying. I was lacking trust; how could I trust in God if I hadn't seen him, but I couldn't trust man in whom I had seen.

Not everyone was bad and not everyone was out to hurt us, only God could help me overcome this. I made a choice that day I need and believe in God with everything.

I was given much time a lone separated from my home and my former lifestyle and friends and in that I had the privilege of having a closer walk with God.

As I had prepared for the evening hours continually being reminded not to take life for granted, because you never know when.

And when I took a break there were many sad faces that I had came face to face with and deep-down I had asked that God give me something to uplift them as he had done me. None of us have to stand alone he will be there if you allow him he really does care.

Families were loosing their homes, transportation, friends, family and even their jobs over tragedy. Satan had them in bondage and many couldn't see the light.

I returned to Joshua's room to find him sleeping peacefully, oh what a relief!

He began to move I said a few words and immediately he was back asleep. I loved him so much, only he would ever know how much. We had a closeness that hadn't been shared in a very long time.

This was one of those evening I crossed the room pulling down some covers to lay on a cot, I hadn't wanted to sleep in a long while.

After seeing him rest made me feel better and I did fall asleep for about 30 minutes. Joshua was making sound and I awoke and raised up it was then I had seen a nurse leaving. I stood up and followed her out and she said she had given him his medicine and I began to cry and why? I was suppose to do that for him. She patted me on the shoulders and said it's alright you need to rest and she sent me back to bed her name was Fern. And she said as I began to turn Mom we know how much you love and care for him; I said I hope so because I feel like I'm not doing enough for him. She replied if all nurses were like you there wouldn't be a need for nurses. I smiled and said you think? I'm doing what is needed of me. She said, I know.

I re-entered his room to see that he was awake, I told him that he was doing great. It was early Friday mourning and he had a big day. As I look at it now everyday had been a big day.

I continually tried comforting techniques sometimes they worked and other times they didn't it all depended on him.

As a newborn babe in Christ we try everything to pacify before God can really show us the simplest is what works. Joshua was relaxed and had smiled as I gave him a sponge bath. I had assured him that in watching him that I had really understood what Jesus had done for us.

Whatever God was asking of us, I would see it through and yes I'm doing it.

My cries and my plea were going out consistently. I couldn't turn or depend on anyone else to get me through this; this was something I had to be obedient and willing to do.

To lean, learn, and understand isn't always easy but sometimes that's what it takes for us to leave a testimony for all to remember.

All of Joshua's medicines had increased and he'd even had patches to give him more of a consistency. Joshua seemed to be doing alright as the hours were passing by it was just minutes before the therapists had arrived he began to really move around. I had said if he didn't want therapy to move as they were about to enter and he did.

I felt that Joshua was saying that he had enough and didn't want to keep fighting it.

I loved him so much and wanted him to be as comfortable as he could be, even if the therapists became agitated with me.

When the therapists had came in more than ever he was stirring around and I had told them he had another difficult night and that I didn't think that was a good time for him. Within minutes of them leaving Joshua calmed down, it was quite odd at times sharing this kind of communication with him. Nevertheless I considered being his voice speaking and was finishing out his last request.

I had read the little study guide that I had faithfully carried and it had said that it would be 2 years before could complete what he had given. I was confused and had asked Lord are we going to go through this 2 years before he receives a complete recovery? And will I be able to withstand all of the tests that will be given?

I didn't receive an answer right then, not the way I had expected. Everyday I was being prepared for what would take place our destiny. I cherished every moment that I had been given with him.

Others that had came to visit had suggested leaving for a day but I couldn't think of being away from him not even for more than a few minutes.

Joshua more than ever before continually said the word oww and had tears coming down. I wondered where he hurt and when I reported it to the attending nurse or nurses they had said that Joshua had dry eyes and eventually the tears would go away. His pain has marred me for life, I felt helpless both inside and out.

I had to remember God breathed life back into him, and it was up to him to decide if we could keep him or have to give him back to our heavenly Creator.

Oww to me is an indication of pain regardless of what others had said. As I watched Joshua attentively he yawned. I was like wow this is great this is another positive response.

I told the nurse and she refused to write it down, I asked why and she said that she didn't have time.

No matter what I was looking forward to the day we would be going home soon! I was happy and sad at the same time, he had been through so much would the move be too much for him.

The day was long and it was around 4:00p.m. the therapists came in and had asked if they could do one session with him. I accepted watching every step and the way they handled him. Joshua had finished his therapy with flying colors for the day and they had said there good-byes and planned on seeing him the next day.

Joshua had done so great I was so proud of him as he rested in his bed Donna and Chris came in and she said knock knock and Joshua turned his head towards her and smiled at her this was one of the biggest presents that she could've got.

I had hoped to bring Joshua home by Donna's birthday. However she received this wonderful surprise, something that I couldn't give her but God did and it would stay with her for a lifetime.

She was hurting and God loved her as much as he did us and allowed Joshua to do for her what he hadn't done before, and this is something that she will never forget.

I hadn't seen Donna smile like that in a long time!

What we had experienced was a gift from God, and it was a privilege to witness it. We were in the midst of the super-natural and there are no words to describe it, I can only utter it with my lips.

I wished Donna a happy birthday and she said yes it was, she received her present early.

We had dinner in Joshua's room that kept me at ease; just in case he needed anything I could be there to assist him.

Everything seemed to be going quite smoothly visiting hours would soon be over and I had agreed to walk them down. We prayed with Joshua in agreement and I told him I would be back in just a few minutes.

We had stood outside for a few minutes and then I felt it necessary to get back to his room.

I knew the shifts would be changing soon and I wanted to know who I would be working with. We said our good-byes and I hurriedly walked back to Joshua's room upon entering the 6th Floor I was quickly informed that Judy would be our nurse. How could they do this she

A Legacy of Faith in 55 Days

had already tried to take away his life and they wanted us to work with her again? I became angry and said no she is not going to come near my boy and I had spoke aloud.

I had requested another nurse and was denied, I spoke loudly when I had said why I didn't want her in there with him. I was told that she didn't have to come in she would give me the medicine to give to him at the door. I immediately calmed and was better with that alternative rather than letting her near Joshua again. Time had past and it was getting later in the evening (around 9:00p.m.) then I was greeted by the hospital administrator. I was pulled into a conference room with a tape recorder going and they said that they would no longer oblige by my request and that nurse Judy was to be in our room and work with me side by side.

She had already made her mind up and I wasn't going to do anything to be separated from him, I left her company full of emotion and said this is going to be another long night. I quickly returned to be beside Joshua's side.

His nurse almost immediately began to delay the administration of his medicines. I'll never know why she had appeared to be so cold and evil towards us we hadn't done anything to her, may God have mercy on her for what she was doing.

At one point throughout the night she had even thought that I was asleep as she had entered in, and immediately walked back out. I followed right behind her and let her know that she needed to give him his medicine and she said she already did. I said no you didn't I was right there waiting to see if you would and you've refused it once again.

I had asked the one nurse to check her pockets and she refused and then nurse Judy went to assist another patient, I waited but she wasn't planning on coming out of that room any time soon. This situation was really playing on me mentally and I didn't want to react foolishly, again walking away to reunite with Joshua again.

He had already been through so many tests and trials this was too much for him to keep fighting. We had went from having a great evening to an evening of devastation. She had waited so long in between giving him his medicine that Joshua began heavily breathing and posturing uncontrollably. I began to cry Joshua would have a good day or days and then we would have someone like Judy to take it away from us.

Joshua's glow that he had was gone. The patches that he had was coming off because he was sweating so bad, there wasn't anything more that I could do to help him. I tried to do everything to comfort him but nothing seemed to be helping. I was so sad and mad, I yelled you're killing him and she said tone it down or she was calling security. I said go ahead they need to report this on you. I was going through the pain and agony of seeing him tried as he already had.

Satan wanted me to feel like God had turned his back, because God was going to use our testimony to help others who have faced a horrific tragedy.

HEAVEN

A Legacy of Faith in 55 Days

Lord Jesus, I am weak and I'm not able to do this without you I pleaded. I don't want to leave him and I don't want to let go. Please Lord don't let it end like this.

Joshua was stirring all night long and we were both exhausted by mourning.

As staff had heard the problems and challenges that we had faced, not one had said anything encouraging or comforting to us that day. There was a staff meeting with all whom were involved with us and no one was to comment about our situation. I was devastated. We were made to stay and the only thing we wanted was to go home and feel safe.

No one said anything when they came into our room. I had been given a song in the early days and I was reminded of all the miracles that had taken place; through his face, to his eyes, to his nose all the way down through the toes.

Oh Joshua please hold on, don't let go as I held his hand. Moments past and I told him I was taking a few minutes away; I had planned on going down to the Chapel to pray. I was crushed as I walked away, I arrived at the Chapel falling to my knees weeping again as I had prayed aloud. I was lost for words but my tears were flowing continuously. I had believed we were going to be walking out together not leaving without him, to be hand in hand.

I sat in the Chapel floor trying to pull myself together and asked God to give me another sign. I had to know what was going on I couldn't continue with the way I was feeling. I had went outside and found a place to sit next to the garden and it was a beautiful sight the sun was shining and the birds were singing there seemed to be a melody in the air. As I was in my chosen spot it was then as I had continued to cry that I heard Joshua's voice speaking to me; he said, Mom you can't be in the room when I cross over. I said what, he said, Mom you can't be in the room when I cross over, nobody can. I said why not? Before hearing him answer I said I'm not leaving without you. But he said, it would be too much for me to stay with him when he went.

All of us were still holding on and Joshua was in a mix to stay or go, and if we were there he would think he had disappointed us, and that it was God's will, we would have to let him go.

This was a lot to except especially after the night we had just had, but for the first time I wanted to understand.

God had blessed me so much to be a witness and a part of something so big, I was scared after hearing this and immediately head back to be with him.

Jesus Christ was my comforter and guide the entire time.

I had to find a way to tell others I just didn't know when. Upon entering Joshua's room everyone was surrounding his bed trying to find words to comfort him. Joshua was extremely agitated and what he was doing had an effect on everyone.

We had said our goodbyes and everyone planning to come and visit with us again real soon. I pulled Donna to the side and shared with her the voice that I had heard downstairs in the garden. I didn't quite understand what I had been given and I was nervous and scared at the same time.

She had pulled me close as I began to shower once again with tears how could I ever go on without him? I said I can't, but God said that I can!

She held me until I stopped crying and said that she would stay with us, if I wanted her too. I said no that I would be alright they had stayed around for quite a long time and then they too had to leave.

Joshua and I were left alone again and I had shared with him what had been spoken to me downstairs. I believe he already knew it would take this in order for me to see the big picture God had in store for us.

I was angry when I first heard but after watching him daily minute by minute and hour by hour, I knew and believed in my heart God knew what he was doing. In our early days I wasn't prepared as I was now, and God took the extra time not to give me too much at any one time.

I visited with him as long as I could before taking another break, before leaving him again. I was stunned with the news that had been given and was questioning it once again.

We were down to our last days had God planned on taking him that night? I wasn't sure.

I made my way downstairs and had went to the same spot, as I sat there it was again the same voice and the same words with nobody can. Nobody can what, and then he said be in the room when I cross over. And I said why not?

Again it was the same answer that I had received earlier, we would hold onto him being in there with him. I had been given the same message twice in one day the second being more specific than the first.

That is Jesus way of doing things he always confirms more than once what he's going to do. Having him speak to me twice in the same manner I was no longer confused and unsure. I knew that it was he speaking to me and that he was preparing me for what was to come. And I had to tell the others even though I didn't want to.

SAYING GOOD-BYE

Everyone had been gone just a couple of hours as I headed back to Joshua's room to call Donna and tell her the news. I phoned Donna first and told her to tell everyone that they needed to come back up, it was very important. The calls were made to both sides of our families I wasn't sure if God had planned on taking him that night, but I had to do what was right and prepare them.

Donna made the necessary calls to share with everyone my request to have them come back that night. I couldn't speak with anyone else at the time I had the biggest lump in my throat and had very few words. There were many families that had comforted me while I was waiting for mine to be with me.

It was within the hour everyone had come to be with us again, I had shared with them what had been shared with me. My eyes were like a river flowing with tears, my heart was torn and in my mind I was thinking I've only been given 14 years, I knew that he was going to leave me.

Everyone please pray, with me. I had requested each of them to please tell Joshua one by one that whatever he and Jesus had decided was alright with us. I already knew what that decision was. I wouldn't be taking him home no matter how much I wanted to.

Reminding everyone that Joshua had endured more at 14 years old than that of a hundred year old. Joshua's monitor was continually going off a constant reminder an alarming sound.

Time was passing as each had visited alternating break times so someone would be with him. When I was asked when he started reacting like this, I was a little stunned he had been but not as aggressive as he was now. I had been guilty of protecting them from what I had seen in his last days and that was Joshua struggling and having much difficulty. In my eyes Joshua was doing great because I had seen and witnessed and always keep in remembrance what God had brought him from and what he had done for us.

It's not always easy for others to understand, if they could grasp a little it would leave them with a legacy. Everyone had made arrangements to stay the night, just in case they had to say good-bye.

I had said if he goes I want him in my arms, I found it very difficult to say it was the deepest pain I had ever felt. I wasn't giving up, but in my heart I felt that time would come. I was going against those words that had been given to me in the garden and so was everyone else. It's easily to do when you love someone so much.

I will always remember the progress that he had made, not ever taking anything we had experienced for granted. God used Joshua to give to us a wonderful remembrance of everything he was able to do when doctors had said that he couldn't or wouldn't. We were so blessed!

Even the charge nurse had planned to stay the night what a surprise, I would find that it was a blessing in disguise. God sees and knows everything before were aware.

The continual care for Joshua became more difficult for he was resisting the assistance and the administering of his medicines became very complicated.

I know that he was trying to tell us that he had enough, yet we wanted to bring him home.

Each of us had our moments and we had commented on the stain glass remembering the portrait of the mother handing her child back. One never wants to think that we may have to give them back but it is he that gave to us.

Each of us had prayed calling upon God with our individual requests, wiping away the many tears that we shed that night.

We had said how proud we were; and what ever he wanted would be alright with us.

The hours were passing as everyone had stayed with us, trying to lean into Jesus understanding isn't always easy. Everyone was lifting me up and I was quite encouraged. I was tired of hiding the rough days, it was good for others to see just a little of what we had experienced.

I had been asked to meet with Joshua's doctor and the charge nurse in the conference room, I agreed. It was three doors away from Joshua's room and everyone had agreed to stay with him while I had went to this meeting. I definitely knew what it was like to feel humbled and crumbled at the same time.

I was being prepared for Code Blue with them thinking he wouldn't make it through the evening. I had tears flowing like a river and there wasn't anything anyone could say or do to take them away.

I had made a request that Joshua have as much medicine as possible to calm him, not anymore than medically necessary. I didn't want to see him suffer because of me thinking selfishly.

We had went through the list of his medicines and care plan to, to sign in agreement was the most difficult thing that I had to do. I was thinking of him and placing him first not me.

I left the room feeling really overwhelmed all of my family waiting and standing by. I shared with them the possibility of Code Blue I was hugged and was told everything would be alright.

I went to Joshua and continued to cry and said I'm not going to be able to do this without you. My heart ached really bad and there was very little that I could say.

It was really getting late everyone was trying to find there own little space to lay there head for they had planned to stay. I lay at the foot of Joshua's bed waiting patiently if he had taken his last breath.

I was given nurse Judy for the evening and wondered why, I had already received enough from her in the weeks prior. I couldn't dispute it Joshua was very critical I had to do my best to deal with her because of the necessity of staying with him.

Everyone was aware of what she had done to us previously and they were extremely nice to her hoping that she wouldn't do to us what she had done ever again.

Our evening progressed and it was really late, Joshua was really agitated and he needed his medicine. I pleaded with her to give it to him but was denied because of the window once again. I went head to head with her tired of being nice, Why are you doing this to him, he's all that I have can't you see that? I began to cry I've been with him everyday to see that he gets better I said, he won't if you take it away from him Judy. Give it to him now, I insisted.

She left immediately and called for Security they came to remove me it was about 4:25a. m. I can't leave now he'll leave me. I was escorted out and shouted out for the head nurse Pat. Joshua was really bad everyone was trying to calm him as him monitor went off and was really loud. I spoke aloud please Joshua don't leave, not this way I screamed.

I was so afraid in just a few minutes he could've left me, but God was with us and didn't allow it to end this way.

I was away from him, as Pat came around the corner I explained as quickly as I could and pleaded with her to help me and explain it to security while I quickly turned back to reunite with him. I said it's ok I'm here Joshua, I'm here. Security left and Pat came in the room to administer medicine and talk with us. She knew the incidence that had happened and said other families were concerned and I needed to be quiet about things. I agreed as she was there with us for the rest of the mourning to assist us. I was so happy that Pat had been there for us . God knew and sent us protection if he hadn't I may have never had closure to such a horrific experience.

I had a lot of resentment building up in my heart for all of the things that had happened to us. Later, I would have those walls of perdition broke down to have a lasting testimony for all to remember.

I have Jesus Christ as my personal Saviour and he is #1 in my life and he gave me the the ability to leave a good name that is all that matters.

Mourning came and Joshua was still with us, we were so blessed.

A Legacy of Faith in 55 Days

Everyone began to leave and had made plans to come again to visit with us. My mom and sister had stayed and that had given me the chance to take a much needed shower. I was relieved and yet very anxious over all of the excitement. I had asked them to take turns reading scripture to him while I was given the opportunity to prepare for another day with him. Joshua's monitor was randomly making sounds and I moved quickly to be beside him.

I know that every mother wants to care for there child as long as they can, as I did.

It was around 10:00a.m. And day 48 Donna and mom also needed rest they were getting sleepy. I gave those hugs and kisses and knew that I would see them later on.

During this time I needed more than anyone to have the ability to understand and to comprehend why we were faced with the many challenges that we had. And day by day Jesus came to me so sweetly and explained it to me.

Joshua was so restless and seemed so uncomfortable I wanted so bad to comfort him but I wasn't sure what I could do that would work for him.

As each minute slowly passed, causing a deeper pain than what I already had.

I managed to break away for a few moments, as I had a genuine desire to understand and went to the Chapel to pray.

Joshua had been placed on oxygen again and it was at a higher level than what it had ever been.

Somehow I had allowed all of the negativity that I had heard get into my spirit and for a short time it was very devastating. I was troubled by everything I didn't want to eat, sleep, or talk to anyone.

I had became short tempered with so many, could they even see how badly I was hurting?

When I began to realize what had happened and the way I had been given such a blessed miracle, I was able to take back what God had given to us and that was victory.

I returned to Joshua's room feeling comforted that Jesus had came to me to help me. I shared with Joshua the joy that I had been given to have him and that I would do whatever it takes to finish what God had intended for us.

What Joshua had done for me and what God allowed for me to see wasn't meant for everyone; this was a very special time for me.

There were many that had wanted to continue giving Joshua tests but that wasn't part of God's plan so it didn't happen the way others had intended.

I had never known what it was like to live by faith until now. I had scripture to read daily and in learning passages it strengthened me and helped me to overcome what we had been facing.

Joshua began to stir around once again and I tried to quote as many scriptures that I could to him; remembering they were given for me also.

It was getting late and I started to prepare for his evening schedule, I also wondered how long I could keep going. I knew that it wasn't me that was taking care of everything as scheduled it was the angels that had accompanied me. To this day when I think about all that had been done I'm still very much amazed. Never forgetting what had been given for us because he loved us so much.

I had the opportunity to sit back and watch him rest so peacefully for a little while, I was rejoicing and torn at the same time. My heart ached as my life had began to change during our stay. God had a plan for me and this was the chosen time for me to fulfill the call that he had for me.

A parable from the word that as Jesus walked on this earth if he had not been willing to sacrifice his life that we may have life than everything that he had done to glorify God would have been done in vain for man to see and not for God. As Jesus was prepared by our heavenly father to face the vengeance of man, I too was being prepared to face the trials, affliction, and suffering that man can place on one that is innocent.

I was a child of the King and he loved me as much as he did his other sons and daughters that has always served him.

I was ready to come home I didn't want to be in the presence of our enemy any longer. Yet I knew that I couldn't leave until God changed the scene or called Joshua home.

I cried almost continuously as I watched Joshua fight for his life, what more could I do, why would they allow him to struggle like he had? Why couldn't they care for him as I had instead of wanting to give up on him as many times as they had? I was hurting and very tired from all of the vigorous activities and continually changing of his schedule.

I had left Joshua for a little while going to the Chapel in desperation. I had heard a voice as I knelt down to pray and it said, "Put me first" I thought I had. I know that when I don't I feel like I am swimming in a world of doubt. I had a lot of learning that comes with growing when your stepping out, having a genuine desire to do things God's way.

I quietly left the Chapel making my way outside; I sat beneath the stars asking God to take him as I pleaded to understand. There had been many requests that I had made to God and when it was according to his plans he filled each one. Why was I pleading for him to take Joshua from me, I felt Joshua was in pain and it was more than I could face and know how to comfort him. He had already proved himself and didn't need to any longer.

This was the first time in my life that I realized that God's love was much greater than mine.

God hadn't changed from day one, nor his plan that he had for us. I had made a pack there was no going back or changing my mind. I would see that we would finish all that he had intended for us. Moments passed and I returned to Joshua's room.

I had the opportunity to speak with one as I was going back to Joshua's room. It was around 2:00a.m. and at this time of night everything seems more quiet. Through the words that this person spoke they were in fear of loosing there home, there job, and possibly the family with this horrific setback. This was the least that I was thinking at a time like this but I insisted that we pray together and put the entire situation in Gods hands and that is what we did.

I believed in what we had asked and although I didn't know how everything would go, Jesus would see to it that we wouldn't be in need of any one thing. We had prayed in agreement, trusting in him that everything would be ok.

We were given the grace to endure the whole situation.

I slowly entered into Joshua's room not wanting him to ever think that he had to go through anything alone. "Lord give me the strength to hold on until you call him home"! I was quickly reminded of the voice that I had previously heard, sharing with others and not being in the room when Joshua crossed over. I'm not sure I can do it, God knew eventually I would place him back into his hands.

A part of me felt that we had been abandoned and that I was doing everything wrong or else Joshua wouldn't have to fight for his life as he had been. Why do we have to go through this if you are with us I asked? My answer came later in much scripture reading the great many heroes of some of the biggest Bible stories ever given. To leave a name like Jesus, Moses, Joseph, Joshua, Paul, and Stephen wow!

Mourning had finally came I loved seeing the sunlight shine after having an evening filled with darkness. I couldn't wait to visit with his doctor as she came in, I pleaded with her to allow me to bring him home, if he was going to leave me I wanted him at home where he had always felt safe and secure she had agreed. I thanked her as I cried, she said there were necessary steps that we had to take but it wouldn't be long, she would make the necessary arrangements both of us knew that we didn't have a lot of time.

I had a continual comforter as we had gone through such a difficult and trying time in our lives.

There were so many preparations to make, the lists seemed endless. Yet this was something that we had been waiting for and planning for from the very beginning.

If I would've had my way after her saying that we could leave, we would've been home by that evening. If that had been God's way I'm sure we would've left almost immediately after arriving.

Joshua was extremely agitated and I was overwhelmed. Some of the caregivers had chose not to follow the doctor's instruction and that left us helpless. Both of us had endured the trials and afflictions by others carelessness.

But, to have the vision to carry out the legacy of faith is priceless. I tried harder to focus on the positive as opposed to the negative. I wanted to feel as if all the pressures had lifted, not as if I was drowning in affliction.

It is through God's grace that he have us the strength and courage to continue.

There had been many lives that had been touched throughout our experience.

I had a lot of mixed emotion, feeling like I was holding on by a loose string. Yet God had me under the shadow of his wing, his ways are so mysterious.

Joshua didn't do well with therapy and his therapist had said he won't last, within the next 24 hours. How could they speak so openly with me standing next to them like that? I wasn't bold enough to say anything not wanting to cause any interference to stay next to him. It wasn't there call to make and God showed me that by allowing him to stay. Every minute was so crucial because the feeling of coming to an end was very near.

I couldn't imagine what it would be like for Joshua to take his last breath without me being next to him. Everything had changed and it wasn't the way I had planned it. I had to remember that God seen ahead and had our best interest at hand.

As I had received comfort and forgiveness I had to learn that all over again even when placed in this circumstance. I had to show others that through anything God gives us the ability to sustain. Not allowing my heart to be hardened from all of the afflictions. I had even managed to come face to face with those that I had offended or that had offended me and apologized for being so short tempered with them and for the wrongfulness towards them that I had expressed to others that would listen.

I had openly said to those that had been my enemy that I forgave them for everything. I had even called the driver of the van in whom hit my son and told her that I forgave her, I didn't make much conversation with her at the time but I felt that she needed to know as well as I needed to heal and this is part of the healing process. Jesus Christ interventions not mine.

What God had given us was not meant for the rest of my days to be sorrow upon sorrow, but to have joy and peace and an expected end.

The staff had a very difficult time with administering his medicine it was like a tight vacuum with no movement. To rebuke the storm and know what your saying will get you through any tribulation.

Joshua had been given a little mirror that had said Ps. 118:26 – This is the day that the Lord has made, we will rejoice and be glad it is. (KJV) It was difficult to do at a time like this but he said he would take care of us and he did.

Family had came to visit with us again, the sadness that swept across everyone's face as his monitor continually kept sounding off. I tried sitting patiently in the waiting room while everyone took there turn visiting but every 15 to 30 seconds I found myself running back. How long would I keep doing this, had I really gave him back? Everyone was so hurt and discouraged, oh what a time it was. Hours had past everyone was leaving with our visitation ending. Everyone had shared the same pain, tears of agony sweeping each face.

The pain Mary must have felt to have seen and witnessed them crucifying her son, I imagined as I wept.

How could I ever face a day without having Joshua in my life? We had fourteen years and now I realize that wasn't a whole lot of time. We always think that were going to make things up and have more time, if you wait to long you've missed out on life.

I was at my weakest point, deep down I had felt like I had given up. I hadn't because I was still facing each day as they came. I had a desire to be a follower but if this is what it was like I couldn't keep doing it. I said I can't, but he said I can! And everyday that I'd been given I did.

Through everything I turned to Jesus for an answer and not to man. Our evening passing as Joshua continually stirring, and every minute felt like it was eternity. I had very little hope of what a new day may bring.

Our mourning came being day 49, how much longer would we have to wait?

Lord, "I'm confused, I'm not sure now what you plan to do." If Joshua was going to go please let it be in peace and not like this as I had seen.

I know with all my heart that I was given this extra time to have the ability to testify for what God had done. I was being renewed and was given a new foundation for my life and to share the plan that he had for me.

I had said that Joshua was in God's hands and that he would take care of him and he did. Every minute and hour seemed to be moving very slowly, yet I had a song still flowing in my heart. I was living by faith and can honestly say I know what it is like to have a relationship with Jesus Christ as my Saviour and he walks beside me everyday. It is the most awesome experience to know what it is like to be a Christian and have someone so great as he is watching your every move. God's promise is to all of those who repent, ask him to come in believe, and trust in him, he is the one who watches over each of our lives, Amen.

I was working for the Lord and being rebellious anymore. What an awesome feeling to know that you are being used by him. And that he has confidence in you to complete the work that he had planned for you.

I wasn't sure why things had went the way they had, I too was amused at our experiences. It was left up to me to continue being obedient and to fulfill Gods commandment that he had given us. We had received in abundance all that we had ever asked.

God's chosen few, one to lift him up and give him praise no matter what we were going through.

It was mid-afternoon and we had received a visitor unexpectedly. It was a time that I wasn't too happy to see or be around anyone particularly her. Our conversation was very brief especially after she had stated that she knew what I was experiencing. I quickly disagreed, how could she? She wanted details, I had very little words for her and she had suggested leaving. I couldn't wait, I was glad she chose not to stay.

Shortly after she left I had thought upon the words that she had said, yes she knew what I was feeling. In her heart she too was grieving she had a little girl in who had been very ill since birth and had near death experiences many times. She would never know what it would be like to share normal living with this little girl. I started to cry how could I have been so short with her. Lord Jesus please forgive me, I said. The next time I see her let me ask her for her forgiveness and he did.

We weren't the only ones that was hurting there are millions who have special needs. Jesus is so good to reach out to us in whom call upon him and believe that he can take care of everything.

I didn't have much time but I managed to take a small break. With every opportunity making my way to the Chapel being thankful for everything that we had been given. In that Chapel was the most beautiful stained glass picture that I have ever witnessed. A continual reminder of a mother's love reaching out to one that is a restorer, a healer, a comforter to all.

When God is in the picture he makes provisions and preparations that will provide you with everything that you will need to continue your journey.

A Legacy of Faith in 55 Days

God needed both of us to finish the work that he had given to us.

I quickly returned to Joshua's room knowing that the therapists would be in to see him any minute. As I stepped in they were already with him, they had said they just stepped in. I said I know as I had been watching the clock and answering hastily. And then I heard that voice again, (be ye angry, and sin not). Lord help me with this because I don't want to offend them. Remembering not the former things, nor considering the old. We had been given another day, praise him and don't complain.

In such a little time Jesus had brought me a long way. I wanted to be a good example as those that he had chosen before me.

I had been delivered from a worldly lifestyle, humbled to my knees there wasn't anything that I wanted to repeat.

The therapists had left as I stayed with Joshua. I told him that there had been so many that had been waiting for him to come home. I had been right and everyone that had doubted was wrong. No that isn't the way God works at all.

I finally managed to get the courage and ask God what he really wanted from me, "the answer came immediately it was to surrender, to quit trying to do it all. If I really trusted him like I said then I would have to give him the entire situation and not just a little. No matter how resistant I had been. I was like the widow who had spent all that she had trying other solutions, but then realizing that him being so mighty he was greater than any issue. If she could but touch the hem of his garment then she would be healed. I had to trust in him as she had completely. He would never leave me, nor forsake me, being my continual stay through everything.

Our journey was ending, there was no more that I could do. I had to give in and then that is when I seen the beauty as he had intended. As long as there's breath, than there's hope for life even when your feeling compassed in a cloud of doubt. We were in our last days and not everyone had the opportunity to come and visit. I felt that there was good reason for some that were unable to make it. God was having his will and way everyday. There is much listening that goes with every instruction that Jesus Christ gives.

Keeping in mind that if there is any negativity that comes from a situation, taking away your blessing then it is coming from Satan who is always out to kill, steal, and destroy what God has planned for us. One has to know the difference between the spirits. When you have Jesus in your life its not a phase that passes by.

Our priorities had gone hay wire until God came along and rewired. God gives all that you need for each day as it reads in Matthew 6:34 (KJV).

REUNION

We had a few days if everything had went according to plan, he would be home by Thursday. Everyone that had received the news eagerly leaving to share this with others that they had spoke too. In all of this time I wanted others to tell him that whatever he had decided it was alright, yet I found that I didn't have the heart to tell him how I really felt about him wanting to leave me in all of that time.

I had to tell him aloud and more than once that I had understood. I was given that opportunity as everything had quieted down once again for the evening.

I tried to describe what heaven would be like in my eyes, but I was having difficulty not understanding the beauty or peace of it completely. It must not be difficult for those that have received the glance to stay in such a heavenly place. To make the decision to leave those in whom they dearly love.

How many loved ones did I have waiting for him to take his hand and welcome him in? I had also asked him not to forget about me and that I had hoped that when the time was right he would come for me and welcome me in those pearly gates, as I held him close and cried. There is no place that I would rather be than to see the one who died for me. I told Joshua not to be afraid and that I knew that he had seen the light as our evening was passing by.

It was early mourning when I quietly arose to go to the bathroom, upon entering and turning on the light I closed the door and the lights completely went out. I was away from the switch and very scared, within seconds that seemed much longer the lights reappeared. Why did this happen the way it did? My answer came that when you cross over for a minute you are scared, within seconds you are received and everything is as glorious as it can be. "A moment of darkness before heavens light" oh how great that must be.

I came out uniting with Joshua and told him that it was alright. It would be for a minute but he would be received into God's light.

Joshua's body was de-toxing all of the medicines that he had. It was like he was being cleansed nothing of man for heaven would do. Something was going on while I was in his room, how much longer I wasn't sure.

I prepared for our day and then I gave myself a break taking a few minutes away. I was walking with fear not sure what I was feeling and or experiencing. Why would God want to use me as a testimony as he did? Through willingness and obedience is what is needed, to this day I still have difficulty explaining.

I found my way outside to my favorite resting place; it was there I was given another sign. There were about a 1,000 birds that came out of nowhere and covered the skies. I had seen this once but twice in the same day what did it mean.

I believe the enemy had meant to take him but God allowed me to have the opportunity to give him back and know that he was safe before our time had ended. There wouldn't be anything negative that would come from this not if I could help it.

I had been given so many signs, that weren't even written. What Jesus did for me is endless.

As I started to walk back this was the first time that all of the fear and anxiety was finally gone. I entered Joshua's room confirming to him everything that had been given. I told him that it was alright and that I knew that there would be a day I would see him again without a spot or blemish.

I asked him to be my guardian angel to stay by my side, and see to it that I would finish the work that needed to be done. I smiled knowing that we were given a good and expected end. Our hours passing and I enjoyed every minute before I knew the day was over and we again received visitors.

It was Donna and Chris that was visiting and they had informed me they had prepared our house for Joshua's return. I was relieved this was needed. There was a lot of calls to be made and preparation to bring him home by Thursday, all of us doing our part continually. Hold on Joshua we have just a couple more days as this day had ended.

There were so many prayers that had went up for him not just from one, but in both young and old.

Joshua was leaving and left a name and a face for all to remember. He was the boy that they had said was D.O.A. but God came by and surpassed everyone's understanding.

For all the ties were broke that once had us bound. What a way to leave a good name.

Everyday that we had been given was a conditioning process to help us through and to see the end. The evening had came and this was the first time that I had an urge to separate from him, watching the continual struggle was crushing and taking the breath right out of me. I believe this was God's way of saying I had seen enough and that we wouldn't have to endure much longer than we already had.

Joshua was tired of fighting and didn't want me to continue holding on, but he wouldn't leave unless I had said that he could. No matter how hard it had been for him.

I was faced with the ultimate sacrifice my son's life, how could I ever give him back to our heavenly Creator? To save lives it would no longer be in question.

Everything seemed to be in slow mode, as the minutes of the evening gradually past. He had been faithful now it was up to me to do the same.

I was so sleepy and yet staying beside him and watching every breath as the mourning came.

As we began to take on another day I had kept the therapists from working with him. Joshua had enough and it was up to me to tell them. "Not today let him rest, I said."

I told Joshua that I was going to take a break, I didn't know the day or hour but I'd hoped he wouldn't do anything until I got back.

I went down stairs and sat for a while, I couldn't help from watch the birds again they were doing something different that I had never seen. There was a bird that seemed to be having some difficulty with flying. This bird was encouraged by many other birds that were surrounding him, taking there time with him and showing him how to fly over and over again. This bird was lagging behind he wanted to fly away but was afraid. I wondered if that's how people are when Jesus sends his angels down to help them fly away.

I just knew that any minute that bird would feel comfortable with his wings and fly away, I had watched and waited but nothing had happened. I had to head back. I didn't understand it completely but before the day ended God would see to it that I would. I thought about that bird all day was he going to stay or was he going to have the courage to fly away?

Joshua was so close to death or flying away but he wasn't sure if it was ok to leave so he stayed.

I returned to Joshua as I watched him slowing down, but his heart was still pounding. I had a difficult time being with him at this time because he seemed as if he didn't want me to touch him or be in the room with him.

He had reacted as it were bothering him for anyone to share his room these last hours.

A part of me was numb preparing for what was to come. This was very upsetting knowing deep down that he was leaving me, I had vowed that whatever it takes I would do it and I meant it.

I told him that I would always remember what God had gave and would share it with as many that would listen.

Donna and Chris had accompanied us with visitation; this was very difficult for them. They had a look upon there face and didn't know what to say.

I took the time to read his cards that had surrounded him, I began to cry.

Donna grabbed me once again and held me tight, I too was afraid. I had said, "I don't feel like I've done enough, and she said that I've done more than enough it was alright. She said that I'd been the perfect mom; I had done more than what I was called to do. Why didn't I feel like it?

Joshua had said the same exact thing just the day before the accident took place, was it coincidence? God had confirmed to me that he had seen and heard everything through the words that she had just spoke. This let me know that I hadn't failed at being a good mom.

God had given him back to me as he had the widow in 1 Kings 17. Although I didn't bring him home with me, I did keep all of the wonderful memories that I had received.

Jesus had moved in such a precious way I will never forget what he gave!

Donna had offered to stay the night, but I refused and said no "she should go home, we will be alright."

I wasn't sure how much more time we had but I had remembered the voice and what Joshua had done and knew deep down I would be alright.

We had decided to take a small break and I knew that they would soon be leaving.

As we sat and talked for a few minutes I couldn't help from notice to my right, the little bird that I had saw earlier was still around having difficulty flying away. He was encouraged by other birds to leave as some already had.

I told Donna and Chris about that bird, and I also told them what I thought it meant. It had been around all day and doing the same thing, being so encouraged by others to fly away.

They didn't think that I was crazy, maybe it did mean something. I felt the angels were there side by side Joshua ready and waiting for him to take that final step. As much as he wanted to leave this world he was still holding on afraid of the un-known. There was anything that I could say that would take that painful look away. Joshua had gone through so much for all of us the only way he would let go is when I let go.

If I did I knew that there would be a day that I would see him again. The only way that I could separate from him is if someone was sent to help me, and Jesus knew that.

Donna and Chris had left with the intent on coming again the following day; I returned to Joshua's room, it was very upsetting to see him so rigid. I tried caring for him but he acted as if he didn't want me touching him. I knew that it wouldn't be long. I was so thankful for all of the extra time that I had been given.

Joshua had yielded his vessel that I may have light and God loved me so much that he didn't take him until he knew I would someday say Lord you can use me as you have with him.

I had a peace that remained with me continually although what I had experienced and witnessed wasn't always easy. As scripture reads in II Corinthians 4:18- While we look not at the things which are seen, but at the things which are not seen: for the things which are seen are temporal, but the things which are not seen are eternal.

I tried to sing a melody but there wasn't anything that I could remember. I just pulled up a chair close to him and held his hand. I didn't ask or seek a medical explanation what God had given us was more than anyone else could ever say, more importantly not allowing anyone to take our victory away.

Many lives and destinations were changed because God breathed life back into him and he gave us the ability to witness it. No one could deny a miracle had taken place it had definitely been heaven sent.

I believe Joshua was prepared ahead of time and was willing to do whatever it took to bring praise to our heavenly father's name. (The Great I AM)

Be it known that is what is asked of each of us.

We continued through out the night letting the darkness pass us by, deep down in my heart I knew that it was almost time. I wondered why it was taking so long if he planned to soon call heaven his new home.

Mourning came and I looked forward to the daylight of another day. I took a break and paced the floors waiting with anticipation it was now day 54. Everyday had started and ended with prayer to encourage, strengthen and prepare us for what lied ahead. I was worked with by God in such a special way, to this day it still amazes me for all the time he took and patience he had with me. He made sure that I would be where I needed to be to bring victory to his great name, which is a wonderful blessing.

Daily the hospital seemed loud, but today was different than the other days that we had. Everything and everyone seemed quiet around us seemingly peaceful than what we had.

It's important to remember daily to think of the positive things to say. All of the arrangements had been made if everything went all right he would be home by Thursday.

We had many visitors throughout this day, and I continually shared with everyone that we would be home by Thursday. I said it with excitement knowing that even if Joshua had chose heaven to become his new home that was very exciting also.

I knew that Joshua had been in Gods hands from the very beginning.

I was asked if I wanted to start removing some of his personal items from the room and send them home with Donna and Chris. I agreed knowing that we had an entire room filled with letters, mementos, stuffed animals and flowers. All of them given by Joshua's family and friends.

After all the lessor of these things would mean it would be easier when it was time to leave.

The day past by quickly with much anticipation with family and friends, one of the last of our visitors was my niece to let be know that her best friend would be there for the evening. Her friends son had surgery the previous mourning and that was good for both of us to have company throughout the evening. I hadn't had any intentions on extensive visitation because our time had been so critical; both of us had different needs. However, it was definite that God had intervened.

Everyone had made there way to saying good-bye with the plans to see us again the following day. We shared in prayer leaving with good words and lots of hugs knowing that we were so loved.

We had received help continually because of Gods great mercy.

Time had past and I had told Joshua that I was breaking away to take a break, as I left having feeling overwhelmed. I couldn't wait to get to my chosen spot as I walked crying out to God. I said, Lord if you want me to leave him you're going to have to carry me through this otherwise I can't do it! I can't leave him, it's tearing me up to see him continually go through this. I was preparing to say my final goodbye; I had to keep in mind that there would be a day that I would reunite with him again.

I had cried many tears throughout our ordeal and this was the ending I started to slowly walk back to his room.

As I walked in Joshua's room and I made my way to lie beside him one more time, I said over and over how much I loved him my hand resting with his. He had moved continually sun up to sun down not relaxing any.

Joshua's nurse came in and asked me to remove myself from beside him. I moved with many tears flowing, it was time for his medicine but it wasn't working. I looked his nurse in the eyes and asked if he would take the best care of him that he could? I wouldn't be able to stay until the end, we had been given so much but as Mary I wasn't able to continue enduring.

I said again please do all that you can all that you've been trained to do to comfort him. I said this is the most difficult thing that I've ever had to do; deep down I don't want to leave him. His nurse said I can only imagine what you are going through. And he said that all of the staff was there for me if I needed anything. I asked for a few more minutes as I said goodbye for the last time.

Joshua was breathing heavily that meant he still had life in him, but he was struggling. I gave one last kiss on his forehead and kissed his hand and told him I was doing this out of love. I knew this is what he wanted and Gods time. I longed for the day that he would come back for me, but I too would have to be willing to endure until the end. I made my way to leave his room heading towards the waiting room, finding a place to sit and wait as God comforted me during this time. I wasn't able to stay and watch him take his last breath.

I kept in my heart that we had received an answered prayer from the very beginning and that nothing would ever change my mind.

I was renewed in my spirit and I knew everything would be alright. There is victory over every storm. I felt weak but my God gave me strength. Joshua was about to have a day of rest no more tests.

I felt the urge to leave our floor and go visit with Beth my niece's best friend.

I arrived on the 7th Floor and asked which room they were in. I was directed around the corner and as I went to enter into the room her little boy Patrick greeted me with a heavenly smile.

I asked the little boys mom if it would be alright to visit with them a while. She was so nice and didn't realize at the time how helpful she was.

We were practically strangers yet I was conversing with her like I'd known her for years. I had asked if we could pray together for her young son, if everything went alright he would be released the next day she said. As I looked across her son's bed there rested another baby his name was Donald.

I wondered why he was so quiet yet he moved so vigorously, my friend filled me in on his condition. Donald was born without a voice; he had been born premature and had other conditions that had kept him from developing like a normal, healthy child. He was 11 months old and was very tiny in comparison with other infants his age. My heart was full of compassion as I looked at him lye so helplessly. Deep down I was quickly reminded of how blessed I had been to have so many perfect years with my son. I had life long memories of watching Joshua grow and be considered a healthy and normal kid.

Moments had past and Donald's mom had stepped in and asked what I was doing as she moved quickly to be next to him. I could tell she was scared as I had been and assured her that I was just visiting and that I too had been faced with difficulty. She looked at me and instantly knew who I was; she stated you're Joshua's mom. I said yes I am! She had let me know that she had heard our story and she too was praying for us. I was relieved knowing how many people that I had spoken too and that our testimony had touched others. I asked her if we could pray with her also; it was important to encourage her as I had been. She accepted. Her heart was heavy and I could feel it, she needed a touch from heaven and that is what we had asked for her. There were many sniffles and release of tears as we spoke in agreement aloud knowing that God was there for each of us having no limitations.

She openly shared Donald was her 5th baby and I smiled and said you must be proud. She ended her sentence by saying that her other four children had died. None of them had made it to the age of two.

My heart sank and I probably frowned. I couldn't imagine the grief that she had carried deep down. She had practically lived at the hospital the last 6 years due to so many complications. She said she couldn't leave because every time she did even when it was for a little while she would return to receive more bad news.

Her heart was heavy, she didn't have anyone family or friends to help or comfort her, she had felt that the choices that she had made in life was coming back to haunt her. I listened carefully and when I had the opportunity to speak I said Jesus knows everything, and even when you feel like you can't carry the load or handle any more pain he steps in and can make everything right again. I told her that what God had done for me he would do for her if she would let him. Many couldn't understand the strength and the courage that I had expressed, but when God handles the situation it's not always easy for others to understand. It wasn't me it was him carrying me.

Our conversation had ended and I had planned to take a walk, Beth had planned to take one with me and then she had noticed a spot on her pants. I had told her that I had a change of clothes that I could lend and that I would be right back with them. I returned to the 6th Floor stopping at the nurse's station. I had asked Fern the one who cared for him that evening to step in and grab some sweat pants that I had on the end of my bed. She came back and said that she thought that Joshua would go sometime throughout that evening and I said I know, I had been already told. She was so good to us I felt comfortable having her watch after him as I had prepared myself to leave again.

I returned to the 7th Floor feeling like I was walking on clouds. I handed Beth the sweats and waited for her to change. I had stood in that room knowing that I had done all that I could do. I was in the hands of mercy and not dis-pleasing to the Great I Am anymore.

Beth and I had decided to walk downstairs it was around 9:00 p.m. she asked if I was alright, I said I would be once it was over. She looked at me and I said I don't know the extent or what will become of this but I know that God does. I know that God breathed life back into him and that everyone remembers our story from the beginning.

She had said that I was strong, I said no Beth I am nothing it is Jesus who strengthens me. Moments after she had to return to her son's room I waited outside until she had the opportunity to return.

There were two ladies that I had the opportunity to meet as we sat sharing our stories. These ladies were there waiting for a loved one to recover, he had been in numerous times for

A Legacy of Faith in 55 Days

the removal of cancer. They had a difficult time watching his health deteriorate. I pointed to Jesus during our conversation; to me there was no other solution than to confide in Jesus about everything.

I believed the angels were coming to get Joshua, I shared with them. I didn't know the hour but I was sure that it would be soon. I continually expressed God's mercy and his love that he had shown to us and then I shared with them the song that Jesus gave to me to strengthen me throughout our hospital stay. They were pleased to hear such a sweet melody they said.

Beth returned and I introduced her to these woman and said she is my friend.

One of the ladies had said that she was watching three men that appeared to be ghosts walking towards the entrance of the hospital. She began to cry and asked if we could see them, I said no although I tried. I believed it was angels working that evening not just for me but there would be others that would soon be with there Maker. They were heaven sent!

Shortly after Beth and I excused ourselves and I walked towards the Garden that is where I wanted to be. As we had made our way around the corner there was a cool breeze that swept our face. Throughout our ordeal God had given us many signs and wonders to hold onto and I would share those experiences with Beth that evening.

I was scared this was the closest that I would be in the super natural realm without being in his heavenly presence. We trusted in everything that we had been given that evening, it was quite breathe taking to say the least, everything seemed to calm and we started to head back it was now around 11:00p.m. I was really feeling tired, I hadn't slept peacefully or even wanted to until now.

Beth walked back with me to Joshua's floor I told her that I would be sleeping on the sofa for that evening as I had done our first evening that we had arrived

Beth sat with me until mid-night and then I said I must sleep, I can't keep my eyes open. She said if I needed anything that I knew where she would be and I thanked her for being so kind to stay with me.

I went around the corner and told the nurses where I would be and to come and get me when it was over. They had to see the sincerity and truth as I looked at them and spoke those last words. One had remembered with her own experience when she lost her grandmother that she knew before anyone else did.

I was given a blanket and I went back to rest my head. Within minutes I was sound asleep, hours past and I was awoke by two nurses that were standing over me, They said, Jelana it's over I quickly arose and said what time is it?

They had said it was 5:02 A.M. I was thinking clearly and new that was the same time that I had arrived at the hospital of day one. I asked when did he pass? She said between 4:25 and 4:30 A.M.

That was the same time that I had arrived at the scene the day the accident took place. God already knew I wouldn't have had the ability to share this story with you if it had ended any sooner.

It was Wednesday mourning the same day that the accident took place, I know none of it was quincidence it's God's mysterious ways of doing things.

I was given 55 extra days to care for Joshua and learn a new life having Jesus Christ in my life. I can't imagine living a life without him being #1 in it.

I asked to walk back and be with him, I told them I needed a few minutes and then I would call my sister. They had planned to call his dad while I had my visitation.

I walked into to see him lye so peacefully and at ease, no more struggles, no more pain, no more suffering for anyone. I gave him a kiss and sat beside him to hold his hand, I said thank you. I know that I'm going to see you again only next time you will be happy and content, the way I had always remembered. You've been my hero from the very beginning.

I had to remember the tears of grief that had been showed, are not to be compared to the debt of love I owe. God had taken good care of us.

Seeing Joshua at peace put me at ease, I wanted to continue caring for him like I had always done. I gave him one last bath and fixed his hair, and dressed him before others came to see him. I called my sister Donna and shared with her Joshua had past, she said she would be up soon and tell the others the news. I knew from that point on I didn't have much more time to be with him. As I sat again and held his hand, feeling the warmth from him, I was keeping in mind Jesus great love that he had for us.

I had music playing softly as family began to arrive, Joshua had a blue shirt on that was as bright as the sunny skies. Everyone was gathering around and was given the time to say there good-byes. Many people visited to share there sympathy and even then, God was working through us to strengthen and encourage others.

Joshua's doctor had made it in to visit and said "You've been the perfect mom" I looked at her and knew that Joshua had just said that to me the day before the accident and that reassured me within everything was going to be alright.

As many came to visit I would share with them scripture as it was given to uplift and encourage through there many challenges for one day.

A Legacy of Faith in 55 Days

The time came when it was a little after 9:00 A.M. transportation had came to take Joshua away. I made sure that we had everything but there was one thing that had troubled me Joshua had a small Bible that had been with him and wasn't present with him now. We searched his bed one last time and there it was beneath him, I was so relieved. All of us were leaving together, not leaving one behind including Joshua he left before we did.

God had me in the palm of his hands for the rest of that day, because even after leaving there would still be preparations that had to be made.

Everyone had followed behind as we had left, my way was different than there's and we wind up being separated. Yet at some point we come together like judgment some will be cast away others get to stay.

Eventually all of us came together at the same intersection and the decision was made to come to my house to help with the funeral arrangements. My sister Donna had followed closed behind and low and behold I stop in the middle of the road and ask if she will bring my dog Bear home. I needed something to be familiar as I planned to enter my house. She agreed and I was pleased.

As I arrived home, I stepped out of my vehicle in relief. My attention was quickly drawn to my front yard; it hadn't been attended to in quite some time. I had always done it, sometimes even in caregivers if certain ones don't do it than it won't get done the way you prefer it. I couldn't wait to step inside; my house seemed like a mansion after living in a 8 x 12 room for two months.

I had walked front to back realizing that the largest room in the house had been set up to bring Joshua home. Everyone started to arrive wanting to help yet not knowing what to do. Donna brought Bear and he was very excited to see me. We would soon go to the funeral home to make the necessary arrangements for his showings.

As we arrived to the Funeral home I was asked who would be speaking, I quickly answered me. I wasn't sure what I was going to say but I knew that God had planned it or else I wouldn't have had the boldness to speak so openly and to agree on something that I had never done previously.

The local newspaper had made the announcement that day and many of Joshua's friends would be over by that evening. I was guided every second, minute and hour of that day and the days to come.

As we returned home the phone began to ring and the children began to come. I didn't turn anyone away, for all had heard so much they needed to hear some encouraging words and remember that God had done so much for all of us.

So many tears and I knew all so well that pain that they were feeling. I hugged them and said prayers with each one continually.

As we made our way outside I began to work on my yard, many of the kids offered to help me. I eagerly accepted, with that many hands in no time at all we would have the yard happy and singing like it once did but now it's with a new melody.

As the day progressed more kids continued to come by, there were some that were angry because of the ugly rumors that they had heard. I let them know that I had done all that I could do, Joshua was and had been the light of my life and that there wasn't anything more that was in my hands to do. I let them know that the biggest part of what they heard was lye, if they didn't hear it from me then they shouldn't believe it. I answered each question that the children had and they began to relax.

It's not my ability to stand with such strength but my God who loves and cares for me sustained me through all of the actions, accusations, and conversations of others or else it would've been enough to destroy me completely.

Satan was on a rampage to destroy me because he knew the impact of sharing such a great testimony would have with many.

I believed in my heart those that spoke falsely and those trying to bring shame and hurt to me God would deal with them directly and left it in his hands to deal with and he has. I had to seek forgiveness in my heart for the wrongfulness of others or else, I would never be able to complete what God had called me to do.

I hadn't planned on having any overnight visitors but as the evening continued I had a multitude of kids. They stayed with me and they encouraged me, we prayed and prepared ourselves for Joshua's ceremony.

And then I was quickly reminded that in the beginning of our hospital stay, I had said that when we come home I would have a sleepover for all of Joshua's friends. God had already planted and prepared before I ever asked.

Jesus intended for us to lift one another up, especially when we are weak.

The children began to get hungry so I ordered pizza. We had sat around the campfire sharing our memories of Joshua one by one. As I listened and watched each of them I had to apologize to them. I had made judgment towards them without knowing them. Joshua had some really great friends.

Many of the children that were there that evening had came to visit with us many times during our hospital stay, they remembered seeing him get better during the recovery.

I looked up and there was the most beautiful orange red star that appeared, it was the brightest in the sky. What is even more bizarre that when I would go into the house the star would disappear and when I would come back out it would reappear. It was Joshua's light shining to us, I know that for everyone that dies and makes it to heaven they are numbered by the light that appears in the sky. I loved knowing that he was watching over me and that he cared for me deeply. To be given this understanding so soon, especially that evening.

There were so many children that continued to arrive, well into the early mourning hours. With every opportunity we gathered hands and made a circle lifting up Jesus for what he gave, and learning how to pray. Joshua had many friends he was well liked by everyone, all ages took to him. He was one that could get you to smile even when you felt like frowning. All of us took it to heart to remember him, not just me because he was my son, but everyone because he was a friend to them.

Our evening past and mourning came we were preparing for the day that would be spent at the funeral home. Everyone started to leave gathering there things knowing that later we would be together again.

As the day past all of us met once again with Joshua being the center of our attention. I didn't prepare as some would do for our hours of visitation, I was given a few moments alone before everyone entered and for the last time I fixed his hair and once again said a prayer. Joshua's appearance was different than what we had been given, just the day before seeing him and holding onto our precious fourteen years. The transformation had taken place that let me know that Joshua wasn't there anymore, he had already ascended that was just the outer shell.

I held his hand and felt the warmth that God was sending to let me know that I wasn't alone. I also placed the little Bible in his hand that he had continually held during our journey. I had asked him to remember my request that I had given that when I'm finished doing God's will that he will come and get me, that I to can call heaven my new home.

I then was able to open the doors and allow the others to come in. During this time I didn't desire to take a break making a point to stay beside him. I greeted everyone and comforted those who were mourning over him. Some of Joshua's friends were having a very difficult time seeing him in a casket, but I assured them as it had been given to me that Joshua is no longer there but in heaven where he wanted to be.

God gave me a continual peace because in my heart and mind, mine eyes were stayed upon him. I thanked everyone for coming each with different characteristics especially the kids. Yet Joshua didn't look on the outer appearance, he looked at the heart. As God does each one of us, not making a difference between us. It is he who uniquely created and molded each of us.

On many different occasions I was asked who would be speaking, or giving the eulogy. I answered me accordingly. I wasn't sure what I was going to say or what it would be but Jesus was my guide entirely. With every child I invited them over for fellowship afterwards, this was necessary for them to receive healing by Jesus and to put closure of some of there uncertainty. Some had said that not all of the kids were Joshua's friends, but if they knew

Joshua the way I did they would surely know that it only took Joshua 5 minutes to call someone his friend. It was important for them to see the good as Joshua and I did and to always remember the good no matter what they had heard or what someone else had said.

There were many hours that past and soon the visitation was over, everyone would be going home. There were many of the adults that were amazed thinking that at some point I would have to shatter, God was with me and unless you have had the same experience giving him the whole situation you can't possibly understand it. God had me in the palm of his hand.

I know that I wouldn't be where I'm at today, especially moving forward if I didn't trust and confide in him with every step that I take.

Some had even thought that I was in shock and that I hadn't comprehended what had happened to us yet. What they hadn't seen was the many tears of grief that had been shed previously, or in the days to come. God was my rock, my amour, my shelter, and my shield. There was no one else that I could confide in with the sorrow that I had felt other than God because he knew it all to well when he gave his only son.

We can be over comers if we allow him to take control of the entire situation. The visitation had ended and it was time to leave, many of the children wanted to ride with me. There were a lot of them that found there own way, because I was limited in space. We were given the opportunity to continue in fellowship and in prayer once I was able to return home.

This time there was twice as many kids as there was the previous night. Some had difference of opinions but they had put them aside all having Joshua on there mind. Some had feeling of guilt and were hurting deeply inside and wanted to take there life, but I quickly reminded them of the 10 Commandments and said you won't be spending eternity with him if you choose to do that. We choose our destination.

I had shared with them first hand I was aware of Joshua's experiences in the past. I had shared with them that I knew that Joshua had made things right just weeks prior to the accident. And then I explained why. I had seen a difference in Joshua's character and his lifestyle and couldn't pin point what it was but it was definitely for the better, I didn't understand it because prior to the accident I didn't have Jesus being #1 in my life. Joshua no longer wanted to hang out with those that he use to call his friends, he would ask me to tell them he wasn't allowed or wasn't there when they would call or frequently visit. I know now that it was Jesus that took hold of his life and that made everything right. Jesus will help keep you separated, if he is the one your seeking to please. And if they needed more I told them God would have not intervened and breathed life back into him, if Joshua hadn't been the one who was saved. I believe Joshua's wish was to see me saved and God used Joshua to get me to tell his story to as many people that would listen.

Having Jesus in your life makes all of the difference.

The children were preparing throughout the evening to sing a song for him for his funeral; each one participating was more than willing.

I watched them carefully throughout the evening the many groups that had been formed, each of them separating throughout the given space. I began to cry and I longed to sing or hold Joshua one more time. The children began to gather around and gave me hugs one by one, reassuring me everything was going to be ok. Adam Joshua's best friend said you'll see him again, I knodded my head as the tears continued to roll down. I was given first hand to see the heart of all of Joshua's friends.

All of them worked together to keep things in order. Even when it came to his room, his cousin and her best friend put it back together again. All of the children made the entire circumstance as comfortable as they could, even when we had went to the grocery store to gather food to feed all of them.

Once again we were given the star for the evening, what a great way to know that our Comforter is always there for those who need him most. I had a friend and her husband stop by to see if I was alright, and they were amazed to see all of the kids in my back yard. God had given and even though they thought I may need help with having so many, I didn't have a problem with any of them. My friend had made mention that I had a glow, but her husband couldn't see it. She said it was a halo shining directly over me, I smiled and said God is with me. They soon left knowing they would see me the following day and asked if I would still be giving the eulogy, I said yes and we prayed before they left. I never thought I would hear anyone say that to me again but I did.

There were many parents who had stopped by to check on there kids and was reassured as my friend that everyone and everything was going great.

Our evening past and we were well into mourning; two of the girls that had stayed the evening had been frightened and came to get me. Joshua's television had come on in his room without anyone being in there to turn it on. They were scared and we hurried back to his room to see what was playing, it was a Christian Broadcast Program that was confirming the message of healing given to these children previously and spoke by me. God was moving and having his way planting the seeds with them so early. As many children that could were in aww hearing the message they heard being repeated.

Many were tired because they hadn't slept all evening and for some they had been up for two days. They couldn't forget the message even though it was time to start gathering there belongings and picking up the areas. It gave them all the more reason to keep on talking, keeping it in remembrance.

Joshua's television came on repeatedly almost a year after his passing to give me a message and prepare me for the day. I was so blessed to have Jesus stay beside me. This also assured me that Joshua was well prepared of having Jesus on his side, well before any of us was.

We were so blessed to have been given an extra 55 days, and that in a since was a point of celebration that Joshua had made it to heaven and to keep in mind what had been continually said not my will, but thine instead.

Each of us can be used by God we have to be willing. He asks of us to offer ourselves nothing else. To have confidence and trust will get you to the finish line every time.

They had rehearsed there song one last time, knowing this would be the last gift they could give him before having to say good-bye.

I made my way getting ready not knowing how much more I was able to withstand. The time had come to be at the funeral home once again, I had taken a recorder to tape the sermon. I took a moment to hold Joshua's hand and I began to pray silently, I didn't feel I could do it but I felt the warmth once again, I knew Jesus stood with me and that he was there to help me.

Our service started in prayer and I began with the verse of John 3:16 it was a beautiful message about love, and forgiveness that none of us know how much time we are given. We shouldn't wait until it's too late to make mends. Joshua and I had a beautiful bond, as I can imagine God did with his only son. Joshua gave his life that I may see light and that I could share it with many. It's important not to hold onto the past, or look into the future but to have and look forward to one day at a time as Jesus did.

I didn't do anything for recognition; I did it because the Lord had need of it.

There were many sniffles and lots of tears; God gives comfort and understanding when no one else feels they can endure. Gods amazing grace will get you through everything.

I had played a song that was so dear to me it was about God healing a nation when there pain seemed so great. The children began to sing with having the message "All for one, or nothing at all" it was so beautiful, and the service ended once again in prayer. I was given the strength to greet those passing, knowing there was such a pain in there heart that only God could repair.

They were prepared to close his casket when I was asked if I wanted to take anything with me. I reached for the little Bible that he had but it seemed as he wanted to keep it with him. I left it with him knowing that it was better for me because we had depended heavily on the scripture to get us through it. I took one memento leaving everything else, which had been given from the adults and children.

A Legacy of Faith in 55 Days

I'm not sure why but after the service, I chose to drive separately. I had many children wanting to ride with me. And it was up to me to see that all of the children who had rode there bikes would have the opportunity to be with us at the grave side.

Everyone was trying to be brave but I could see the pain they carried in there eyes. As we proceeded in the ceremony everyone gathered at a stand still until all had arrived at the grave site. I allowed a preacher to end the service with final words, and I had asked if everyone would join in and sing "Amazing Grace" before they planned to leave.

I was given a peace and serenity that I can't explain as everyone began to leave. Gods love was greater than I could've ever imagined.

There were many that had planned to gather in my yard once again for fellowship both young and old. Satan was mad and caused a division between the family after arriving. I couldn't turn anyone away no matter what the circumstance. I had asked many of the children that arrived into my home to protect and share with them the reason for others actions. I simply said I had family that was hurting and they needed to vent a little. We would pray for the entire situation and allow God to move because we couldn't.

Our evening past everyone comforting and confiding in one another, I began to feel really tired. I hadn't slept peacefully in many weeks. I had about 72 hours sleep in 55 days. I had felt that during our stay if I had turned my back, or closed my eyes that Joshua would be gone, I couldn't do anything for any long length of time. The children prayed with me and that was the first time that I had went and slept in my bed, it was a great feeling.

Mourning arrived with the beautiful sunlight and all of the kids began to say there good-byes.

It was Sunday a day of rest and I really felt it. Everyone was leaving very happy and content. I knew it wouldn't be long before the phone would begin to ring others continue to check in on me.

I had been through a lot but Jesus had never left me. My mom had stopped by to apologize; I told her that it was alright. We sat on the porch and I continually shared with her the peace that I had felt. As she was watching me closely and then she said Jelana you have the most beautiful glow all around you. I said I know Jesus is with me, my friend Doris had told me she had seen the same glow just two nights earlier. I was amazed, I knew Jesus loved me but he was letting them see that he was in me.

Our visitation ended and I stayed close around the house, feeling for the first time content to be home. As each day passing God continued to work with me, he gave me an understanding as I read scripture and that strengthened me and allowed me to have joy and happiness.

I knew that it was important to get into church; I had to get grounded to have good roots. My home church that I had chose was one that Joshua and I had attended together in times past. My church was built by trinity believing in God, the Son, and the Holy Ghost, together this created the unity that I needed. I felt like I was home the first time I had the opportunity to walk through the doors. I knew God had a plan for me and this was the church that he needed me in.

I had taken the time to write a very special Thank You note to all who were close to Joshua and kept us in there prayers continually. We had it published in the local paper as we had uplifted God for keeping his hand upon us.

Not long after I started attending I became a member and got baptized offering my life to my Lord Jesus Christ. I made it a point to take just one day at time and accept what God had planned for me.

It has been a tremendous ministry he has opened my eyes to so many peoples needs.

I've had the opportunity to work with the homeless, and help find them permanent shelter. I've had the opportunity to supply children with glasses or else they wouldn't have the gift of reading. I've had the opportunity to work with the "Special Children" or else they would've never received visitors. I've had the opportunity to feed many on a limited income. And now I've been given the opportunity to work with and teach children. That they can come together and hear the many great things that Jesus has given to each of us that love him.

My life with Jesus has been so rewarding but the greatest gift he has given was his life for me.

I am so blessed to have been given this opportunity to share with you, the Legacy of Faith in 55 days that I hope all will remember.

On the dark days that I feel like I can't see the light it is he who quickly warms me and reminds me that I am still his.

It's been almost three years since Joshua's accident, and I still live for Jesus remembering what he delivered me from. Joshua's room is filled with mementos of those who offered something.

Everyday that I pray, I ask the Lord to direct my path and to lead my way. I never want to have the humble experience that I had to bring me to my knees as I did Wednesday May 23, 2001.

In memory of Joshua the one who meant so much. Remembered by family and friends and loved so much.

I look forward to the day that the heavens will open and the angels will say, you get to be with Jesus and reunite with Joshua again. Eternity is forever and a day.

Joshua believed in me and the one that believed in him gave me the ability to finish. Thank you Lord Jesus

Every mark that Joshua had was recorded for medical documentation, the list of doctor's, nurses, and therapists that would be assisting us upon our leaving was given and the list of medicines and cleaning supplies needed.

It was God that allowed me the memory to record our 55 day stay. I had family stay with Joshua as I made the necessary arrangements, not leaving him unattended.

Everyone was there for me and had said if I need anything at all to call them. What I had need of couldn't come from any of them.

ABOUT THE AUTHOR

Three years ago in May a mothers son was involved in a critical automobile accident.

Many lives were touched, but the mother tells how her life was changed. I made a decision, a commitment, to share with as many people that I could, of our miracles that took place. A vow kept whether it was life or death.

I want to know that I've done all that I was asked before facing the great "I am."

I know that his love is greater than one could ever imagine.

I will never forget the news I received, or the words that echoed tragedy.

God was a very present help, and throughout it all he never left. He continually extends his mercy, and leaves us with hope to continue our journey.

Memoirs of our last days, of a mom and her son together.